HERE'S A PRETT

Here's a pretty mess!
In a month, or less,
I must die without a wedding!
Let the bitter tears I'm shedding
Witness my distress,
Here's a pretty mess!
(from *The Mikado*, W.S. Gilbert)

ABOUT THE AUTHOR

David Bathurst has taken part in all thirteen of the surviving Gilbert & Sullivan operas, singing with ten different operatic societies varying tremendously in resources and abilities, and taking a mixture of principal and chorus roles. He has written five other books on a variety of topics. He also enjoys "straight" choral singing, and belongs to a church choir which specialises in Renaissance polyphony, as well as an *a cappella* quartet performing everything from madrigals to Flanders & Swann. Whilst not writing or singing, he enjoys long-distance walking, and has walked all the national trails of England and Wales. A solicitor by profession, he lives just outside Chichester in West Sussex.

BY THE SAME AUTHOR

The Selsey Tram – Phillimore, 1992
Six Of The Best! – Romansmead, 1994
The Jennings Companion – Summersdale in association with Romansmead, 1995
Financial Penalties – Collection And Enforcement In Magistrates' Courts – Barry Rose, 1996
Around Chichester In Old Photographs – Sutton Publishing, 1997

HERE'S A PRETTY MESS!

A new guide to Gilbert & Sullivan opera for the amateur
performer and enthusiast

By DAVID BATHURST

Illustrated by TERENCE WHITLOCK

with best wishes

1998

Romansmead Publications

First published in 1998 by

Romansmead Publications
46 Mosse Gardens
Fishbourne
Chichester
West Sussex PO19 3PQ

Printed in England by Antony Rowe Ltd, Bumper's Farm, Chippenham, Wilts SN14 6LH

ISBN 0-9523936-5-4

British Library Cataloguing-in-Publication Data.
A catalogue record for this book is available from the British Library.

CONTENTS

ACKNOWLEDGEMENTS

The author wishes to acknowledge the kind permission given to him to quote from various other texts. These are marked with an asterisk in the bibliography section at the end of this book.

The author also wishes to thank all those who have assisted him in the preparation and printing of this book, particularly Terence Whitlock for his superb illustrations and Jackie Martin at Antony Rowe Ltd. for her invaluable help.

David Bathurst

Chichester 1998

INTRODUCTION

The operas of W.S. Gilbert and Arthur Sullivan have become an integral part of English musical and literary heritage. The well-known expressions "A policeman's lot is not a happy one," "short sharp shock" and "to let the punishment fit the crime" all originate from the pen of the lyricist Gilbert. Sullivan's rousing melodies have also worked their way into popular culture, from Harold Abrahams' spirited rendition of the Boatswain's song from *H.M.S. Pinafore* in *Chariots of Fire*, to the somewhat inferior reproduction of "A wandering minstrel" from *The Mikado* being enjoyed in the trenches in the First World War by a certain Captain Blackadder.

Written just over one hundred years ago (the publication of this book coincides with the centenary of the last public appearance of the two composers on stage together), the fourteen operas – of which thirteen survive – combine the dazzling wit of one of the foremost humorists of the Victorian age with music written by one of the most talented composers of that time. Much of the humour has certainly dated, but the very fact that the operas are period pieces, reflecting an era that has long gone, adds to their nostalgic charm. Occasionally, however, the listener will detect a witticism or vein of humour which retains its topicality and relevance even today. That the music remains fresh, singable and memorable, with a subtlety and depth in the harmonies and orchestration that are conspicuously absent in many more recent musicals, is undeniable by even the greatest fans of such twentieth-century musical offerings as *Nick And Nora* or *Fings Ain't Wot They Used T'Be*.

The backgrounds and indeed personalities of the composers were remarkably different. They led entirely separate lives, and their professional partnership was often sullied by disagreement. Born in 1836 in London, William Schwenk Gilbert's first profession was that of barrister, although he also served as a reservist with the 5th West Yorkshire Militia and the Royal Aberdeenshire Militia. During his time at the Bar, he developed a love for writing humorous articles. Tiring of the law, he joined the staff of a newly-founded magazine entitled *Fun*, which was to be the perfect vehicle for his writing endeavours. His most noteworthy contribution to the magazine was a series of comic ballads which came to be known as the *Bab Ballads*. During the 1860's, whilst writing for *Fun*, he also produced a considerable amount of material for the theatre and became known to many of the foremost impresarios of that time. Though capable of great generosity, he was prone to irascibility and had a wit which was often acid in its sharpness. Arthur Seymour Sullivan, by nature a much more delicate, sensitive man, was born in 1842, also in London. He entered the Chapel Royal as a chorister and later studied at the Royal Academy of Music, continuing his studies in Leipzig. In his twenties he held numerous prestigious appointments, including that of resident organist at the Royal Opera House and Professor of Composition at the Royal Academy of Music. It was a certain F.C. Burnand who persuaded him to branch into operetta by asking him to compose the music for a burlesque he was writing, entitled *Cox And Box*. The work, when performed, was a huge success.

With the increasing demand for quality musical entertainment, it was perhaps inevitable that some theatrical director somewhere would commission a joint work from Gilbert and Sullivan. Around 1869 or 1870 they were introduced to each other for the first time – although both had seen performances of the other's work before that – and it was one John Hollingshead, director of the Gaiety Theatre in London, who commissioned what was to be their first joint work. Entitled *Thespis*, it opened at the Gaiety on Boxing Day 1871 and ran for 63 performances. After its opening run finished it was never revived, and cannot now be performed as it was written because the music is lost. After *Thespis* finished, more than three years passed before the opening of the earliest surviving opera of the partnership, *Trial By Jury*, commissioned by the impresario Richard D'Oyly Carte. Inspired by the success of their work, Gilbert and Sullivan went on to write another dozen operas. Their last really successful offering was *The Gondoliers* in 1889. Thereafter, a combination of factors saw the partnership disintegrate, and although they wrote two further operas together, these were both comparative failures.

After *The Grand Duke* which appeared in 1896 the collaboration stopped completely and Gilbert and Sullivan had nothing more to do with each other. They were last seen on a stage together in the autumn of 1898 at a revival of one of their operas. They took a bow at the final curtain and exited without speaking to each other. There was no real animosity between them; they simply led separate lives and moved in different circles. Sullivan died in 1900, two years after their last stage appearance together. Gilbert lived on until 1911, losing his life whilst trying to save a lady friend from drowning in his lake at Grim's Dyke. Despite the fact that the professional collaboration ceased some years before Sullivan's death, Gilbert is reputed to have confessed in 1903 that "A Gilbert is no use without a Sullivan, and I can't find one." These two very different individuals found immortality only when they worked together, and their combined works have become institutions. Indeed, it is common, when speaking of Gilbert and Sullivan opera, to refer to it as "G & S," and this practice will be adopted throughout this book. To talk of Gilbert without Sullivan, or vice versa, seems as inconceivable as to talk of Laurel without Hardy, or Marks without Spencer.

A visit to a professional performance of a G & S opera, ideally involving members of the D'Oyly Carte Opera Company, or sight of the expertly-produced George Walker videos of the operas, will show G & S at its best. Such productions will combine highly-trained singers and actors, expensive and perfectly-fitting costumes, scenery that is built and assembled by professionals, and directors with an eye for the strictest detail and a flair for breathtaking creativity. In all these aspects the quality of the performances will reflect the professional polish that went into the original productions. There is, however, another and far more prevalent type of G & S production. This is the amateur production, in which enthusiastic individuals give up possibly five or six precious hours of their leisure time per week for several months in preparation for the performance of one of the operas for the delectation of the local populace.

Amateur G & S, amongst operatic societies as well as ad hoc groups, is thriving; as Ian Bradley, author of *The Complete Annotated Gilbert & Sullivan*, admirably puts it, "There are few evenings in the winter months when the sound of singing policemen or pirates isn't wafting out of some church room or village hall." The number of amateur G & S productions in rehearsal at any one time in this country alone is vast; whilst amateur operatic societies may take a well-deserved break over Christmas and in the summer months, the majority of weekday evenings, and many weekends too, will see rehearsals for forthcoming G & S shows going on all across England and beyond. The standards will vary dramatically, from societies whose professional outlook and standards enable them to recruit some of the best singers and actors in the locality, to those which through lack of talent, recruiting skills and organisation possess all the professional polish of a mud-caked rubber boot.

This book is all about the world of amateur G & S, and is primarily intended for the prospective amateur performer of a G & S opera. You, the reader, may be new to the whole world of G & S and amateur operatics; new simply to a particular opera having already performed in one or more of the others; or a seasoned G & S performer who is looking forward to a second, third or fourth production of one of the operas and who will enjoy being reminded of past endeavours besides those still to come. By the end, it is hoped that you will have a far greater insight into the work you are performing, as well as those things you might expect from taking part in the production as a whole.

It is also hoped that the book will serve as a helpful introduction for students either of G & S or amateur operatics, and an enjoyable and nostalgic read for past performers or spectators of amateur G & S. Each chapter takes a different opera in turn; all thirteen surviving operas are covered, beginning with *Trial By Jury* and finishing with *The Grand Duke*. An appendix covers the "lost" opera, *Thespis*, and two works by Sullivan, *Cox And Box* and *The Zoo*, which are often performed alongside a G & S opera. Each chapter opens with a brief historical introduction to the opera in question, and an outline of the plot. This is then followed by a detailed, if somewhat irreverent, journey through the opera, highlighting potential sources of difficulty, challenge, enjoyment or hilarity for the amateur performer. Opportunity will be taken, as each opera is described, to acquaint the new performer (and reacquaint the more experienced campaigner!) with some of the quirkier, and often comical, aspects of taking part in a G & S show, although some could be said to be true of any amateur production. They include, to name but just a few, the cut and thrust of principal auditions; misbehaving props; collapsing scenery; ill-fitting costume and ill-applied make-up; restless and somnolent spectators; ill-chosen ad-libs; sudden attacks of stage amnesia; hurriedly-planned curtain calls; interminable thank-you speeches; chaotic band calls; tenors who are less than competent at hitting the high notes; unsubtle fishing for compliments; over-optimistic rehearsal schedules and dance routines; officious rehearsal hall caretakers; and associated joys of the amateur G & S performer such as esoteric quizzes and humiliating singing competitions.

Numerous books about Gilbert and Sullivan – both the composers and their works – have been written. The author believes, however, that in departing from the traditional factual or academic study of the operas, and delving into the world of G & S as performed by amateurs, this book is unique. It is perhaps surprising that this should be so. In an age in which professional performers of G & S must compete with ever more sophisticated and technically awesome varieties of entertainment, the amateur stage seems the only way in which, certainly in Great Britain, the operas can be sure of holding their own in the twenty-first century. The book is, in a sense, a tribute to all those who by their dedication, enthusiasm, stoicism and, at times, masochism, have helped to keep G & S alive in the parish rooms, church halls and town halls of Great Britain, and indeed overseas, for over one hundred years. May their descendants still be doing the same a century from now – assuming that there are still some parish rooms, church halls and town halls that have not been turned into theme pubs or "drive-thru" pizza palaces.

NOTE

A study of the textbooks on G & S will reveal that there is divided opinion on whether their works should be described as operas or operettas. The author has chosen to describe the works as operas throughout the text, but as a matter of convenience rather than an expression of his own opinion!

Trial By Jury is the earliest surviving Gilbert & Sullivan opera, and undoubtedly one of the most popular. This farcical enactment of a "breach of promise" legal action in front of a jury of twelve good men and true (or in a society which is short of men, perhaps nine and therefore illegally constituted) will be especially popular with the producer of a less talented amateur group. Anxious to avoid the tiresome inconvenience of persuading his cast to move about, he can install the jurymen and members of the public in their places at the outset, and keep them there for the duration. He will thereby be saved the trouble of choreographing elaborate routines, which in turn will save the society's followers from their usual fate, to wit a choreographic offering which in terms of grace and elegance compares somewhat less favourably with the movement of rush-hour traffic on the Hanger Lane Gyratory System.

Three years had passed since the opening of *Thespis*, Gilbert and Sullivan's first joint work, and for which the music has now disappeared. Its mixed reviews and comparatively modest box office returns had not convinced the public, or more importantly the impresarios, that Gilbert and Sullivan were meant for each other. During those three years Gilbert had continued to write, and Sullivan had continued to compose, each entirely independently of the other. It then so happened that in January 1875 a well-known impresario named Richard D'Oyly Carte was looking for a short musical entertainment to accompany a production of Offenbach's opera *La Perichole*. By coincidence, Gilbert had the libretto of an opera to offer Carte. He had written it for one Madame Parepa Rosa as part of a Drury Lane opera season, but she died in 1874 before it could be staged. Carte liked the libretto and suggested that Sullivan should set it to music. It took Sullivan just three weeks to finish the job, and on 25th March 1875 *Trial By Jury* opened at the Royalty Theatre in London. Such was the enthusiasm for the show that in its first two years it was performed 300 times. Its initial run at the Royalty consisted of 131 performances; it then opened at the Opera Comique off the Strand in 1876, and in the United States in the autumn of that year. The timing of the first performance of the opera was 10.15 p.m. The reason for the late hour of the performance was that it had opened in a triple bill, not only with *La Perichole* but also a farce entitled *Cryptoconchoidsyphonostomata* (not a G & S work), suggestive not so much of musical entertainment as a mental disease brought on by attempting too many crossword puzzles to fill the idle gaps during lengthy technical rehearsals.

Trial By Jury is quite unlike the other G & S operas. It has no overture, but rushes almost straight into a rousing chorus. It has no spoken dialogue at all (although one very brief vocal exchange is usually ad-libbed into the Judge's song) and unlike the other operas, each of which is long enough to provide a full evening's entertainment, it lasts just 40 minutes. The brevity of the opera offers great flexibility for the amateur company, which may decide to stage it merely as an appetiser to be followed by a performance of one of the shorter full-length operas such as *H.M.S. Pinafore*. If so, the more ambitious and limelight-loving soloists may magnanimously leave the modest parts of *Trial By Jury* to the second eleven, congratulating themselves on having the foresight and generosity of spirit to encourage the fostering of new talent amongst the lower echelons of the society. Alternatively, it may be the main event in an evening's programme that could include parlour songs, old-time music-hall favourites, other similar pieces of nostalgia, and the perennial standby, "songs from the shows." Regardless of the exact content of this musical pot-pourri, the company's elite will content themselves with the centre stage in the main event, and then inwardly cringe as inexperienced and aged members alike endeavour to impress unfussy audiences by squawking through ill-chosen items from *The Desert Song* or mounting a bloody assault on *The Holy City*.

The essential humour of *Trial By Jury* is derived from the fact that while the setting and indeed the costumes of the players have all the solemnity, majesty and decorum of a real-life Court of Justice, the trial itself is a farce. The Judge, jury and Usher are patently biased and the legal dispute is argued and resolved in an entirely non-legalistic fashion. A journal entitled *The Athenaeum*, when reviewing the work, commented that "Mr Gilbert's aim has been to ridicule the sentimental influences which in breach of promise cases are sometimes allowed to interfere with the course of justice." The solemnity and decorum are, however, integral features in the work; it has been said that the opera is a genial satirisation of ordinary English character types and institutions. Gilbert was insistent that the principals should not submit to extravagance or caricature, and would-be soloists should pay heed to the words of Rutland Barrington, one of the greatest G & S performers of all time: "On many occasions I have seen it distorted almost out of recognition by artists who insist on being funny." Gilbert, who drilled his soloists and chorus to the very smallest detail, had no time himself for such performers; after one rendition of the opera he remarked: "There is a man in the chorus – a funny man who is the bane of comic opera. He has overacted right through rehearsals, and although I told the jurymen not to make up with wigs etc. he nevertheless took it upon himself to appear last night in a grotesque flaxen wig. He

13

occupies a place in the jury box close to the footlights and is therefore extremely conspicuous. I suggest that he be put in the back row at the end furthest from the stage, then his exaggeration will not be important." This is not a step to be taken lightly; a modern-day producer of an amateur company who is tempted to suggest that something similar be done to a cast member will have to carefully consider that member's standing and influence in the society before making his views known. He will know that at stake is not only his own immediate popularity as producer but his chances of fulfilling a lifetime's ambition by directing the society through its next production of *How To Succeed In Business Without Really Trying*.

The show is a joy for the indolent stage manager, as the scenery and lighting are unchanging throughout. Indeed, the need for special scenery can be dispensed with altogether if it is possible to utilise an appropriately old-fashioned court room for the production, and in fact a number of genuine court houses have been used for performances of the opera. Gilbert, who for a time practised as a barrister himself, had in mind an exact copy of Clerkenwell Sessions House for his original scene. Fortunate chorus members will be cast as bridesmaids with rich satin, lace and bouquets, or jurymen, complete with mutton chop whiskers and checks, or lawyers in traditional wigs and gowns; the less fortunate will be consigned to the ranks of the general public, which in any G & S opera is a splendid catch-all for producers in the lucky position of having a few chorus members too many. Amateur performers who tire of nepotism when principal or chorus roles are cast will derive little comfort from Sullivan, whose brother Fred was given the part of the Judge and who undoubtedly would have gone on to take many more roles in G & S opera but for his untimely death in 1877. Incidentally, Fred was an architect and must have generated more than a few groans when he said that even on stage he was still drawing big houses.

The story of *Trial By Jury* is very straightforward. Angelina, the Plaintiff (soprano), represented by Counsel (tenor or soprano), is suing Edwin, the Defendant (tenor) for breach of promise of marriage. Led on by the Usher (bass-baritone) and Foreman of the Jury (baritone), both the jury and the public are totally on her side. Edwin's defence is that he is a human being whose tastes, likes and dislikes change. He suggests marrying Angelina today and then marrying his new woman on the following day. Counsel objects to this proposal, so instead Edwin suggests that, unpleasant fellow that he is, Angelina would not want him anyway. The Judge (baritone) resolves the problem by offering to marry Angelina himself. She accepts and all ends happily.

14

The show opens with a chorus ("Hark, the hour of ten is sounding") in which the assembled jurymen and members of the public inform the audience of the nature of the court hearing and the parties involved in it. Good diction is therefore essential, since otherwise the audience might be left not understanding what is happening for the rest of the opera. In order to justify his existence if nothing else, the musical director may frequently remind the cast of the necessity for good enunciation, seemingly forgetting that half the audience will have seen the show before and know the story anyway, and the other half will not worry about the plot as long as the tunes are good and the show is over before the pubs close. The Usher then appears, and sings a solo with choral interjections ("Now, jurymen, hear my advice"); he makes it clear that his sympathies lie with the Plaintiff. Much of the humour of the song arises from his continual calling for "Silence in court" which develops into a running theme during the opera, and any Usher sensing an awkward hiatus in some part of the proceedings could well do worse than to fill it with a brusque call for quiet, however subdued the atmosphere happens to be at the time. The Usher's solo leads into the entrance of the villain of the piece, the Defendant Edwin. To his opening recitative "Is this the court of the Exchequer" the chorus are supposed to respond "It is" in perfect unison. However, the crisp reply will often be spoilt by chorus members either omitting to sing anything, or holding on to the "is" long after they should have stopped, apparently unable to interpret correctly the anguished signalling of the conductor. A musical director will not last long with any amateur society if he assumes that, when waving his hands manically in the air, his charges realise that he is conducting them as opposed to attempting to remove a colony of ants from his shirtsleeves. Having announced himself and (in recitative) endeavoured to endear himself to the hostile crowd, the Defendant explains the history of his love life in an aria with chorus ("When first my old, old love I knew"). In early rehearsals, his repeated use of the words "Tink-a-tank" as his refrain will seem meaningless. It will later become clear that he is supposed to be accompanying himself on the guitar and the refrain is an attempt to augment this in words. As the show nears, he may be blessed with a real guitar and offered copious tuition from guitar players within the society, but when the orchestral accompaniment is added he may well still be unable to strum it without producing a succession of cacophonous discords which even Peter Maxwell Davies would dismiss as excessively jarring to the ears. After he has finished, the chorus berate him in fatherly fashion with a brief ensemble section ("Oh, I was like that when a lad"); it finishes not with "Tra-la-la" (although more indolent chorus members may sing this anyway) but the particularly apt "Trial-a-law!" The Usher silences them and in recitative announces the arrival of the Judge. As the Judge enters, the jurymen, lawyers and public hail him in a solemn mock-Handelian chorus ("All hail, great Judge"); graciously, the Judge acknowledges their display of homage and indicates he would like to tell them how he rose to his exalted professional position. In a splendid pastiche of grand opera, Sullivan gives the chorus a full page of music in which they explain to the audience "He'll tell us how he came to be a judge...hush, hush he speaks" whilst the Judge in vain tries to get a word in edgeways. In the end, further cries of "Silence in court" are needed to bring the court to order. As they acclaim the Judge, the chorus sing "May each decree as statute rank, and never be reversed in Banc." "Banc" here means a superior court of the common law, but audiences in northern England with a keen ear and no programme glossary may wonder why or how a judicial decision can come to be reviewed amongst the sophisticated equipment and sleek furnishings of the T.S.B. or the National Westminster.

At last, the Judge can provide his potted autobiography in song, with chorus. The song ("When I, good friends, was called to the Bar, I'd an appetite fresh and hearty") is, when well sung and well acted, one of the gems of the opera, however much its title may to the more waggish amateur opera buffs connote a summons to the food counter of the Dog & Duck to place orders for soup and sausage sandwiches. Every eye of the jurymen should be focused on the Judge as he sings to them about his rise to the judicial heights; when the jurymen echo his words in chorus they should turn gleefully and supportively to each other before, as one, turning attentively to the Judge for the continuance of his orations. Much of the humour in the Judge's song is derived from his recounting to his adoring listeners that he was once guilty of precisely the same conduct which has brought Edwin to court, the unlucky lady being the elderly ugly daughter of a wealthy lawyer. After his words "The rich attorney my character high tried vainly to disparage" it is common for the chorus (or those in the chorus who remember) to cry "No!" This, with the Judge's "He did!" in reply, offers the only spoken words in the opera, although its origin is in the mists of tradition rather than in any of the current vocal scores. The Judge is the first in the line of comic principal parts in the G & S operas which have in more recent times become known as the "John Reed" roles after that D'Oyly Carte stalwart who both on stage and on gramophone has delighted countless G & S enthusiasts. Those who prefer the video to the gramophone will observe Frankie Howerd offering a rather more radical interpretation of the Judge's role, which might lead some amateur performers to believe that it will suffice merely to speak the words rather than be put to the inconvenience of having to learn the music as well.

Counsel for the Plaintiff enters and in a recitative and brief song for Usher and jurymen ("Swear thou the jury") the jury is sworn in; the command by the Usher "Kneel, jurymen, oh, kneel" begs the classic G & S trivia question "Who is the Irish juryman in *Trial By Jury*?" With traditionally exaggerated cries of pain and discomfort the jurymen drop to their knees, perhaps disappearing from view beneath the top of the jury desks. On the syllable "tru" from the words "truly try" a trill is perhaps unwisely written in for the chorus, and amongst less talented groups this may provoke a sound which is more reminiscent of a posse of Tarzan impressionists than a chorus line. After the jury have been sworn, there is a further recitative for Counsel and Usher ("Where is the Plaintiff?") in which Angelina is invited into court, and again the imaginative producer can enjoy creating an echo effect as Angelina is called for by name. The echo was included in an 1884 prompt book and is also mentioned in the vocal score. In D'Oyly Carte productions the Defendant would perform the echo, singing with his back to the audience, but the vocal score suggests it be executed behind the scene; accordingly, there is no reason why it should not be performed by somebody off stage with no other part to play in the show at all. It might, perhaps, be a useful warm-up for the more precious of the male soloists in *H.M.S. Pinafore* which is to follow later in the evening; otherwise it may simply be entrusted to the backstage assistant with the much heavier responsibility of putting the urn on for the cast's interval tea. Whoever does it will have a hard task to imitate exactly the Usher's jump from F above middle C to the F below it, particularly if the Usher chooses to include all the intervening notes and continue down a second octave for good measure, and only too late does the echoer discover that on plumbing the lower reaches of his voice he is actually incapable of hitting the bottom.

The bridesmaids dance in, singing a chorus of acclamation for the Plaintiff ("Comes the broken flower"); Audrey Williamson suggests that they should offer a "sharp decorative contrast to the everyday court atmosphere." They are followed by the Plaintiff who in her solo of introduction ("O'er the season vernal") repeats the music the girls have just sung. The male chorus will be expected to drool lustfully over the glittering array of female talent that is set before them, which will place considerable strain on their acting abilities in more geriatric societies. A nice little piece of comic business is included in the libretto, whereby the Judge, taking a fancy to the First Bridesmaid, writes her a *billet-doux* which she then places in her bosom; when the Plaintiff appears, the Usher is commanded to relieve the First Bridesmaid of the letter and hand it to the Plaintiff who places it in her own bosom. Since the audience will not see the contents of the note, the Judge has free rein to be as suggestive and imaginative as he wishes. Some Judges, anxious enough about remembering their lines and not wanting to upset the producer, will only pretend to write on the paper or endorse it with such anodyne sentiments as "You look lovely." Others will, in a burst of overconfidence, tend to the other extreme with suitably lewd references to bodily endowments. Meanwhile, the would-be wags may make reference to the split in the seat of the trousers worn by the juryman standing second from the left, or enquiry of the Plaintiff as to whether she knows that the gentleman playing the Defendant has just left his wife and has taken up with a dinner lady from Grange Road Comprehensive and her three teenage children.

The Judge expresses his admiration for the Plaintiff in an ensemble section with solos ("Oh, never, never, never"), and the Foreman, on behalf of the jury, echoes these sentiments. The role of the Foreman is not dissimilar to the role of the cymbals player in an orchestra; he has remarkably little to do, and if he is not careful he will find himself coming off the stage at the end of the performance having omitted to do any of it. The jury have another trill to execute on the word "make" as in "would make you ours" thereby providing further incitement to murder by musical director as each member decides for themselves how long the trill should last. Those who remain alive accuse the Defendant of being a monster and threaten substantial damages. The Usher cuts right across the final utterance of the word "damages" so that only "dam" is heard; this is another clever piece of Gilbertian writing which neatly presages the use of the word "damme" in *H.M.S. Pinafore*, written three years later. Incidentally, there is an even smaller part than the Foreman in *Trial By Jury*, namely that of the Associate; he appears in the list of *dramatis personae* and in some editions of the libretto the Judge is directed to address to him his words of admiration for the Plaintiff. His role during the rest of the opera is unclear but with no solo singing it is in obvious role for the tone-deaf performer who for political reasons has to be allocated a named part. Such an expedient is unlikely to be possible in most other G & S shows; if the producer wishes to continue to work with the company he will have to hope that rehearsals and performances of *Trial By Jury* have given him sufficient time to convince the performer of the not inconsiderable attractions of the operatic society in the next town, rivalled only by the joys of backpacking in Outer Mongolia.

With the opera already half over, Counsel for the Plaintiff is only now in a position to make his opening address. Counsel, incidentally, may be played by a man or a woman; since only one major part in the opera is written specifically for a woman, there may be merit in casting a female in that role, notwithstanding the objections from those who point to the paucity of female counsel in 1875. The address, by way of a solo with chorus ("With a sense of deep emotion"), predictably underlines the mental anguish suffered by Angelina as a result of Edwin's callous behaviour. The music for the first two verses of the song is identical, and, as with other G & S songs with repetitious musical material for different words, it is all too easy to transpose the words so that they make no sense whatsoever. Choruses are frequently invited in G & S opera – as they are invited here – to repeat what the soloist has just sung, and the biggest sin a chorus can commit is to sing the correct words back after the soloist has sung the incorrect words. This, of course, will not stop some chorus members doing it all the same.

Angelina, overcome by her advocate's flowery address, begins staggering around the stage; this prompts the Judge to introduce the next (ensemble) number by helpfully singing "That she is reeling is plain to see." Both Foreman and Judge invite her to "recline on me" and with the Plaintiff consequently cuddling up to a Judge who is more amorous than solicitous, the Defendant becomes once more the target for the jury's vitriol. Undeterred, he offers his testimony in the form of a brisk solo, with ladies' chorus ("Oh, gentlemen, listen, I pray"). Of course the Judge will be paying far more attention to the Plaintiff's physical attributes to be listening to what he has to say, and the jury will also ignore him. A nice touch is for the Foreman to distribute some reading material for the jurymen to peruse – provision of copies of *The Beano* may add some humour to the already absurd scene – while the Defendant explains the rationale behind his action. However, ears prick up when he suggests marrying Angelina, as promised, that day, and then on the following day he will marry his current girlfriend or "the other" as he calls her. Another recitative section follows in which the Judge, who is visibly bored by the whole court proceeding, expresses agreement with this suggestion, remarking "that seems a reasonable proposition." Counsel, however, objects, and with a display of grovelling deference – "but I submit, m'Lud, with all submission" – describes marrying two wives at once as Burglaree. Some producers may substitute the word "Bigamee" which makes rather more sense. Counsel then refers to legal authority for his submission, and will certainly generate a smile by producing a very old, very thick, leatherbound dust-covered book, and making great play of clearing his throat and blowing off the dust before pronouncing it to be a "rather serious crime" to marry two wives at a time. There follows a big ensemble number ("A nice dilemma") in which all in the court room reflect on the

19

apparent impasse that has been reached. Theoretically, this is G & S at its best; a topsy-turvy situation but with the musical complexity of a grand opera chorus. The different opinions as to the desired outcome are reflected in awesome counterpoint until suddenly there gushes forth a succession of block chords, sung *fortissimo* in ten-part harmony. When sung well, this ranks as one of the highlights of the production. Unfortunately, it is all too easy to sing it extremely badly; the chorus may be simply unable to cope with Sullivan's contrapuntal niceties, particularly the syncopated rhythms. Musical directors will encourage choruses faced with syncopations to sniff on the silent downbeats: "Sniff-a nice sniff-dilem-sniff-ma we-sniff-have here-sniff-a nice-sniff-dilem..." and so on. In winter, when snivelly colds are abundant, such a technique could actually be particularly useful in curbing nose-blowings and other mucous outpourings.

It is now time for Angelina to turn on the charm, and in a duet with the Defendant, followed by a chorus ("I love him, I love him"), she tries to make out that his brutish behaviour has not blighted her affection for him. Edwin replies that he is a smoker, a drinker and disposed to domestic violence, all of which, he says, makes him a totally unsuitable husband for her. An 1884 direction suggests that the jury should either disappear or be engaged in other activity as he sings. In a sequence which combines recitative and chorus ("The question, gentlemen") the Judge suggests that Edwin should be given a few drinks so the effect of liquor on him can be accurately gauged, a suggestion with which Edwin is quite agreeable. Inevitably, Counsel voices strong objections on the Plaintiff's behalf. The Judge however has no intention of prolonging the trial and commands the lawyers to set off for home, while the poor Usher is invited, by the exigencies of rhyme, to set off to "Russher." At the same time the Judge picks up all the books and papers on his desk and tosses them indiscriminately about the stage. Care is of course needed when taking this step, not merely because a badly-aimed legal tome may decapitate the second violin, but because the separation of a book from its austere brown-paper cover may reveal that it is not Queens Bench Reports 1870 but rather the less legally helpful Super Value Book Club edition of the collected works of Danielle Steel.

Once his desk is bereft of reading material, the Judge will invite the lawyers to put their briefs upon the shelf – non-lawyers in the cast or audience may regard this as a strange place to deposit their underwear – then proposes his own solution by way of an offer of marriage to the Plaintiff. With barely two minutes of running time of the opera to go, it would be a most unreasonable Plaintiff who refused such an offer, and as the Judge leaves the Bench and comes down to the floor of the court, she is happy to accept his warm embrace. The ensemble finale ("Oh, joy unbounded") follows immediately; the opera ends with a reprise of the final section of the Judge's song, the company expressing admiration for the Judge who in turn provides Edwin with a financial reward for effectively giving Angelina up to him. Everyone seems happy; everyone, that is, save the stage manager whose eye may rest on at least one edition of the lyrics and see "JUDGE and PLAINTIFF dance back on to the Bench – the BRIDESMAIDS take the eight garlands of roses from behind the Judge's desk (where one end of them is fastened) and draw them across floor of Court, so that they radiate from the desk. Two plaster Cupids in bar wigs descend from flies. Red fire." In fact, following the discontinuance of these directions by the D'Oyly Carte Opera Company in the 1920's they are rarely, if ever, followed today. The original "trick change" was even more elaborate – "At the last 'And a good Judge too' the gong is struck for the quick change to Fairyland. The canopy revolves. The fan pieces behind the Judge fall. Two revolving pieces on either side of the Judge come round. The rise comes up and covers bench front. The Judge's Associate's desks open, the chamber flats are taken away and wings pushed on. Cloth in front of benches and jury box are let down and masking for same pushed on. Red fire." And only a twenty-minute interval afterwards to rig up *H.M.S. Pinafore*.

"He's much better at his lines on the prompt's bingo night"

2 THE ROLLICKING, ROLLICKING BUN

It was only natural that after the success of *Trial By Jury* Richard D'Oyly Carte should wish to tempt Gilbert and Sullivan to collaborate on a further work. Gilbert would only consider this if money were available up front. As a result, Carte sought and fortunately managed to find four backers for a Comedy Opera Company which was established in 1876. Assured of ready money, Gilbert and Sullivan began work on a new opera based on Gilbert's story *An Elixir of Love*. This was in fact a burlesque on Donizetti's opera *L'Elisir D'Amore* in which a magic love potion was distributed, with interesting results. The new work by Gilbert and Sullivan was to be known as *The Sorcerer*. It opened on 17th November 1877 in a double bill with *Dora's Dream* (not a G & S work) at the Opera Comique, which Carte had hired as his new company's first home. It was hardly the most prestigious venue. The theatre itself was approached by an underground passage, and the wall at the back of the stage was a party wall with the Globe Theatre next door. Those who took part in, or witnessed, early performances of *The Sorcerer* there would doubtless sympathise with those who, a century later, must rehearse and sometimes perform G & S opera in overbooked halls, not knowing on any one night whether the noise in the next room will emanate from the village youth club games evening or the Parents and Friends of St Cuthbert's Under Fives Group's quarterly discotheque and fish-and-chip supper.

The Sorcerer is the earliest surviving full-length G & S opera with dialogue, and Leslie Baily describes it as a "solid base on which Gilbert and Sullivan were to build their castles of fantasy for the next twenty years." It is still considerably briefer than other G & S works, and a double bill with *Trial By Jury* is certainly feasible. The trivia buff may care to note that it is the only full-length G & S opera not to be blessed with an alternative title. As with *Trial By Jury* the plot hardly requires the brain of an Einstein to untangle. It could be described simply as a sequence of results from a single premise and anyone who comes to this show after reading a   John Le Carre novel will experience the same feeling as Charles Blondin might encounter if, having crossed the Niagara Falls by tightrope, he were asked to traverse the London to Southend railway line by means of the footbridge outside Gidea Park.

Perhaps what is most interesting about *The Sorcerer* from a historical perspective is that one sees Gilbert beginning to establish certain character types which would recur in subsequent operas. He made a policy of engaging actors who he felt could play these types successfully, and would then transfer each type to the next opera. There was no room for overacting or forced humour; Gilbert firmly believed that the humour was already there, and would emerge through the characters believing throughout in the "perfect sincerity of their words and actions." Starting as he did from scratch, Gilbert could afford himself the luxury of engaging only people who would not spoil the ensemble by self-assertion. One is tempted to ask whether any G & S producer since Gilbert has been quite so fortunate. For the part of John Wellington Wells, the Sorcerer himself, Gilbert did not want a current star; he required a man who could articulate his words with great precision and clarity. Bypassing established professional singers, he took on a young man named George Grossmith. Grossmith, a former Bow Street press reporter, went on to take almost all the comic baritone roles in subsequent G & S operas. For the secondary comic role, Dr Daly, Gilbert chose Rutland Barrington, who slotted in as another, albeit lesser, comic baritone figure. When surprise was expressed that this inexperienced and virtually unknown actor had been cast in the role, Gilbert replied "He's a staid, stolid swine, and that's what I want."

Audience numbers varied from one performance to the next; the backers blew hot and cold, glowing with enthusiasm for a possible further opera when houses were good, and threatening the cast with the sack if the houses were poor. The show's initial run was 175 performances, finishing in May 1878 after three months of declining audiences. It was revived, with a number of changes, in 1884 for a 150-performance run, and was regularly performed by the D'Oyly Carte Company until the outbreak of the Second World War. Following the wartime destruction of the scenery and costumes used in *The Sorcerer*, the Company did not stage it again until 1971, and performed it only spasmodically until its closure in 1982. It has never enjoyed much success in the States. Rather like *Patience* and *Ruddigore, The Sorcerer* is one of those G & S operas which rely, for regular airings, on specialist G & S societies which aim to keep the operas going more or less in rotation, rather than societies which mix G & S with non-G & S works and whose concern is to produce money-spinners. The G & S enthusiast within the latter category will shoot his hand ceilingwards at show selection meetings and point to the fact that "we haven't done *The Sorcerer* since 1968 and it's got some lovely tunes in it." The hard-nosed society treasurer will immediately respond that that show in 1968 was in real terms the least successful show in the society's history with a matinee audience of precisely ten people, three of whom were asleep before page eight. Five minutes later, the meeting will have resolved to stage *The Mikado* for the fourth time in the past thirteen years; this will be especially convenient for the producer, who has long wanted to stage *The Mikado* in an Icelandic setting, and equally useful for the assistant secretary who suddenly remembers that the genuine Samurai swords borrowed from the town museum for the previous production may still be sitting in his old golf bag in the cupboard under the stairs.

The story can be summarised briefly. Alexis Pointdextre (tenor) is betrothed to Aline Sangazure (soprano) and wishes all his fellow inhabitants of the village of Ploverleigh to enjoy similar happiness by falling in love. He engages the services of a Sorcerer, John Wellington Wells (baritone), to concoct a love-potion which when tasted will cause the taster to fall in love with the first person of the opposite sex whom he or she sees, providing that person has also tasted the potion, and the love will instantly be returned. Unfortunately things do not work out as planned. Alexis' father, the exalted Sir Marmaduke (bass), in love with Aline's mother Lady Sangazure (contralto), falls in love instead with lowly Mrs Partlet, the pew-opener (mezzo-soprano). Mrs Partlet's daughter Constance (soprano), herself in love with Dr Daly, the vicar (baritone), finds herself thrown together with the stone-deaf Notary (bass). Lady Sangazure acquires a sudden passion for the horrified Mr Wells, and worst of all, Aline becomes besotted with Dr Daly. Only Mr Wells' disappearance into the hands of Ahrimanes, the personification of evil, can undo the effects of the potion. Mr Wells duly obliges, and all are united with their real loves.

The curtain opens with a view of Sir Marmaduke's Elizabethan mansion in Ploverleigh, where the villagers are seen making merry. The action begins with a joyful chorus ("Ring forth, ye bells") which helpfully explains the cause of their revelry, namely the betrothal of Alexis to Aline. The setting could hardly be more homely, with no indication of the black magic that is to come. Charles Hayter describes the scene as "jollily English," with the village's gentry and peasant folk all enjoying the scene. What is required, Audrey Williamson asserts, is "a bright blend of colour, patterned movement, dances where required, the general effect of a country estate in summer and rural festivity." All but one of the G & S operas begin with a chorus which in many ways is very convenient. When rehearsals reach the run-through stage the producer can rely on at least a few chorus members arriving at rehearsal on time, thereby allowing him to make some semblance of a start. At the performance itself, the soloist with delusions of grandeur, who believes that the audience has come to listen to him and nobody else, can instruct the chorus to "Warm the audience up for me, will you;" he will be seemingly oblivious of the fact that hardened chorus members will be grateful if there is an audience of any kind, whatever their temperature. Best of all, a loud full-blooded chorus number can mask the noise made by late audience arrivals. Of course, many professional theatres do make it a rule that no latecoming audience member can be admitted until "a suitable break occurs" which may be anything from 10 minutes to the first interval. Front-of-house staff in amateur productions may be more willing to allow any tardy customer to clomp noisily into the auditorium, either through unawareness of how much importance or influence within the society or local community the late arrival may possess, or in an anxious attempt to convey quickly to the cast that there really are more people in the audience than there are on stage.

The chorus exit, and Mrs Partlet appears with her daughter. Mrs Partlet's occupation, that of pew-opener, might foil the contestants on *What's My Line* but gives the audience a clue as to her humble status in the village community. Following solicitous enquiry in recitative ("Constance, my daughter") Constance tells of her love for the vicar, Dr Daly, in a solo ("When he is here"), and then in dialogue. The vicar is not directed to enter until the dialogue has finished, but thoughtful producers will, at Constance's words "Hush mother! He is here!" allow him to proceed along the back of the stage by bicycle. This of course presupposes that a suitably antiquated machine is available, that there is sufficient room for the rider to mount it in the wings and begin pedalling before the front wheel comes into view, and that the brakes are functioning. Failure to stop the machine in time may result in a collision with Alexis, waiting to come on stage, and a black tyre mark being irrevocably imprinted upon his clothing, causing serious damage to the tenor's credibility and confidence, to say nothing of his immaculate cream-coloured jodhpurs.

Dr Daly is the only clergyman to play a significant part in a G & S opera (The Archbishop of Titipu is just *one* of Pooh-Bah's many titles in *The Mikado*!). Dr Daly was the only clergyman for whom Gilbert **dared** to write a major part in any of the operas; he would have been well aware of the potential hostility to introducing a man of the cloth into a comic opera. Lewis Carroll was one noted objector. However, Dr Daly's opening recitative ("The air is charged") and subsequent song, in which he reflects on his former popularity and eligibility ("Time was when love and I"), establish him as a thoughtful but very likeable character, without the buffoonery or chicanery which characterises many of the other G & S baritone roles. His entrance is accompanied by pastoral birdsong in the orchestra, and all his subsequent music and dialogue indicate that his character should be portrayed as a homely sympathetic individual, and certainly not as a "silly ass." In his ensuing dialogue with Mrs Partlet he raises the hopes of Constance by saying he looks forward to "marrying her myself" and then dashes those hopes by continuing, after a discreet pause, "to some strapping fellow in her own rank of life." Like any "dramatic pause" in G & S opera, the pause needs to be long enough to excite Constance, but not so long that the audience think he has forgotten the next line and the prompt feels obliged to add her dulcet tones to the proceedings. Fits of amnesia are not unknown in even the most professional production. How the forgetful thespian extracts himself from the difficulty depends to a degree on his own unflappability and capability for repartee, but also to a degree on the composition of the audience and personality of the producer. In some productions, a simple enjoinment to the other performers, "You carry on, I'll come in when I remember what the hell I'm supposed to be saying" will achieve the biggest laugh of the evening and add to the jocundity of the after-show drinking session. With other productions, such humour will be sadly misplaced, and the reproachful stares that attend him as he stands in the queue for the washbasin afterwards provide as good an indication as any that his best chance of getting even a small role next year is in the High Street bakery.

The disappointed Constance exits with her mother, who promises that they will "try again" at a more fitting time. Dr Daly soliloquises briefly, suggesting that he does in fact have more than a passing fancy for Constance. At that moment, however, Sir Marmaduke Pointdextre appears with his son Alexis. After a brief recitative ("Sir Marmaduke – my dear young friend Alexis") in which Dr Daly offers his congratulations, Dr Daly extends further good wishes in an absurdly polite conversation with Sir Marmaduke, to a background of solemn music in mock-Purcellian style. After Dr Daly leaves, Sir Marmaduke and Alexis talk together, Alexis informing his father that he is "welling over with limpid joy; no sicklying taint of sorrow overlies the lucid lake of liquid love on which, hand in hand, Aline and I are to drift into eternity." One suspects that Gilbert, who was more cynical than most in matters appertaining to love, had his tongue firmly in his cheek when writing these lines, and the modern Alexis may find his audience either chuckling at their oversentimentality, or reaching for the nearest convenient sickbag. Sir Marmaduke, far from feeling queasy, is shocked; he reminds his son that he (Sir Marmaduke) was once in love with Lady Sangazure, the future mother-in-law of Alexis, but conventions of their society precluded their expressing their love as vivaciously as they might have liked. Both he and Alexis leave the stage. Alexis, incidentally, is a member of the Grenadier Guards, and indeed *The Sorcerer* is not the only G & S opera in which at least one guardsman makes an appearance. Any soloist with aspirations to play the part of Alexis and also that of the Duke, Colonel or Major in *Patience*, Private Willis in *Iolanthe* and Fitzbattleaxe in *Utopia Limited* should seriously consider investing in a custom-made guardsman's uniform. Failure to do so may be regretted as the soloist ambles on to the stage with a red tunic which reaches to the knee, and a sword belt which is so loose that the sword when released trails along the ground and creates an interesting new floor pattern on the Town Hall stage. Worse still are ill-fitting boots, which whilst enhancing the authority and manliness of the wearer give him at the same time the gracefulness and pedal finesse of a drunken baboon.

Aline now appears, together with an admiring female chorus, and after her pleasant ballad of rejoicing over her forthcoming nuptials ("Oh, happy young heart") she is joined on stage by her mother who in a brief recitative ("My child, I join") hints at her own disappointment in love. She is described as a "lady of ancient lineage" and is the first, and perhaps the most benign, of that formidable Gilbertian type, the elderly lovesick contralto. Hers is also the only major solo role in a G & S opera other than *Trial By Jury* to contain no spoken dialogue. Following her recitative, the brigade of yokels march on and acclaim Alexis who himself enters and embraces Aline. There is a short recitative for them both ("Oh, my adored one") after which they withdraw from centre stage, allowing Sir Marmaduke to reappear. He and Lady Sangazure then sing a duet expressing their love for each other ("Welcome joy, adieu to sadness"). The couple, in keeping with the strict rules of etiquette in which they have been brought up, sing to each other with perfect decorum and politeness, the gavotte-style music reflecting the old-fashioned gentility which both characters affect to project. It is only in asides that they frantically declaim their own true feelings, which are far wilder and more passionate than they would dare to express openly. Assuming that any damage done by Dr Daly's bicycle has been cleared up, another challenge now awaits the production team. It is time for the sealing and signing of the marriage contract. The Notary enters and in his song, with chorus ("All is prepared"), he invites the signatories Alexis and Aline to approach the table. Sullivan allows the table-carriers just three bars of music, before the singing begins, to put the table in position; if the table is not in place by the time the Notary opens his mouth, the song is a nonsense. Inevitably the technical rehearsal for a production will reveal that the transporting of any object on to the stage takes far longer than supposed in earlier practices, and if the table is a particularly cumbersome one the signatories may find themselves approaching not the table but fresh air. Alexis and Aline duly sign the contract amidst further mock-Handelian music which would not seem out of place in a wedding service. Much of the wedding and indeed non-wedding music of G & S is indeed eminently suitable for real-life marriage ceremonies involving members of amateur societies. "Bridegroom and bride" and "When a merry maiden marries" from *The Gondoliers* will, for example, be more than acceptable before, during or after the ceremony. However, some G & S choruses demand more careful examination before being deployed in this way. One such example is the opening chorus in *The Grand Duke* which begins promisingly enough ("Won't it be a pretty wedding") but continues with the comment that "her bouquet is simply frightful" and finishes less than optimistically: "Man and maid, for aye united, till divorce or death shall part them!"

The Notary's song leads on into an exuberant chorus in which the villagers acclaim the couple, Sullivan cleverly combining the men's earlier chorus of acclamation for Alexis, and the girls' earlier chorus for Aline. Everybody, plus table, then leaves the stage save the young lovers, the yokels perhaps providing an arch of pitchforks to honour their prospective union. In the ensuing dialogue and song ("Love feeds on every kind of food") Alexis speaks and sings gushingly of the benefits which love and marriage may bring to those of every social class, but does so in a pompous and pious manner which does little to endear him to the audience or, one would have thought, his betrothed. He then announces that he has engaged the services of J.W. Wells & Co, a firm of Family Sorcerers which has invented a love-potion, the effect of which will be to enable all its samplers to "learn the secret of pure and lasting happiness" through falling in love. Brushing aside Aline's objections, he calls to a Page named Hercules to fetch Mr Wells himself. In early productions of the opera this part was played by a young Henry Lytton, who went on to become one of the great G & S performers of his time; it is still traditional today for the part to be played by a small boy who thereby may receive his first taste of amateur operatics. Whether the experience of going along to a meeting of an amateur G & S company for the first time is pleasurable or hateful will of course depend on the personality of the society and the individual. Some societies, in an effort to extend the hand of welcome to anybody under the age of 85, will be so effusive in their greeting that by the end of the evening the new recruit will not only have successfully auditioned for the society with the first two lines of the National Anthem, but will have been stood two rounds in the Red Lion, paid £5 for next week's pub skittles night, parted with £20 for next month's annual dinner dance, and will have agreed to join the set-painting team starting with an eight o'clock session on Sunday morning in a barn thirteen miles and two muddy fields away. By contrast, the unlucky would-be new recruit may be plonked anonymously in a chair, forced to share a copy of the score with an unwilling neighbour, and then during the coffee break stand impotently in a corner of the room, the indifference of the established members towards him convincing him that he must have trodden in something unpleasant on his way in.

The Sorcerer himself, full name John Wellington Wells, now appears. He is described by Alan Jefferson as possessing a "lively cheapjack manner which endears him to the audience" and it is traditional for him to have a Cockney accent; moreover, modern players of the role may seek to emulate the adult Henry Lytton in his portrayal of Mr Wells, and don a bald wig and mutton chop whiskers for the part. By way of introducing himself and his sinister wares, Mr Wells immediately delivers a long speech and possibly the hardest patter song in the entire G & S repertoire ("My name is John Wellington Wells"). Whilst the Lord Chancellor's Nightmare Song in *Iolanthe* tells a story of sorts, and has become such a classic that even non-devotees of G & S can probably recall some of the words, Mr Wells' song is a veritable jumble of unrelated phrases and ideas. (One phrase which does appear more than once is the address of Mr Wells' business, namely "Seventy Simmery Axe." It sounds an unlikely address, and indeed it is, for the "Simmery" is actually shorthand for "St Mary.") The patter song, requiring the singer to get his tongue round a great many words to be sung often at high speed, became one of the hallmarks of the Grossmith roles. A musical director with a grudge against the actor playing the role in a modern performance can render the song almost impossible to sing by beginning with an overenthusiastic tempo. Nonetheless, providing some words are spewed into the public arena, and the little orchestral interludes are spiced with some fancy footwork, the performer is guaranteed to receive rapturous applause. In the ensuing dialogue, Mr Wells then extols the wonders of his product. He states that any drinker of it will lose consciousness for a period of 12 hours then on waking will fall in love with the first lady he meets who has also tasted it, and his affection will be at once returned. Moreover it is compounded on the strictest principles; it has no effect on married people at all. Having obtained a teapot into which the potion will be poured, Alexis agrees to buy sufficient quantities of the potion to affect the whole village. He is able to obtain a substantial discount through his membership of the Army & Navy Stores; it would be a pity if the producer did not either alternatively or in addition allow him the luxury of an American Express Gold Card. Mr Wells' inevitable "That'll do nicely" in reply will surely raise a few laughs from the audience, unless of course they recall the same two actors perform an identical exchange in last year's production of *The Mikado*, and, indeed, every performance of *The Sorcerer* and *The Mikado* since the dreaded advertising slogan was born.

After suitable words of warning, Mr Wells then proceeds with the Incantation during which, to suitably tense music ("Sprites of earth and air") for the three principals and chorus, the potion will be charged with the magic powers that are required to produce the desired effect. If cleverly done, this scene is not for the faint-hearted. It is the only G & S scene where pyrotechnics on any scale are called for. The stage will darken, loud flashes and bangs will startle the audience, and demonic figures will enter and race menacingly round the stage. Children may be enlisted to play the parts of demons, their nimble feet and piercing screams being regarded as more conducive to the atmosphere of tension and uncertainty than a cluster of ageing troubadours whose biggest contact hitherto with the forces of demonry has been a flutter on the Derby. Audrey Williamson writes that "expert collaboration of the stage electricians, and some imaginative feeling for lighting" are required. Unfortunately, the fates may conspire not only against the calm of Ploverleigh but the blood pressure of the production team. Since it is unlikely that the musical director will wish to entrust the chorus parts solely to the on-stage juvenile demons, some singing from the off-stage adult chorus, out of sight of the conductor's baton, could be necessary. The result may be that hours of disciplined rehearsal disintegrate into a veritable Babel of late entries, aggravated by feeble attempts of half a dozen would-be conductors in the chorus to get fellow singers to follow their various beats. It is possible that explosive effects will require licences; helpful warning signs may be posted indicating that explosions will occur during the production, which could result in those of a nervous disposition spending much of the show with their ears permanently blocked. It is only when the show finishes without the mildest bang that it is revealed that one of the demons tripped over the wiring and disconnected it before the performance even started. Alternatively, the effects may be of such magnitude that the fire alarms and/or smoke alarms will scream into action, and the audience, instead of quivering before Mr Wells' mastery of the forces of Satanic darkness, will be standing shivering in the car park outside.

With the contents of the teapot duly charged, the tension eases, although an enthusiastic reception is guaranteed for the performer who can imitate Grossmith's "squatter's run" by chugging backwards round the stage holding the teapot and making a noise like a railway engine. The stage is

31

lit once more and the villagers reappear to begin the feast in honour of the betrothed couple. A lively chorus ("Now to the banquet we press") is in fact the start of the Act 1 finale. The conveyance of both food and crockery on to the stage may pose even greater logistical demands than those presented by the conveyance of the Notary's table earlier on in the Act. Nonetheless, performers will be delighted to tuck into all the culinary delights which the chorus proclaim in song, from muffins and toast to mustard and cress. One of the foods mentioned is a type of teacake called the "gay Sally Lunn," a lady who, like Juryman O'Neill, could form the basis of any number of trick questions to enliven a G & S quiz night. Another comestible which is serenaded is the "rollicking, rollicking bun," which sounds appetising enough but is a potentially lethal banana skin for those prone to spoonerisms. The timescale available for the chorus to enjoy the food is seriously limited, and certainly not long enough for those who have dashed to the theatre from work, with no time in the interim for anything but an individual apricot pie.

It is of course at the feast that the villagers will drink the tea that is laced with Mr Wells' potion. Dr Daly is designated tea-maker, and the villagers join in a Teacup Brindisi, or toast, before enjoying the fateful brew. Two considerations now come into play which will tax the producer's nerve endings still further. The first is to ensure that the teacups are collected without delay and without breakage after their contents have been consumed. In most productions these contents will be merely notional. Indeed, assuming a chorus of thirty and a teapot capable of holding ten cupfuls, that is only to be expected, and only the most puristic of spectators will be put out when he sees a serving wench pouring what is quite obviously non-existent liquid from a pot which is quite obviously empty. The reason for the prompt collection of crockery is that as Alexis and Aline sing a sentimental duet ("Oh love, true love") the effects of the laced tea begin to be felt, and in the final ensemble section ("Oh, marvellous illusion") all the tea drinkers (i.e. everybody save Alexis, Aline and Mr Wells) fall to the ground. This presents the second difficulty for the producer, which is to ensure that each person lands in such a way as to guarantee proximity to their post-potion partner. Incidentally, it may be noted that as the potion begins to take hold on them, the performers are instructed by the stage directions to "stagger about the stage as if under the influence of a narcotic." Cynical producers may feel this is simply another way of saying "Carry on as you were."

Act 2 takes place on the same spot 12 hours later, at midnight. Alexis, Aline and Mr Wells enter to find all the tea drinkers slumbering; it will hopefully not be asking too much to expect that they will have remembered where they finished Act 1 and repositioned themselves accordingly after their interval tipples. In a trio ("Tis twelve, I think") they look forward to the time, now imminent, when the full effects of the potion will manifest themselves, while Mr Wells explains that Sir Marmaduke, Dr Daly, the Notary and Lady Sangazure have been respectably put to bed.

As the trio sing and then exit, the villagers begin to awaken and sing a chorus thick with suddenly-adopted West Country accents ("Why, where be oi, and what be oi a doin'?") in which they first express bewilderment and then all the symptoms of having fallen in love with their somnolent neighbours. Intriguingly, all of the villagers – at least, all of those on the set – appear to be unmarried, for the potion has worked its spell on each one of them. In a boisterous dance, the villagers enjoy cavorting with their new partners. The more unfortunate pairings which the potion has provoked is to be a running (and some might say, rather laboured) theme throughout the second Act and will eventually backfire on Alexis, its instigator. To begin with, Constance tearfully enters, escorted by the ancient Notary. In a waltz song, with chorus, immediately following the dance ("Dear friends, take pity on my lot"), she bemoans her unhappy situation – hardly what the potion manufacturers could have had in mind! – which is compounded by the fact that her new lover is very deaf and can hardly make out a word of what she is saying. A nice touch is for the Notary, who carries an ear-trumpet, to hobble feebly round the stage seeking clarification of his changed circumstances from any chorus member who can give it, with an exasperated Constance on his arm. Alexis however, notices nothing amiss, and in his ensuing recitative and chorus ("Oh joy, oh joy, the charm works well") he and the company rejoice over the effects of the potion. All but Alexis and Aline leave the scene. In dialogue, Alexis continues to speak highly of "the good that will become of these ill-assorted unions," and one suspects that Gilbert had more than the ghost of an ironic smile on his face when he wrote Alexis' line "The young and lively spouse will cheer the declining days of her aged partner with comic songs unceasing." It is inevitable that Sullivan's singable and memorable tunes will remain in the performer's mind long after he has left the rehearsal hall or theatre, and those non-devotees with whom he or she lives may well be subjected to frequent renditions of them. This may be tolerable in short bursts or if, on the basis that the spouse or cohabitee is aspiring to be canonised, he or she has rashly agreed to test the performer on his lines. It may be less bearable in the middle of a four-mile tailback on the M62 or as a means of gauging cooking time for soft-boiled eggs.

Alexis tells Aline that in order to ensure his (never mind her!) complete happiness, he and his beloved should drink the potion themselves so that they may be assured of each other's love for ever. Upon Aline's refusal to do this, Alexis expresses his petulant disappointment in his second big solo number ("Thou hast the power thy vaunted love"). This number, like others in the opera, is in fact a typical Victorian drawing-room ballad the like of which would have been heard at many musical evenings. The lyrics are both poetic and dramatic, with music that calls upon the tenor to show off his full vocal range. After the song, Dr Daly appears in a state of some sadness; although one assumes that he has taken the potion, he announces that all the villagers have found partners, and nobody is left for him. Sir Marmaduke, by contrast, has found a partner; it is not Lady Sangazure but rather the humble Mrs Partlet. She informs Alexis that socially she is not "heverythink" that could be desired, but she can confer on his father a "true, tender and lovin' `art." Although he accepts the situation, Alexis is clearly unimpressed, but Aline and Dr Daly remind Sir Marmaduke that her penchant for personal cleanliness is much more important than beauty. This conversation leads neatly into one of the loveliest musical numbers in the opera, a quintet in which all express delight for the couple ("I rejoice that it's decided"); there is a solo verse for each and then an unaccompanied ensemble refrain in madrigal style, with some exquisite harmonisation. Blendability is therefore essential. The sublimeness of the music is neatly offset against the vaguely ridiculous lyrics: "She will tend him, nurse him, mend him, air his linen, dry his tears." Everybody then exits and Mr Wells appears. He begins with a solo in which he laments the difficulties his magic-making has caused ("Oh, I have wrought much evil with my spells"); the solo becomes a duet when Lady Sangazure appears. Horrified, he realises that she – having taken the potion – is going to fall in love with him (even though one infers that he himself has not tasted it) and in the hilarious sequence that follows he attempts to ward off her advances, initially by talking about his disgusting habits and then by telling her of a (non-existent) fiancee of exquisite beauty. She is overcome with anguish to be told that the girl has "light brown hair" whilst her own is "as white as snow." Modern-day audiences and performers with a liking for a *double-entendre* will enjoy a chuckle at the lines "Hate me! I drop my H's - have through life!" "Love me! I'll drop them too!" Later, Mr Wells makes reference to his frequenting One Tree Hill and (to achieve a suitable rhyme) Rosherville, and it would be a churlish producer who did not allow these locations, meaningless to most of today's audiences (One Tree Hill was located in London, Rosherville was a pleasure garden in Kent), to be altered to something more local or topical. Even if no locations which rhyme with "Hill" spring to mind, a dutiful laugh might be raised amongst audiences by Mr Wells singing "Hate me! I like to watch *The Bill*!"

After a spirited exit by Mr Wells, with a devastated Lady Sangazure in hot pursuit, the tempo and the hilarity subside as Aline enters. In a recitative ("Alexis! Doubt me not") she decides to drink the potion in response to the command of her beloved, and then does so, reflecting on her selflessness in a brief aria ("The fearful deed is done"). Dr Daly then enters, accompanying himself on the flageolet; ideally he should not need the support of an instrument in the orchestra, but should it be necessary, it is all the more important that his lips and fingers should move in time with it. In another charming but sorrowful solo ("Oh, my voice is sad and low") he glumly reflects that "every maiden in the village is engaged to So-and-so." Since both he and Aline have taken the potion, his entrance could not be more untimely; Aline immediately falls in love with him and they sing a joyful love duet ("Oh, joyous boon"). Just as it is curious that Lady Sangazure should fall in love with Mr Wells, who has not tasted the potion, the audience may be puzzled that what has taken twelve hours to work on Aline's fellow villagers should for the heroine be effective in just a couple of pages of vocal score. Alexis appears and begins a powerful musical sequence, in the style of grand opera, with a recitative ("Aline, my only love"). He is delighted to see that Aline has tasted the potion, but his delight turns to anger when he sees the result it has produced. In duet, Aline and Dr Daly try to reason with him; his response is firstly to spurn Aline, conveniently forgetting that it was entirely at his behest that she consumed the potion, and secondly to summon all the villagers so that they may know of her perfidious behaviour. The full company appear and in a dramatic chorus demand to know what is going on. In recitative ("Prepare for sad surprises") Alexis informs the villagers what has happened, and is on the point of placing a curse on Aline when Dr Daly interposes. In dialogue the vicar explains the circumstances to Alexis in such reasonable and conciliatory terms – he offers to bury his sorrow "in the congenial gloom of a Colonial Bishopric" – that Alexis at last is shamed into accepting that his scheme has been a disaster. Mr Wells tells them the only way of getting rid of the effects of the potion is either for him or Alexis to yield up his life to Ahrimanes. Helpful programme notes will explain that this individual is the personification of evil in Persian theology, the spiritual enemy of mankind and in eternal conflict with Ormuzd, the angel of light and goodness, but those with neither notes nor a grounding in such matters may still be forgiven for wondering if it is not in fact the latest foreign outlet to acquire a site on the out-of-town retail park.

Mr Wells reasonably states that it would cause his professional colleagues some inconvenience if he were to make the supreme sacrifice, and Alexis properly offers to do so instead. Aline, however, complains that this would leave her without a love to be restored to. The situation seems to be deadlocked, so in a recitative which starts off the Act 2 finale ("Or he or I must die") Mr Wells elects to leave the decision to the villagers. They are unanimous in the belief that he should be the one to yield his life, and accordingly he withdraws to a trapdoor to prepare for his descent to the forces of evil. It seems somewhat unjust and unfortunate a fate for an honest Cockney tradesman who was only carrying out the wishes of one of the villagers; no other principal character in the G & S operas is consigned to such a miserable end, even in the tragic finale to *The Yeomen Of The Guard*, where the pathos, almost completely absent here, is acute. A gong sound is the cue for the company to leave their present partners and rejoin their old lovers, with Constance joining Dr Daly, Sir Marmaduke pairing with Lady Sangazure, the Notary going to Mrs Partlet and of course Alexis linking with Aline. The chorus also waste no time in making a corresponding change. Indeed, the ease with which everybody finds partners makes one wonder whether the potion was really necessary at all. The musical finale, a straight reprise of "Now to the banquet we press" is a simple but jolly end to the opera. There is still time, however, for one more piece of pyrotechnics and a further headache for the stage crew, namely the release of Mr Wells through the trapdoor amid red fire. Cautious producers will simply ask for a blackout, a flash and perhaps a couple of rolls of thunder from the sound effects team, with just Mr Wells' hat left on stage when the lights come up again; the blackout must of course be long enough to give the actor sufficient time to hurry off by means of a side exit. Those not already exhausted by the demands of the Incantation scene will endeavour to create a realistic impression of Mr Wells disappearing through the trapdoor into a blanket of smoke and brimstone. They will be unlucky if the trapdoor gets stuck, thus prompting an exultant cry, an echo from the days of Henry Lytton, that hell is now full. Any producer for whom the Incantation scene has also misfired will doubtless believe he is already there.

The St George Flag effect on the good ship Pinafore
was slightly marred when Denis forgot his red hankie
and was forced to improvise

H.M.S. Pinafore, the third surviving G & S opera, is the earliest full-length opera to be produced by the partnership which continues to enjoy success today. It seemed from the start that Gilbert was confident that the work would do well. It was just after Christmas 1877 that he sent Sullivan the sketch of his proposed work, having "very little doubt" that Sullivan would be pleased. He would surely also have been in no doubt that the British people, being an island race with a proud naval history, would warm to an opera with a seafaring theme and set on the deck of a Portsmouth-based warship. In keeping with the best naval tradition, rehearsals were organised with ruthless efficiency and painstaking attention to detail; amateur performers who dread the late-night technical or dress rehearsal might like to note that Gilbert was at the theatre until 3.30 a.m. following the dress rehearsal – and then went to his club for supper.

There is a considerable dose of satire in the opera, although it is magnificent entertainment value in itself. Rather as he had done in *The Sorcerer*, Gilbert poked fun at those who believed that absolute human equality could be achieved; to this end, he endeavoured to demonstrate the hopelessness of any attempt to break down social conventions based on the constraints of class, the impossibility of equal treatment in a profession where some people must give orders and others obey them, and the manner in which people were perceived and judged simply on the basis of their social standing. In particular, Gilbert highlighted the absurdity of the First Sea Lord who could work his way up to this position with no nautical experience at all!

The opera opened on 25th May 1878 at the Opera Comique and, perhaps largely because of that year's sweltering summer weather, audiences were initially disappointing. However, the inclusion of some of the tunes in a summer promenade concert at Covent Garden resulted in something of an explosion of interest in the work, and thereafter audience numbers greatly increased. The opening run consisted of 571 performances. In December 1879, a special production of the opera for children was launched. 1879 was also a significant year for amateur G & S, being the first year in which a G & S opera was seen on the amateur stage. *H.M.S. Pinafore* was the work chosen for the production at Kingston-upon-Thames. Unlike *The Sorcerer*, the opera was hugely successful in the States. After opening in Boston in November 1878, something akin to *Pinafore*-mania hit the U.S.A., the lack of copyright restrictions allowing numerous pirate performances which took greater liberties with the script than any modern amateur company would dare to try to get away with. Finally an "authentic" version was produced in New York in December 1879. By then the Comedy Opera Company had disbanded; Carte, whose relationship with his backers had never been consistently cordial, had been instrumental in the drafting of a complex legal arrangement which effectively gave him sole control of the Company's financial matters from the beginning of August 1879 following the expiry of the Company's lease on the Opera Comique. On the night of July 31st the backers attempted to exact revenge by interrupting a live performance of the opera in order to seize some scenery from the theatre for a rival production they were mounting. Predictably this was not a huge success. The opening run of *H.M.S. Pinafore* again saw audiences enjoying the talents of George Grossmith and Rutland Barrington. In one rehearsal, Gilbert asked Barrington to sit on the skylight of the deck "pensively," whereupon the prop collapsed. Gilbert's immediate retort was "That's EXpensively." Gilbert did not confine his wit to his star performers. One member of the cast, having been asked to repeat a particular piece of business once too often for his liking, said to Gilbert "I have been on the stage quite long enough." Gilbert's response was to say "Quite" and dismiss him on the spot. On other occasion, when a revival of the opera was in preparation, a lady was displeased about her position in a particular scene; when she complained to Gilbert that she always took centre stage in Italian opera she was told "Madam, this is not Italian opera; it is only a low burlesque of the worst kind."

Burlesque or not, *H.M.S. Pinafore* remains one of the most popular of the G & S operas today, on both sides of the Atlantic. Certain other aspects of the opera, beside its splendid music and memorable songs, make it particularly appealing to amateurs. Firstly it is one of the shortest two-Act G & S operas, so performers can generally rely on audience members not gazing meaningfully at their watches every five minutes as the time of the last bus to Strawberry Hill creeps inexorably closer. It can be (and often is) coupled with *Trial By Jury* thereby creating not only a full evening's entertainment, but, with two operas supposedly for the price of one, providing the perfect pretext for a marked increase in ticket charges. Secondly, no scenery changes are needed; all the action takes place on board the good ship Pinafore. An unambitious stage manager could simply decorate an otherwise empty stage with some ropes and then paint a few ships on the backcloth; if the previous year's show was *The Pirates Of Penzance*, it may be possible to use the suitably maritime backcloth from that production. Thirdly, it is one of the easiest operas to costume for male chorus members and, indeed, most of the male principals. A set of white sailor suits and straw hats will be easy to hire and easy to put on, with no change necessary. The male cast will doubtless be just as relieved as the wardrobe team, particularly if the previous production has been some richly-costumed extravaganza such as *The Merry Widow*, where hapless troupers have had to change from hearty Pontevedrian peasants to urbane embassy flunkeys in three minutes and the forty square feet of dressing room has become a quivering mass of greasepaint-stained smocks and Velcro-patched breeches.

The story of *H.M.S. Pinafore* , with the alternative title *The Lass That Loved A Sailor*, is simple. Ralph Rackstraw (tenor), a humble sailor on board the aforementioned vessel, is in love with Josephine (soprano), the daughter of the ship's Captain Corcoran (baritone). Josephine is, in turn, promised to Sir Joseph Porter K.C.B, the First Lord of the Admiralty (baritone). The union between Ralph – supported by the Boatswain (baritone) and Carpenter (bass) – and Josephine is doomed because of their class difference, so the couple decide to elope. Tipped off by the unpopular Dick Deadeye (bass), the Captain catches them in the act of escaping and Ralph is committed to solitary confinement, until Mrs Cripps, always known as Little Buttercup, a Portsmouth bumboat woman (contralto), announces that she mixed Ralph and the Captain at birth and that Ralph is therefore the rightful Captain. With Sir Joseph unwilling to marry the daughter of one who has turned out to be a common sailor, there are no obstacles to Ralph marrying her instead. Sir Joseph settles for Hebe (mezzo-soprano), his first cousin. Incidentally Hebe was played in the original production by Jessie Bond, who went on to take a number of significant roles in later productions.

Before the action commences, there is an overture, which like all the G & S overtures is a pot-pourri of tunes that will be heard again as the story progresses. Whatever show is being performed, the overture may have been preceded by the National Anthem, depending upon the respect which the musical director, the committee and the public (usually in that order) may have for the monarchy. The overture to *H.M.S. Pinafore* begins with a brief roll of drums, and it may occur to the more mischievous M.D. who has *not* just guided his band through the National Anthem to prolong this drum roll. This may cause the unsuspecting patron to spring to his feet in deference to the sovereign, and as Sullivan's rollicking nautical tune begins it will be in somewhat self-conscious fashion that he resumes his seat, particularly if his minor *faux pas* has generated an outburst of titters from a popcorn-chomping juvenile in the row behind.

The opera opens on the quarterdeck of the vessel H.M.S. Pinafore by day, with the sailors supposedly "discovered cleaning brass, splicing rope etc." Since, however, the Scouting or indeed naval days of most of the cast are either long forgotten or non-existent, it is improbable that any splicing will take place. Instead, the gentlemen of the chorus entrusted with rope work will confine themselves to clasping part of a coil of rope and fiddling impotently with it for as long as it takes the instrumental introduction to finish and the singing to start. Moreover, since it is unlikely that there will be any brass to clean, those to whom polishing duties have been delegated will apply their cleansing skills to any other available surface, of which the most popular is the floor of the performance hall, however assiduously Mr Crump, the janitor, has already polished it earlier in the day. Duties come to an abrupt end as the sailors identify themselves in song ("We sail the ocean blue").

Assuming that the childish smirks at the line "When the balls whistle free o'er the bright blue sea" have been erased in early rehearsals, the musical director's biggest challenge may be to find sufficient manpower to provide the three-part harmony that is needed for the number. Little Buttercup, a Portsmouth bumboat woman (bumboat being a boat used to carry provisions to vessels), appears at the end of the song. After a brief recitative of invitation to the sailors to sample her wares ("Hail, men o'wars men") she introduces herself and her range of products in a lilting aria ("I'm called Little Buttercup"). The goods she offers are tempting indeed, from watches and knives to gastronomic delights such as treacle and toffee, some or all of which may be produced from her basket as she sings. In an effort to fill the basket, unambitious properties teams may stretch to a couple of tins of Tate & Lyle Golden Syrup and a *papier mache* knife that survived the Christmas pantomime. Alternatively the basket may have become a repository for any stage props which have failed to find homes elsewhere, from the ubiquitous pewter drinking tankards that can be worked into many G & S shows, to the rubber parrot that the producer vetoed in last year's production of *The Pirates Of Penzance* but which was never claimed by its heartbroken owner and has sat in the props cupboard ever since.

After Little Buttercup has taken a fistful of non-existent cash for the goods she has sold, she traditionally offers the Midshipmite a stick of rock with the words "And that's for you, my little man!" There are no clues to this in the libretto but it was a stock D'Oyly Carte addition and will certainly delight the Midshipmite if nobody else. The part of the Midshipmite, otherwise known as Tom Tucker, is traditionally played by a small boy, and although he has no lines of his own to say, there is no reason why he should not appear with the chorus of sailors whenever they are on stage. Because of the laws governing juvenile performers, it is customary to use two children to alternate in the role. This may boost ticket sales considerably, as assorted parents, guardians, grandparents, aunts and uncles of both boys dutifully make their way to the theatre, and Row D is filled with nostalgic banter as one uncle reminisces to another on how his last appearance on stage was as a tooth fairy at the age of eight. Flattering support will also ooze from the cast who encourage the young performers with such platitudinous remarks as "In a few years' time you'll be up there taking a lead part" whilst knowing in their heart of hearts that when those few years are up, the lead parts are still likely to be taken by a cluster of ageing artistes who have no intention of relinquishing their star billing or their influence until they literally drop off the stage into the orchestra pit.

Little Buttercup gracefully accepts the compliments of the crew, but hints at a darker more mysterious side to her character. As she does so, Dick Deadeye appears. Deadeye is one of the most colourful Gilbertian creations, portrayed in the opera as a typical villain of melodrama as he exposes the futility of well-intentioned attempts to break down barriers of class and social standing, and foils the innocent plans of the two young lovers. However, all that is in the future. For now, he is content merely to introduce himself as an ugly misfit (one might ask why he has not been discharged from the R.N. on medical grounds) who is hated by all his fellow sailors and knows it. His very name suggests that he should appear with an eyepatch, and many producers will also request him to be hunchbacked, although they may have cause to regret this decision if the character playing the role is aiming to maximise audience attention and reaction. Once he has been cast in the role, the more conscientious actor will continue to work on his hunch at every opportunity, which may be both understandable and tolerable within the confines of the garden shed but less so in the Monday morning season-ticket queue at Catford Bridge Station.

Little Buttercup interrupts Deadeye's reflections by querying, in recitative, the identity of a young sailor with faltering footsteps ("Pray, tell me") and the Boatswain informs her, also in recitative, that this is Ralph (pronounced Rafe) Rackstraw, the "smartest lad in all the Fleet." Little Buttercup immediately feels remorse at the mention of the name, although she will not say why at this stage. Ralph sings a haunting recitative with chorus, accompanied by a trilling flute ("The nightingale sighed"), followed by a short aria also with chorus ("A maiden fair to see") in which he declares his love for the Captain's daughter. After he

42

sings "I love, alas, above my station," the chorus respond "He loves a lass above his station" – just one of a number of examples of subtle Gilbertian plays on words which make the operas such a delight. Ralph also remarks that although he knows "the value of a kindly chorus," they are not much use in a crisis, still less so if they fail to respond to his utterance in tune. In the G & S operas, the chorus is given a far more meaningful role within the story than that to which audiences at that time were accustomed. This is emphasized in the dialogue that follows Ralph's solo, in which the hopelessness of his love is acknowledged by the Boatswain and Deadeye; the latter points out that Captains' daughters simply do not marry foremast hands. Here, as in other sections of dialogue in the opera, there are brief spoken interjections for the chorus. Since most of the chorus members will have regarded it as unnecessary to purchase a libretto, they may frequently forget what the interjections are, or indeed when they come. At times of acute outbreaks of amnesia, there may be a deafening silence from the ranks. This may be broken at rehearsal stage by an irate producer who bellows the interjection across the room, or in performance by a helpful conductor who shouts it across the orchestra pit. If the sailors fail to pick up their cue, the conductor's exclamation "Horrible! Horrible!" (which the men are supposed to cry later in Act 1) may provoke mystified listeners to believe he has entered the action himself. They may, of course, conclude that he is passing comment on either the standard of acting or the overpowering after-shave of the first violinist.

Now it is the turn of Captain Corcoran to arrive. He introduces himself with a recitative ("My gallant crew") in typically Handelian style, down to the last "You do us proud, sir!" followed by a decisive "pom-pom" from the orchestra. Then comes the solo with chorus ("I am the Captain of the Pinafore") in which the Captain freely extols his many virtues, including good breeding (he claims never to swear a "big, big D") and a strong constitution. The song is best known for the immortal exchange "What, never?" "Well, hardly ever." This quickly assumed catchphrase status among the opera's many devotees. An American news editor is reputed to have said that he never wanted to hear any of his staff use the expression, and to the incredulous response "What, never?" came the almost inevitable rejoinder "Well, hardly ever." Societies rehearsing *H.M.S. Pinafore* will seize eagerly on any use of the word "never" by the producer or musical director and respond in like fashion ("Tenors, you never get that line right;" "we never start rehearsals on time;" "I've never needed a packet of condoms at the after-show party") until all concerned vow never to say never again. Well, hardly ever.

The sailors exit, leaving just Little Buttercup and the Captain. In a recitative ("Sir, you are sad") Little Buttercup states that she detects the Captain is upset about something, to which the Captain responds that his daughter Josephine is promised to the First Lord, Sir Joseph Porter – "but for some reason she does not seem to tackle kindly to it." Again this section of the recitative ends with a "pom-pom" from the orchestra. In a sung aside to the audience the Captain concludes the recitative by describing Little Buttercup as a "plump and pleasing person," a splendid Gilbertian alliteration but also a somewhat patronising gesture of affection. It is of course quite out of the question that he should seek a loving relationship with her, she being a mere bumboat woman and he a ship's Captain. The two singers exit and Josephine then appears for the first time. She sings a sad lament for the hopelessness of her own love for Ralph ("Sorry her lot who loves too well") after which her father enters and she confides in him about her affections for a humble sailor. The Captain is sympathetic but also insistent that "the line must be drawn somewhere" and makes it clear that a sailor is quite unsuitable as a marriage partner. Another of Gilbert's puns occurs here; as the Captain provides his daughter with a photograph of Sir Joseph, he hopes that the picture will bring her to a more reasonable "frame" of mind. After the dialogue, it is now time for Sir Joseph to appear, and the chorus assemble to greet him in song ("Over the bright blue sea"); the ladies appear initially, and the sailors then enter on tiptoe. Unless a shortage of chorus males has forced the producer to conscript some lady sailors, the female chorus assembly will all be made up of Sir Joseph's sisters, cousins and aunts, each gaily turned out in a variety of bright crinolines. One of these is Hebe, Sir Joseph's first cousin, who has little solo work but contributes significantly to some ensemble sections especially in the Act 1 finale. If ticket sales for the show are slack, then the society's business manager will raise a few sickly grins by exhorting members to drag not only their immediate families along, but "your sisters and your cousins and your aunts" as well. This may of course prompt some wag in the back row of the chorus, who last sold a ticket for one of his society's performances in 1959, to mutter semi-audibly that this is impossible in his case, since he has no cousins and his aunt moved out to Kuala Lumpur two days after he buried his sister in Chipping Ongar.

In recitative with chorus ("Now give three cheers") the captain leads in giving Sir Joseph a hearty welcome, and after this has been offered, the First Lord is among those present. Sir Joseph is not only one of the great "character" parts in the opera – it is one of the George Grossmith roles – but he is the vehicle for the most biting satire in the piece. After his innocuous introduction with chorus ("I am the monarch of the sea") he gives a potted autobiography in song ("When I was a lad I served a term") in which he reveals that prior to becoming First Lord of the Admiralty he had never been to sea at all. This was clearly a dig at the "real" First Lord at the time, W.H. Smith, who was of course the founder of the famous newsagency and who had a similar lack of nautical experience. Although Gilbert denied that his portrayal of Sir Joseph was based on Smith, it would be hard to deny that Smith had in fact given him the inspiration for it. As he said to some of his juvenile performers, "You would naturally think that a person who commanded the entire British Navy would be the most accomplished sailor who could be found, but that is not the way in which things are managed in England."

There follows some dialogue between Sir Joseph and the crew of the Pinafore, in which Sir Joseph exhorts the Captain not to bully or patronise his crew; he tells Ralph that a "British sailor is any man's equal – excepting mine." It is of course easy for Sir Joseph to preach the virtues of equality – to the extent of insisting that the Captain accompanies any order with the words "if you please" – because he knows that nobody will ever be equal to him. The dialogue gives way to a reprise of Sir Joseph's entrance music; in a brief solo, with chorus, he reiterates the virtues of politeness ("For I hold that on the seas") and then leaves the stage, as do the Captain and the ladies. The stage is once again occupied exclusively by the sailors, and there is more dialogue for the chorus to learn, although it is unlikely that the interjections "Well spoke! Well spoke!", "Horrible! Horrible!" "Aye, aye!"(x 2), and "We do" should add greatly to the pressures on the overtaxed brain cells of the male company. Deadeye sums up the futility of Ralph's endeavours, and touches on one of the principal themes of the opera, when he says "When people have to obey other people's orders, equality's out of the question." Ostensibly to cheer him up, Ralph, together with the Boatswain and the Carpenter, sings a song ("A British tar") which Sir Joseph has given to them to perform. This list of supposed attributes of a British sailor is one of the most remarkable musical pieces in the opera. It consists of an unaccompanied contrapuntal trio, a brief choral echo of material already sung in the trio, and a hornpipe in the middle for good measure. The trio can be successfully performed in two ways. The singers can opt for a performance of musical excellence, with a finesse and polish that could remind the audience of the town's masterful close-harmony singers' performance in the Memorial Hall last week. Alternatively, they can try to make it look as though they are getting to grips with a tricky piece of three-part harmony – which, of course, they are – and give the appearance of reaching tentatively for the notes, then exaggerating each note and syllable that is successfully hit. What is not acceptable – although many performers of the trio may beg to differ – is a wholly inaccurate rendition of the piece either on the basis that that is how it is intended to be performed, or on the basis of sheer incompetence. It is possible that while Ralph, and probably the Boatswain, will have had to audition for their parts, the Carpenter (having no solo work as such) will have been selected at random from the chorus on the basis that he happened to catch the producer's eye at the wrong moment. The harassed producer may wisely decide to delegate responsibility for setting the hornpipe to a dedicated choreographer, preferably one with not only a degree in stage management but also a diploma from the Job Academy of Patient Endurance. Hornpipe or no hornpipe, the producer may still wish to coax the chorus through the actions to accompany the declamation of the qualities the British tar should possess, including flashing eye, furling brow, heaving bosom, curling lip and protruding breast. However a moment's reflection will suggest that perhaps, after all, it is better to leave these actions to the trio (who sing about them in rather slower time before the chorus come in) than trust that the chorus will remember at what point they are supposed to be heaving their eyes or flashing their bosoms.

The chorus leave, and only Ralph remains on stage. Josephine appears and in a passionate exchange of dialogue and subsequent duet ("Refrain, audacious tar") she outwardly rejects his proffered advances with disdain, but aside she makes it clear that she would love to accept them. Ralph in turn is forced to acknowledge the situation, but his devotion to her remains unaltered. He describes himself as a "living ganglion of irreconcilable antagonisms," an utterance which is hardly consistent with his simple background, and which in Geoffrey Smith's words, parodies the "literary figure of the lowly swain whose humble expressions of passion sound as if every moment has been spent studying rhetoric." In response to Josephine's statements of rejection, Ralph sings a dramatic recitative ("Can I survive this overbearing") which opens the Act 1 finale. He then summons all the ladies and sailors back on stage and tells them his sad news. The chorus react with dismay; only Deadeye, with his cruel assertion that "I told you so!" remains unsympathetic, and everyone else responds angrily and resolutely to his gloating. Despite their encouragement, Ralph resolves to terminate his now barren existence and having sung a mournful solo anticipating his imminent suicide ("My friends, my leave of life I'm taking") he takes possession of a pistol. The possibility of a loud explosion on stage may cause alarm amongst nervous spectators, especially those who recall the overenthusiastic antics of Calamity Jane in the society's previous production. In fact, as Ralph starts to squeeze the trigger, Josephine arrives; in recitative she commands him to stay his hand then declares her love for him openly. The anxious audience members can relax as the threat of an explosive suicide recedes. Of course, the thoughtful producer will then direct Ralph to toss the gun to a couple of deckhands who will mischievously send three ear-splitting blanks high into the air, causing fingers to retreat once more into the cavernous recesses of the ear for as long as the weapon remains on stage.

A joyous ensemble section ("Oh joy, oh rapture unforeseen") ensues, interspersed with Deadeye's prophecies that the union is doomed. There follows a most difficult piece of singing as the principals whisper to the company of the couple's intention to elope after nightfall ("This very night"). Each principal takes it in turns to add a few syllables before the chorus join in, the sopranos having to spit out a quick succession of quavers. It is Sullivan at his best, painting in music a suspenseful picture of stealthy escape. In a brief recitative Deadeye warns the couple not to proceed, but for his pains is told "Back, vermin, back, you shock us!" Deadeye is then directed to exit, but producers may instead direct that he be thrown summarily from the ship by a couple of burly foremast hands, and that this be accompanied by a splashing sound from off the set. A lively chorus with dance ("Let's give three cheers for the sailor's bride") leads into a reprise of some of the material found in "A British tar" with more lip-curling and bosom-heaving. After the singing has finished there is a brief orchestral playout; even if producers have avoided any chorus dancing so far, a few dainty steps will be almost obligatory at this point, if only to avoid the oft-heard complaint from chorus members that they are "standing there like lemons." Ambitious choreographers may aim for a polished formation dance to round off the first half, whereas more down-to-earth producers, mindful of the fact that the sequence lasts barely 20 seconds, and the three hours of rehearsals necessary to perfect it could be better spent in other ways, will hope that a line of singers running on the spot with their raised arms folded imparts some nautical verisimilitude into the proceedings. With no costume change necessary, for the chorus at any rate, the ensuing interval can be spent in comparatively relaxed fashion; 19 Down of the *Daily Mail* crossword can receive undivided attention, lipstick will be transferred to polystyrene cartons as interval tea and coffee are consumed, and the good-looking wardrobe assistant will hide from the spotty tenor in the back row of the chorus who has been boring her with his attentions ever since she unwisely smiled at him during the party following the last show but three.

For the chorus the interval will in fact be a long one, as the opening numbers in Act 2 are for principals only. The curtains part to reveal the ship's quarterdeck but this time by night. The only occupants of the stage are the Captain and also Little Buttercup, who sits gazing sentimentally at him. Act 2 opens with a solo for the Captain ("Fair moon, to thee I sing") in which, accompanying himself on a mandolin, he soliloquises about his rebellious crew and Sir Joseph's hostile reaction to his daughter's partiality to a common sailor. The song is sung by moonlight, and a round of applause will certainly be due to the lighting team if they manage to achieve a moonlit effect. In the ensuing dialogue, the Captain again expresses his affection for Little Buttercup, but both recognise that their differences in status must prevent their friendship blossoming into romance. However, she warns him that there is a change in store for him; in a duet immediately preceding her departure she uses a series of proverbs to demonstrate that, as the song begins, "Things are seldom what they seem." The Captain responds with a series of proverbs of his own which indicate he has no idea what she is talking about, but in a brief spoken soliloquy after she has exited he seems aware that his own fortunes may be about to change for the worse. Sir Joseph enters and snaps him out of his reverie by speaking regretfully of Josephine's disinterest in him; the Captain presumes this is attributable to her belief that she is unworthy of him, and suggests that Sir Joseph reason with her on the basis of the Admiralty's rule that love levels all ranks. This a somewhat surprising assertion given the Captain's own reservations about Little Buttercup or his daughter's partiality to Ralph! The two men exit, then Josephine enters and sings her second uninterrupted solo, or "Scena," as the score calls it ("The hours creep on apace"). This is, by popular consensus, one of the most technically demanding solos in all the operas, in which Josephine agonises over the choice between maintaining her life of luxury with her father with "rich oriental rugs (and) luxurious sofa pillows" and adopting a life of squalor in a "dark and dingy room in some back street" with an overworked underpaid sailor. For a brief moment Gilbert paints a stark Dickensian picture which suddenly jolts the hitherto carefree audience into a mood of sombre reflectiveness. To this Sullivan adds a truly mesmeric musical sequence, beginning with a recitative and then moving into an aria to be sung *allegro*, climaxing with a succession of sustained high notes on the dramatic words "Oh god of love, god of reason, which of you twain shall

48

my poor heart obey?" It requires a singer of considerable skill to execute the song satisfactorily, and the reward for so doing will be a burst of applause the moment the singer has finished and the orchestra begins a brisk playout. Less talented sopranos, who creep on to the stage to perform the number like a condemned deserter making his way to a firing squad, and caterwaul their way anxiously through the number, will have to wait until the orchestra have finished before receiving a sympathetic ripple from the assembled masses rather reminiscent of that which might be accorded the booby-prize winner in the school sports egg-and-spoon race.

The Captain and Sir Joseph re-enter, and Sir Joseph wastes no time in assuring Josephine that love is a platform on which all ranks meet. Josephine is delighted because this assertion gives her the pretext to pursue her love for Ralph. The happiness and relief of all three is evident in the ensuing trio ("Never mind the why and wherefore") in which each celebrates the position they are in; Sir Joseph has a potential bride, the Captain can look forward to having an exalted son-in-law, and Josephine believes she is free to pursue her real love. It is one of the most frequently performed numbers in the G & S repertoire, and is an obvious candidate for an encore. The idea of an encore – the repetition of the whole or part of a number – dates back to times when recordings were unavailable and audiences had to rely on live performances to absorb particularly tuneful numbers. The tradition has continued, and despite the ability of modern technology to relay to the listener the brightest and best G & S numbers in the privacy of his lounge, car or allotment, live audiences will still be accorded the dubious pleasure of seeing parts of their evening's entertainment being subjected to instant action replays. There are three types of encore. The first is the genuinely skilful well-handled encore, where new material entirely in keeping with the spirit of the piece – either spoken or dramatic – is subtly introduced into the performance. For instance, with the command to "Ring the merry bells on board ship" the performers might copy the D'Oyly Carte artistes and find a formidable variety of imaginary bells to ring. The second is the token anaemic encore, where out of a sense of duty the singers simply repeat the words and actions with no variation whatsoever. That is at least preferable to the third type, where the performers indulge in supposedly comic business which is entirely out of keeping with the spirit of the piece and which satisfies nobody except themselves. The difficulty that performers will have is in knowing whether audience reaction will be such as to justify any encore at all. The decision may well have to be made in advance. If the producer has guessed correctly, the performers will carry a rapturous audience through up to half a dozen renditions of the latter part of the number on a tide of euphoria and hilarity, with the prospect of a rave review in the Argus and the certainty of sell-out houses for the next show. Producers without the same psychic powers will sit in dumbfounded horror as the four reruns of pages one hundred and four (first line, last bar) to the end are greeted with stony silence, broken only by an elderly gentleman in the front row who confides in his neighbour that he thinks something has gone wrong with his hearing aid.

Josephine and Sir Joseph exit, the Captain now convinced that his daughter has been won over to Sir Joseph. He is immediately disabused of this by Deadeye who enters and in a dark duet in a minor key ("Kind Captain, I've important information") informs him that Ralph is about to flee with his daughter. The Captain is grateful for this warning, and indicates he will act upon it with the assistance of the "merry cat o'nine tails." Interestingly, the use of this instrument of correction was abolished just three years after the show was first performed. In the best melodramatic tradition, the Captain uses a boat cloak to effect a disguise with a view to ambushing the eloping couple. Deadeye looks on in satisfaction, and his cry of "They are foiled – foiled – foiled!" may provoke a timely hiss from pantomime fans in the audience. Then, refreshed from their third or fourth cup of interval tea, the sailors of the Pinafore – led by Ralph and the Boatswain – creep stealthily on, meeting up with Josephine and Little Buttercup. A dramatic musical section begins, starting with the sailors' confirmation that they are "Carefully on tiptoe stealing." All at once they are startled by a stamping sound, and a violent chord from the direction of the orchestra pit. When enquiring what it was, they are informed that it was the "cat." Again a stamp and loud chord reverberate around the stage, and again it is explained away as the cat. However, no sooner have the couple resolved to steal away when the Captain pounces and in a brisk solo ("Pretty daughter of mine") demands to know what is going on. Ralph bravely informs his would-be father-in-law of his intended elopement; together with Josephine he demonstrates his determination to have his way, and in a show of pride and self-respect cites the fact that he is an Englishman. This theme is taken up by the Boatswain in his solo, with chorus, which follows. The song, beginning with the words "For he himself has said it," is one of the best tunes in the opera, and a splendid pastiche of a corny English patriotic song. As the Boatswain sings, "He might have been a Roosian, a French or Turk or Proosian, or perhaps Italian!" (This last word is traditionally pronounced Eye-tal-eye-anne!) The Captain is

50

furious when he finds what has happened, and says as much in an angry solo ("In uttering a reprobation") which includes the dreaded words "Why, damme, it's too bad!" By this time the female chorus members have reappeared, followed by Sir Joseph, and all react with horror to this foul language. The author Lewis Carroll was one of those who took great exception to the use of the "big, big D" word, particularly in the special children's performances. Sir Joseph wastes no time in admonishing the Captain, and sends him off "to your cabin with celerity." The word "celerity" means "promptness," but like the Irish juryman in *Trial By Jury*, and the lady serenaded at the Ploverleigh village feast in *The Sorcerer*, the name of the Captain's cabin companion is an obvious subject for a trick question in a G & S quiz evening!

After a spirited encore of "For he is an Englishman" (the Englishman referred to here being Sir Joseph, not Ralph), a section of dialogue follows in which Sir Joseph learns the reason for the Captain's bad language. Outraged, he directs that Ralph be loaded with chains and confined to a dungeon, although not before yet another excruciating pun – "Your position as a topman is a very exalted one." Before Ralph is committed, he has to undergo another punishment – joining in an octet for all the soloists and the chorus. It is actually the only octet in the G & S operas. It is an obvious pastiche on the elaborate grand opera farewells preceding some tragic event, and the situation is in a sense made more absurd by Little Buttercup's hinting that the situation will change when her secret, whatever that may be, is divulged. The octet is of particular interest in that it contains a very early reference to the telephone; the singers lament that "No telephone communicates with his cell." When the opera was premiered, London did not even have a telephone exchange. In the late 1990's, a topical substitute might be "No fax machine communicates with his cell" which also happens to fit the music, or "The Internet can't communicate with his cell," which doesn't.

Little Buttercup graciously allows Ralph to go through the humiliation of being led away, and also permits Sir Joseph to sing a recitative with chorus expressing "My pain and my distress," before, at long last, disclosing the information which would have saved everybody so much time had she provided it a great deal earlier. In her recitative ("Hold! Ere upon your loss") which immediately follows, and in her ensuing solo with chorus ("A many years ago") she reveals that in her youth she mixed up Ralph and the Captain so that Ralph is really the Captain, and the Captain merely a humble sailor. A few moments later, Ralph indeed appears as the Captain, and the Captain as a common tar. It is traditional for the actors to swap clothes before returning, although neither of them are actually supposed to be on stage when Little Buttercup's revelations are announced, and one might ask how they are supposed to know what has happened. One can only speculate that perhaps the ship, although lacking a telephone, is fitted with a loudspeaker system. The well-organised wardrobe team will have an army of willing volunteers available to assist the actors in effecting the change; less fortunate Ralphs and Captains will be left to fend for themselves, and those standing close to the wings as Little Buttercup regales the crew with her baby-farming activities may be treated to a succession of anguished grunts as the 38-waist Captain attempts to don Ralph's 32-waist ducks, and vice versa.

The transformation, of course, alters everything. In the dialogue which follows, Sir Joseph makes it plain that he will have nothing to do with the daughter of a common sailor, saying that although love levels all ranks to a considerable extent, it does not level them as much as that. Hebe offers herself as a marriage partner instead, and after a half-hearted protest he agrees. Josephine, freed from Sir Joseph's attentions, joyfully goes to Ralph, and Little Buttercup is now of course quite acceptable to the erstwhile Captain; not, however, before the latter has remarked to Josephine "It is hard, is it not, my dear?" This is, alas, just one of many quite innocently-penned expressions which have acquired an unfortunate additional meaning over the years, and which may provoke a ripple of sniggering when uttered before the full company for the first time.

The opera ends with a jolly reprise of a selection of tunes already heard (starting with "Oh joy, oh rapture unforeseen") in celebration of the happy pairings which Little Buttercup's revelations have made possible. That most celebrated G & S catchphrase makes a welcome return visit, triggered by the ex-Captain promising to Little Buttercup that "I shall never be untrue to thee." To the inevitable response "What, never?" he candidly proclaims "Well, hardly ever!" The opera ends with the patriotic tones of "He is an Englishman" ringing in the ears of the audience. As they leave, they will perhaps do well not to trouble their heads with difficult questions such as why Ralph, as the new Captain, is quite happy to marry a girl who is nothing more than the daughter of a common sailor; and why if Ralph and the ex-Captain were cribmates (which one assumes they were) and therefore the same age, the ex-Captain should be old enough to be the father of Ralph's beloved, not to mention the intended spouse for his old nurse. It is much easier to do as Gilbert would doubtless do if he were still alive; agree that it is all nonsense, and concede that things like that would never happen in real life. Well, hardly ever.

4 PLACE THEM AT THE BAR

The Pirates Of Penzance is everybody's favourite. It was hugely popular when it was first performed, both in New York and in London; its plethora of splendid tunes has given untold pleasure to operatic societies and their audiences; it has transferred successfully to the Broadway stage and somehow lends itself to novel interpretations, with all the technological wizardry latter-day customers might expect from an evening's entertainment; and, for the amateur actor, it contains possibilities for overacting and tomfoolery which arguably none of the other operas can hope ever to match.

The fifth offering of the partnership has a somewhat bizarre history, and organisers of a G & S quiz night ought not to let slip the opportunity for some first-rate trivia questioning on the opera's origins. It had not always been Gilbert's intention to write an opera specifically about pirates. His translation of Offenbach's *Les Brigands* and his kidnapping by bandits in his own childhood may have influenced him in deciding to write an opera entitled *The Robbers* in which burglars and policemen were involved. However, as his work on the new opera proceeded, and with the real American pirates of *H.M.S. Pinafore* perhaps on his mind, he decided on a story that was not dissimilar to his earlier play *Our Island Home* and which would combine policemen not with burglars but with pirates. The result was the opera which remains so popular today. Its first full performance was at the Fifth Avenue Theatre, New York, on 31st December 1879, hot on the heels of the first "authentic" United States performance of *H.M.S. Pinafore*. By premiering the opera in this way, the writers hoped to avoid a glut of "pirate" performances of *Pirates* and so stave off a repetition of the *H.M.S. Pinafore* problems. In order to secure the British copyright, however, a single British performance of the opera was scheduled for 29th December. It was to be held in Paignton, as touring members of the D'Oyly Carte Company were in the area at the time. It had to be postponed for a day because the opera was still not finished; even when the show did take place, some of the music was missing and there were no costumes to speak of. The cast simply donned their *H.M.S. Pinafore* sailor suits and added some handkerchiefs to make them look a little more like pirates. Whilst the audience of 50 sat and enjoyed the fun, Sullivan was in his New York apartment still completing the music for the "official" opening. Having been somewhat disadvantaged by leaving much of the music behind in England, without the services of a fax machine to assist him, he did not complete the work until 5 a.m. on the day of the first performance. A few hours later he was conducting the orchestra in the final rehearsal! Doubtless revived by a snack of oysters and champagne, he returned to the theatre for the grand opening which was a huge success. Gilbert and Sullivan stayed on in the States, enjoying American society, until March 1880 when they returned to England and, soon afterwards, the opera opened in London. The English premiere of the full opera was at the Opera Comique on 3rd April 1880, and was the first of a continuous London run of 363 performances. It was incidentally during the composers' sojourn in the States that an American woman reputedly asked Gilbert if "Baytch" was still composing, to which Gilbert famously replied: "No; he is by way of *de*composing."

The opera is a sparkling combination of Gilbertian satire and both musical and melodramatic burlesque. Gilbert declared that "treatment of the new opera will be similar to that of *Pinafore*, namely to treat a thoroughly farcical subject in a thoroughly serious manner." Although the satire does not predominate as much as it did in *H.M.S. Pinafore*, it is still present. Gilbert satirised the very Victorian concept of moral duty (the opera has the alternative title *The Slave Of Duty*) and its occasional tendency to override common sense; as in *H.M.S. Pinafore*, he had a dig at the senior officer in the Forces and his total ignorance of his chosen profession; he also satirised the *nouveaux riches* and the fashion for acquiring ancestors effectively by purchase. Melodramatic burlesque abounds, with a host of larger-than-life characters, and sudden and unexpected twists in a farcical plot, including a number of deliberately exaggerated farewell scenes. Moreover, Sullivan's music burlesques grand opera so successfully that the score comes as close to true operatic writing as any of his collaborations with Gilbert. However good his music, he was not always so fortunate with his musicians. He described the lead tenor in early performances as "an idiot...vain and empty-headed. He very nearly upset the piece on his first night as he didn't know his words and forgot his music. We shall, I think, have to get rid of him."

The opera centres round Frederic (tenor), the slave of duty himself. He has reached what he believes to be the end of his pirate apprenticeship, mistakenly arranged for him by Ruth, a Pirate Maid of all Work (contralto). Spurning the affections of Ruth, and the cavortings of his rumbustious Pirate King (bass-baritone) and the Pirate King's Lieutenant Samuel (baritone), he falls in love with Mabel (soprano) who with Edith (soprano), Kate (mezzo-soprano) and their sisters are all daughters of Major-General Stanley (baritone). The pirates sense easy pickings amongst the girls, and accordingly seize them, but let them go after being fooled into thinking that the Major-General is an orphan. Frederic, now out of his apprenticeship, sends the local policemen, led by the less than formidable Sergeant (bass), to deal with the pirates, but a loophole in the terms of his apprenticeship, pointed out by Ruth and the Pirate King, forces him to leave Mabel and return to the pirates. The pirates overcome the police, but Ruth's assertion that they are all fallen noblemen is accepted by the Major-General who freely offers his daughters to them on the basis that they end their piratical careers.

Act 1 opens on a rocky sea-shore on the coast of Cornwall. A G & S trivia quiz question that is worth keeping up one's sleeve is the date on which the action of the opera takes place; it is possible to work it out from the story that follows. (For those who cannot bear to be kept in suspense, the answer is 1st March 1873.) A group of pirates will either be discovered on stage, or will be seen hurrying purposefully on to it, their faces daubed with black make-up, their spotty neckerchiefs adding colour to the ensemble of rough shirts and waistcoats. Black gaiters combined with sensible slip-on shoes will hopefully give the impression of high piratical boots, without the discomfort that will inevitably attend any smaller-footed gentleman who tries to import verisimilitude into the proceedings by borrowing a pair of ill-fitting thigh boots from the girl at number 38.

However they happen to be attired, the pirates will be observed playing cards and drinking, their vessels being topped up by Samuel, the Pirate King's Lieutenant, at regular intervals. Wise producers will instil some discipline into their merriment, perhaps with a well-choreographed dance. Less confident directors will simply invite the gentlemen to behave in an exuberant manner, and leave the form of exuberance to take its own less than predictable course; audiences may therefore be treated to some boisterous ham acting or a few painful bars' self-conscious and obviously forced laughter intermingled with desultory conversation on such topics as the yawning gaps in rows C and D and the unpleasant cat-like screechings emanating from the direction of the substitute first violin. The opening chorus ("Pour, oh, pour the pirate sherry") sets the scene; the fact of consumption of sherry rather than traditional rum will later prove significant, but for now it just seems to fit the music better. In the course of the song Samuel explains that today Frederic, their apprentice, is 21 years old and is therefore free to go his own way in life. Samuel is often referred to as Sam, therefore allowing the producer a minimum of one dutiful laugh per production by an exhortation to him, having delivered one of his few lines, to "say it again, Sam." The Pirate King (hereinafter the King) expresses sadness that Frederic wishes to leave the band, and it comes as some surprise to him and the pirates when Frederic explains that it was an error that led to the apprenticeship in the first place. In a solo ("When Frederic was a little lad") Ruth relates how as Frederic's nurserymaid she mistakenly apprenticed him to a "pirate" instead of a "pilot" as his parents intended (his parents presumably being powerless to rectify the error subsequently). The pirates sit and listen, and try to remember to react on the basis that all this is news to them, even though they will have been told it through several months of rehearsal, not to mention the technical rehearsal, the first dress rehearsal (6.30 p.m. sharp, full costume, no make-up) and final dress rehearsal (7.00 p.m., full costume and make-up, invited audience of the Scratchface Close Over 70's Club).

Frederic, whose sense of duty remains of paramount importance to him, states with regret that he will indeed soon be leaving the band and devoting himself rigorously to their extermination. However, while he is still with them he feels duty-bound to offer them some advice, informing them that as pirates they are too compassionate – for instance, they make a point of never molesting an orphan – and are often victims of their own kind-heartedness. He tries to persuade them to accompany him back to civilisation, and presumably away from piracy, but the King proclaims in song, with chorus ("Oh, better far to live and die"), that it is a "glorious thing" to be a Pirate King. The song gives the King every opportunity to display the brashness and confidence with which his role is traditionally associated; it is not unknown for him to engage in a brisk sword duel with fellow pirates or even the conductor across the orchestra pit, the King with his rapier and the conductor with his rather less fearsome baton purchased from Potts Music Supplies thirty years ago for eight shillings and sixpence.

The pirates and the King dance merrily off stage, leaving Frederic and Ruth. It is clear from both their dialogue and subsequent duet that Ruth, one of Gilbert's assembly of ageing contraltos, is hardly the most beautiful creature on God's earth. However, Frederic has never seen another female, and is in no position to dispute Ruth's claim that she is a "fine woman." Indeed he seems to be on the point of proposing to her when he hears voices. He asks himself if the voices belong to "Custom House," another word for customs men who would of course be on the lookout for smugglers; a few titters may be generated from the audience by substituting the words "the Inland Revenue." In fact the voices belong to a bevy of beautiful maidens. Frederic, looking off, is outraged; he sees that by comparison with them, Ruth is both plain and old. In a mock-melodramatic duet ("Oh, false one") in which music reminiscent of grand opera is combined with ridiculous words ("Upon my innocence you play," "I'm not the one to plot so;" "Your face is lined, your hair is grey," "It's gradually got so!"), Frederic rejects Ruth and sends her away in despair. Now he can turn his attention to the aforementioned maidens. In a recitative ("What shall I do?") he bemoans his lack of decent clothing. Accordingly, as the girls enter the action, he hides himself in the hope of being able to attire himself more respectably before he appears to them. Their chorus of entry, with brief solos for Edith and Kate ("Climbing over rocky mountain") is an ebullient celebration of the joys of the great Cornish outdoors. It is also the only music known to have survived from *Thespis* which has been worked into another G & S opera. The audience's suspension of disbelief may be severely tested at this point; if the female chorus consists more or less exclusively of singers on the downhill side of fifty, and Ruth is played by an attractive and talented young musician, they may well wonder why Frederic does not substantially rewrite (and possibly shorten considerably) the script by deciding to settle for Ruth after all. As it is, Frederic may have to pretend to be transfixed by the procession of elderly troubadours who despite boasting of their hardiness in "scaling rough and rugged passes" look in real life as though they would have difficulty negotiating their way down an aisle in an Asda superstore.

In the dialogue which follows, the girls – who are evidently all sisters – agree that this is a perfect spot for some paddling before their luncheon arrives. Suddenly Frederic appears in their midst, and in a dramatic recitative with chorus ("Stop, ladies, pray") he shocks them all by announcing that he is a pirate who is about to end his association with piracy. He then appeals to them for assistance, informing them that he is "sore at heart." It will not take a person with an excessively high I.Q. to realise that "I, sore at heart," if not enunciated carefully, suggests that Frederic has been engaged in something that the librettist certainly did not intend. Frederic then pleads with the girls in the hope of finding one who will accept his proffered affections. The solo, with chorus, in which he does this ("Oh, is there not one maiden breast") squeezes every last drop of pathos from the situation, although the words can hardly be said to have the same haunting quality as the music ("Oh, is there not one maiden here whose homely face and bad complexion have caused all hopes to disappear of ever winning man's affection?"). The climax of the aria is a top B flat (just under an octave above middle C) but any hope the tenor might have of rapturous applause will be dashed by the fact that the aria leads straight into a musical exchange with the girls' chorus and then the entry of another sister Mabel. She completely steals his limelight by announcing herself with an opening musical flourish that might come straight from the pages of Verdi or Rossini. The lack of applause may not in fact unduly concern the tenor soloist. There has been at least one modern production where Frederic has been portrayed as a rock star, with all the potential for overacting on both his part and that of the girls that such a portrayal suggests. If he carries it off effectively, the girls' drooling admiration for him may extend beyond the stage and into real life, and as a result some genuine romance may follow. Providing both parties are unattached and compatible, such a pairing within a society will delight families and members alike. Unfortunately matters may be less than straightforward; if Frederic is actually aged 51, is married and has three children, he would be well advised to ensure that his sessions with the actress playing Kate, aged 18 and studying for her 'A' levels, are confined to snogs behind the scenery sheds.

After a brief recitative ("Oh sisters, deaf") in which she berates the girls for their apparent indifference to Frederic, Mabel launches immediately into a show-stopping solo, with chorus ("Poor wandering one"), in which she implores him to take her heart. The song is a burlesque of what Sullivan called the "farmyard effects" of Italian grand opera, with a succession of very high staccato notes for the soloist whilst the chorus of girls provide accompaniment underneath. There is opportunity for a cadenza at the end, and assuming that the soloist climbs down safely from it to end on the right note, enthusiastic applause is guaranteed. In a recitative, with solos for Edith and Kate ("What ought we to do?"), the girls discuss the tricky dilemma of being sudden unintentional gooseberries, and they decide to close their eyes and talk about the weather. The ensuing duet ("How beautifully blue the sky") is G & S at its absolute best. There is Sullivan's frequent, and very effective, device of two tunes being sung back to back, and then in duet with one another; there is also the Gilbertian absurdity of a very British discussion amongst the chorus, whilst a passionate love duet continues between Frederic and Mabel. It may seem curious that their passion should have reached such heights when they have only met a few pages back, but with less than two hours to play with, and Mr Crump the janitor coming to lock up the hall at 10.45 sharp, they cannot afford to waste time. The chorus' concern about lack of rain ("Tomorrow it may pour again, I hear the country wants some rain") is echoed by Robin Oakapple in *Ruddigore*, a later G & S work set in Cornwall, when he says "But we do want rain" suggesting that even in the supposed golden Victorian age the good people of the extreme south-west were anxious about sprinkler bans and drought orders.

In a recitative ("Stay, we must not lose our senses") Frederic warns that the pirates may return at any moment, but before the girls can disappear the pirates spring upon them, reflecting in a rousing chorus that "Here's a first-rate opportunity to get married with impunity and indulge in the felicity of unbounded domesticity." The girls, Felicity doubtless no less so than the others, resign themselves to their fate. However, at the start of an ensemble musical section, Mabel reminds the pirates in a fierce recitative ("Hold, monsters") that the girls' (and her) father is a Major-General. The audience can be forgiven for wanting early sight of a man who has succeeded in spawning not only such an impressive array of offspring, but offspring that may be considerably older than he. Samuel adds his voice to the recitative, urging some caution upon the pirates; moments later the Major-General (his full title, according to the list of *dramatis personae*, is Major-General Stanley) appears and embarks upon his big solo of introduction, "I am the very model of a modern Major-General." The Major-General is one of the classic G & S comic roles; his task is made that much harder by having to come on stage and almost immediately sing this very difficult patter song, with its jumble of tongue-twisting words and phrases, such as "I quote in elegiacs all the crimes of Heliogabalus." The aim of the song is to display to the assembled crowd his proficiency in everything except those things demanded by his chosen profession. One of his most renowned characteristics is the ability to rhyme at a moment's notice. The cast could quite easily believe that even the most skilful poet would have difficulty in rhyming "strategy" with anything, but after a succession of knowing glances and a few dutiful exclamations of "That's got him!" he continues "You'll say a better Major-General has never sat a gee," i.e. ridden a horse. When he wants something to rhyme with "Then I can hum a fugue of which I've heard the music's din afore" the chorus will exchange similar knowing glances, only for him to continue "And whistle all the airs from that infernal nonsense *Pinafore!*" (Gilbert correctly predicted that the mention of an earlier G & S opera would earn a hearty laugh from audiences.) This will be the cue for the chorus, charged with the heavy responsibility of repeating his words, to break into a simultaneous hornpipe, and another ungainly exhibition of clumsily folded arms and jogging on the spot which even in *H.M.S. Pinafore* rehearsals the previous year was as redolent of the surging seas as a packet of cod fish fingers.

The Major-General, in the ensuing dialogue, is horrified to learn of the pirates' intentions, but equally he seems to be aware of their weakness, and attempts to fool the pirates into refraining from stealing his daughters from him by pretending to be an orphan. The mention of the word "orphan" leads to a tortuous exchange of dialogue in which the words "orphan" and "often" are confused. For it to be effective, it is essential that the word "often," when spoken by the King for the first time, is pronounced "auffen" or the joke will be entirely lost on the audience. The King could, of course, forestall the entire exchange by briskly responding "Frequently" to the Major-General's inquiry as to the King's experience of orphanhood, and indeed this may be a wise move if it is an elderly matinee audience whose groaning bladders at this late stage in Act 1 are already causing them to shift anxiously and uncomfortably in their seats. The Act 1 finale ("Oh, men of dark and dismal fate") begins with the Major-General's pathetic plea for clemency, and in both his appeal and the tearful response of the pirates there is splendid exaggeration of grand opera pathos, culminating in a ridiculous prolonged trill on the word "orphan" the effect of which can be accentuated by an equally exaggerated display of weeping. No sooner has this subsided than the Major-General admits that he is "telling a terrible story." It is somewhat surprising that the cast do not hear this, given that the musical director will inevitably have urged his soloists to project as much as possible, and it would be a curious theatre whose stage was bigger than its auditorium. The King and his nefarious band must at least pretend to remain in blissful unawareness of the deception; the King boasts that they are not altogether void of feeling, and that life is a poor thing without a "touch of poetry in it." This is a cue for one of the most remarkable moments in the entire collection of operas, as the whole company join to sing a hymn to poetry ("Hail, poetry!") Its unaccompanied block harmony, with vivid contrasts of loud and soft, has all the grandeur and solemnity of a chorus from a sacred oratorio or part of an act of religious worship. The spell is broken by the King who formally releases the girls from their obligations to the pirates, while the Major-General in an aside asserts that it "sometimes is a useful thing to be an orphan boy." Meanwhile, Frederic happily contemplates his marriage to Mabel. The joy of the young couple is marred only by Ruth, who bursts in on the scene and implores Frederic to consider her feelings. Frederic, mindful of her earlier deception, has no qualms about summarily rejecting her, and the finale ends with her exiting in despair. The pirates meanwhile indulge in a wild dance of delight, having agreed (in a reprise of previously-used musical material) to "give up the felicity of unbounded domesticity" and thereby save Felicity, for the time being at least, from the shackles of the kitchen sink and the Moulinex Magimix.

Act 2 takes place in a ruined chapel by moonlight, with a backcloth of ruined Gothic windows; this is the first G & S opera in which a change of scenery is required halfway through. The Major-General is observed sitting pensively and tearfully amongst his offspring; in chorus, with solo from Mabel ("Oh, dry the glistening tear"), the girls do their best to cheer him up whilst Mabel asks him why he is not asleep in bed. At the end of the song Frederic enters, and in dialogue, the Major-General explains that he is overcome with remorse at his deceit. He is particularly conscious of the consequent disgrace he has brought on the family escutcheon, notwithstanding that he has only acquired this escutcheon by purchase having bought the property just a year ago! This was a neat dig by Gilbert at the then fashionable pursuit of "acquiring ancestors" exercised by the *nouveaux riches* of his day. Despite the naggings of his guilty conscience, however, the Major-General is pleased to give Frederic every encouragement in convening a force to eliminate the pirates. After a brief recitative in which he confirms his approval of Frederic's expedition ("Then, Frederic, let your escort lion-hearted") the force appears in the form of a motley collection of policemen who, led by the Sergeant, sing one of the best-known and best-loved choruses in all the G & S operas, "When the foeman bears his steel." In essence, the Sergeant and his colleagues sing of their immense apprehension at the magnitude of their task, while the girls try and lift their spirits with such diplomatic sentiments as "Go to glory and the grave." Sullivan again places two fine tunes back to back and then combines them to provide a chorus worthy of Verdi himself. He reserves his finest skit on grand opera to the end, when it is time for the police to set off to battle. Instead of marching off, they remain on stage singing "We go, we go" whilst the Major-General cries in exasperation "Yes, but you DON'T go!" (A popular variation, and an echo of *H.M.S. Pinafore*, is "But damme, you don't go!") As Ian Bradley puts it, this passage burlesques those grand opera scenes "where people spend a lot of time singing about something that they are just going to do but never seem to get round to doing it." Splendid and amusing though the words and music are throughout the song, there is much scope for additional humour in interpretation. The police may march on to the stage, and inadvertently march off the other side before realising their mistake; the Sergeant may continually stumble on an imaginary object which all the other police negotiate without difficulty; the police may line up on the stage and go into a complex routine involving much bending of the knees; or the constant use of the word "tarantara" (not to be confused with a spider with similar name) as a rallying-cry may lead to each policeman using his truncheon as a kind of trumpet. Since it is unlikely that the amateur performer will have a truncheon about the house, and the supply of stage truncheons will probably not arrive long before show week, a variety of implements may have to be used to rehearse the latter manoeuvre. Whilst lucky societies will contain at least one member who is apparently more than happy to while away a succession of Sunday evenings creating a passable set of imitations of which any *Blue Peter* presenter would be justly proud, a certain degree of improvisation, such as in the form of a rolled-up libretto or a ballpoint pen, may be necessary for those groups where no members boast the same dexterity with sticky-back plastic.

The police march off to thunderous applause, leaving Frederic on stage alone. A recitative immediately follows ("Now for the pirates' lair") in which he eagerly looks forward to atoning for his earlier acts of piracy. As he sings, Ruth and the King enter with pistols, apparently wishing to speak to him. As the recitative continues they reintroduce themselves and use the persuasive influence of their firearms to make Frederic agree to stay and listen to what they have to say. In a spirited trio which immediately follows ("When you had left our pirate fold") they tell him that a "startling paradox" has occurred to them. In a powerful recitative in the middle of the trio, again very much in the style of a sacred oratorio, the King explains this paradox; namely that since Frederic was born on the 29th February, he has actually only celebrated five birthdays notwithstanding that he has lived 21 years. Frederic does some quick mental arithmetic and accepts the truth of the assertion. To begin with, he fails to understand its significance. In the dialogue which follows, however, it is made clear to him that by the terms of his apprenticeship he was bound to remain with the pirates, not until his twenty-first *year* but until his twenty-first *birthday*, which owing to the vagaries of the calendar will not occur for another 67 years! The slave of duty that he is, Frederic feels he must not only return to a piratical existence but also inform Ruth and the King that the Major-General has lied to them about his orphanhood. In a trio full of movement and urgency ("Away, away, my heart's on fire") the three swear revenge upon the soldier, and Ruth and the King hurry off to summon the piratical band. An interesting logistical problem now presents itself to the producer; unless the society performing the show has a generous supply of male chorus members, it is going to be difficult to assemble both a chorus of pirates and a chorus of police which the remainder of the show now demands. Indeed it may be necessary during this middle section of Act 2 to get some of the girls out of their immaculate dresses and into piratical mode. It would perhaps be prudent of the producer to select carefully; whilst some younger chorus members may vie with each other to escape the piercing vibrato of their more senior colleagues, it may be straining the audience's credulity just a little too far when alongside the array of black-toothed, sabre-rattling cutlass-wielding fiends is placed the four-feet-nine-tall Janice Potts whose diminutive build and anxious expression betray all too clearly the fact that her experience of piracy is limited to the removal of a single peppermint bon-bon off the Woolworths Pick and Mix counter at the age of nine.

Frederic remains on stage and is met by Mabel. A dramatic musical sequence for them both commences with a recitative in which she reminds him that "All is prepared; your gallant crew await you." Frederic's tears tell her that all is not quite right; he informs her that he will not reach his 21st birthday, and consequent escape from piratehood, until 1940. Assuming that she has no further interest in him, he begins to make off, but in an impassioned plea ("Stay, Frederic, stay!") Mabel persuades him to remain and, in a classic melodramatic scene, begs him not to leave her to "pine alone and desolate." It is hard to tell which is more absurd; the fact that it is simply Frederic's sense of duty which is effectively destroying their happiness by tearing them apart, or the fact that Mabel promises to remain true to him until 29th February 1940, almost 70 years hence. The sequence ends with an optimistic duet ("Oh, here is love") but even in this high drama Gilbert's cynicism at the institution of marriage shines out: "He will be faithful to his sooth till we are wed, and even after!" Frederic exits but Mabel remains to sing a recitative ("No, I'll be brave") in which she confirms her steadfastness and extends encouragement to her force of police officers. They march in, led by the Sergeant, and in song ("Though in body and in mind") with music that is lifted from "When a foeman bares his steel" they try to address themselves bravely to the task in hand. Mabel then speaks for only the third time in the opera (she has precisely five speeches to learn) concerning the need for them to do their duty; in acknowledging her sentiments, the police traditionally respond to her in plainchant, providing another reminder of Sullivan's skill in weaving sacred-sounding music into a secular setting. The Sergeant then delivers a few spoken lines of encouragement to his men, again responded to in plainchant, before breaking into plainchant himself. The twist is at the end, when he suddenly speaks instead of sings, and the police's final "It is" is sung an octave lower than anything that has gone before, and right at the very bottom of the vocal register. Immediately afterwards the orchestra play the introduction which signals arguably the most famous G & S song of them all, "When a felon's not engaged in his employment." The sentiments in it, sung by the Sergeant and echoed by the chorus, can be summed up in the song's immortal line "A policeman's lot is not a happy one." As well as adding this expression to the English language, the song contains ample opportunities for comic business, as the chorus of police dutifully echo the last few words of each line of music sung by the Sergeant and then join in the refrain at the end of each verse. It is traditional for "not a happy one" to be converted to "not an happy one" and thus to "not a nappy one" which may, in societies that rely on cheap humour for the delectation of the audience, prompt a sudden manifestation of infant underwear. When Rutland Barrington, who sang the solo originally, received enthusiastic applause for his performance, he had the temerity to ask Gilbert to write another verse as an encore to which Gilbert brusquely replied "Encore means sing it again!"

No sooner has the applause died down than the pirates are heard off stage preparing themselves in song for their imminent battle. Their introductory line, "A rollicking band of pirates we who tired of tossing on the sea," may regrettably be of more than passing interest to the connoisseur both of spoonerisms and *double-entendres*. In any event it is to be hoped that the pirates will remember to start their singing on the correct note, as there is no orchestral accompaniment on which to rely; since the entry of the orchestra will expose any inaccuracy in their tuning, it is perhaps better not to depend upon the ageing bass who traditionally supplies the starting notes for the operatic society's round-the-village carol-singing. Having heard the pirates swear revenge "for General Stanley's story" the police feel their obvious course is to hide. This they do, and the pirates make their entrance whilst singing another highly popular chorus ("With cat-like tread") in which they formally proclaim their arrival and claim to make it stealthily and soundlessly. The joke is that far from entering quietly, as the words of the song – "In silence dread our cautious way we feel" – suggest, their entry is extremely noisy, with loud intervening orchestral chords in which their pirate boots can stamp heavily and ear-splittingly on the ground. Samuel produces a sack full of burglarious implements which he describes in a brief solo and then distributes to the gang, before another boisterous chorus of "With cat-like tread" brings the number to a deafening conclusion. All the police can do is nervously watch and wait, vainly attempting to bolster their spirits with a further succession of background "tarantaras." It is not unknown for the pirates to make their entrance through the audience, and additional hilarity can be provided by priming a spectator to allow their wallet or handbag to be snatched from them, and returned to them only after a spirited struggle. Pirates who fail to brief their intended victim in advance may find that their tomfoolery backfires on them, particularly if the individual concerned is the society president's 91-year-old mother whose ability to recover her jewellery box will certainly not be enhanced either by her arthritic ankles or her belief that she has been sitting for two hours watching *The Sound Of Music* and wondering why Julie Andrews is taking so long to put in her first appearance.

Frederic, the King and Ruth enter the scene and in recitative ("Hush, hush, not a word") Frederic orders his fellow-conspirators to hide as the Major-General comes. As the principal pirates plus Ruth exit, and the other pirates hide, he enters and in recitative confesses that his deception renders him unable to sleep. His discomfiture is compounded by his belief that he has heard a noise. The pirates obligingly seek to confirm his suspicions with a resounding "Ha, ha!" but the Major-General remains unaware of any potential trouble and in a charming solo with chorus ("Sighing softly to the river") he serenades the loving yet fickle breeze that he believes to have been the cause of the disturbance. This is one of the most lyrical and reflective of all the G & S comic leads' solos, with the orchestra imitating the flow of a brook. The Major-General's absence from his bed has not gone unnoticed by his daughters. Led by Mabel, the girls, clad in nighties and bearing candles, enter hurriedly and in a chattering chorus ("Now what is this, and what is that") endeavour to find out what has summoned him from his bed. The King, Frederic and Samuel reappear; the pirates suddenly come out of hiding and, at the King's spoken command, seize the Major-General. The scene is now set for a dramatic finale to the opera, with no further spoken dialogue. The Major-General is certain that Frederic will assist him, but Frederic has to refuse, singing "I would if I could but I am not able." At a rehearsal for the London premiere of the show, the actor playing Frederic was absent and Gilbert obligingly filled in at this point by warbling "I'd sing if I could but I am not able!"

The King reminds the Major-General of his deceit, and tells him to prepare for death. Certainly his immediate outlook seems unsettled; Mabel in particular is upset that he is to die "unannealed" – i.e. without having received the last religious rites (and nothing to do with Irish jurymen). Some measure of comfort is afforded by the appearance of the police, but in a short battle the pirates overcome them with ease. Stage fights are never easy to mount, and the police might feel they are doubly disadvantaged in any event by being declared the losers in advance. It has been known for the stage to darken at this point and a display of such Batmanesque captions as THUMP, SPLAT, KERPOW and BIFF to be superimposed over the action. The pirates stand triumphant, stating "We triumph now" but the Sergeant replies that they will not enjoy their triumph for long. This is not because, as the King expects, the police declare themselves to be orphans, but because there is an even stronger claim on their allegiance, namely their love for Queen Victoria. The Sergeant is quite correct; at the sound of the monarch's name, it is the pirates' turn to prostrate themselves. The Major-General wastes no time in ordering the police to "place them at the Bar," which of course means "bring them before the court," but initial rehearsals at least will not be complete without one or more wags calling out "Mine's a whisky and soda" or making some similar reference to the imminent consumption of intoxicating refreshment.

Despite Frederic's ill treatment of her throughout the opera, it is Ruth who now enters and saves the piratical bacon. She informs the Major-General, in another absurd *denouement* (not the first, nor the last time in the G & S operas that a happy ending will have been effected by wildly contrived means) that far from being bloodthirsty ruffians, the pirates are noblemen who have gone wrong. The effect on the Major-General is dramatic; he instantly forgives the pirates and invites them not only to resume their ranks and legislative duties, but also to marry the girls – or such girls as have not been reincarnated as pirates during the course of the action. In a reprise of "Poor wandering one" which ends the opera, Mabel and Edith recall fond

66

farmyard memories from Act 1 to celebrate the surrender of their hearts to the erring peers. The police are apparently left with no girls at all, despite the loving send-off they had received before going – supposedly – into battle with the pirates; for them it is merely a case of returning to the humdrum world of booking cyclists for not showing a light after dark, and drunks for urinating against the statue in the town square. This may seem rough justice, especially when the errant peers could have been quite legitimately arrested and charged with conspiracy to kidnap, false imprisonment, resisting arrest, assaulting a police officer, possession of offensive weapons, violent disorder, and raucous singing with intent to cause a breach of the peace.

Patience is in many ways the most underrated of the G & S operas. Though it lacks the immediate appeal and charisma of *The Pirates Of Penzance* and *H.M.S. Pinafore*, it is generally reckoned to contain one of the finest libretti Gilbert ever wrote. Moreover, although the music is generally less memorable than in some of the other operas, there are plenty of singable and catchy melodies. In some ways, *Patience* is the most enduringly topical of any of the operas. In its dig at the preoccupation with aestheticism during the mid-Victorian age, Gilbert was also poking fun at any ephemeral craze which is intensely fashionable for a while before sliding into oblivion. As Geoffrey Smith points out, "any age can discern its own cult heroes, its preening rock stars or poetic visionaries, and their followers, hysterical with longing and adulation." Dissatisfied with mid-Victorian standards, the aesthetics devoted themselves to the worship of beauty, deriving inspiration from such sources as ancient Greece, the Renaissance, the Middle Ages and the Orient. One of the staunchest advocates of the aesthetic movement was a certain Oxford don named Walter Pater, who in his essays counselled devotees to "seek to live beautifully." Such beautiful living might manifest itself in Japanese fans, Oriental jars and vases, jackets of velvet, silk stockings, large flowing ties, long hair and very affected mannerisms and language. Notable in the aesthetic movement was the Pre-Raphaelite Brotherhood, which dedicated itself to recovering the purity of medieval art which Raphael and the Renaissance had supposedly destroyed. Members of the Brotherhood advocated bright colours, subjects drawn from religion or literature, and a cultivation of a mood of dreamy melancholy. Amongst the most famous aesthetics of the age were Algernon Swinburne and Oscar Wilde, who both helped to inspire the central character in the opera. Gilbert's satire was to be directed not so much at the aesthetic ideal, but at those who exaggerated its salient features, including aesthetic shams who jumped on the bandwagon and thereby attempted to gain some cheap popularity and recognition for themselves, and those who fervently pursued the aesthetics only to reject them when they were no longer considered fashionable. It has to be said that when conversing with Wilde, Gilbert met his match; when Gilbert said to Wilde "I wish I could talk like you – I'd keep my mouth shut and claim it as a virtue," Wilde replied "Ah, that would be selfish. I could deny myself the pleasure of talking, but not to others the pleasure of listening."

Although Gilbert saw the aesthetic movement as a good basis for an opera, he subsequently changed his mind and instead drafted a libretto entitled *The Rival Curates* that satirised the excesses of the Anglo-Catholic movement within the Church of England. One of the characters was to have had the splendid name The Rev. Lawn Tennison! Fearful of accusations of irreverence, Gilbert returned to his original idea. (Gilbert knew his place amongst men of the cloth; on staying one night in a hotel and finding it full of clergymen, it is reported that he said he felt "like a lion in a den of Daniels!") The sixth G & S opera opened at the Opera Comique on 23rd April 1881. The first night was a huge success, with no fewer than eight encores; its opening run of 578 performances was the second longest of all the G & S operas, beaten only by *The Mikado*. On 10th October 1881 it transferred to the new Savoy Theatre, the first English theatre to be lit by electricity and one of the first English theatres to introduce the system of queuing – an entirely new innovation to England – for people waiting outside the theatre for unreserved seats. *Patience* is therefore the first of the G & S operas which could properly be called a Savoy opera, although many people still mistakenly give that epithet to any G & S work. All subsequent G & S operas were premiered at the Savoy. One of the principals in the D'Oyly Carte Company, Julia Gwynne, was constantly fined for giggling on stage, and she is reputed to have suggested to Gilbert that the Savoy Theatre was built from the proceeds of her fines!

Despite being so well-received at the beginning, the popularity of the opera has undoubtedly declined as the twentieth century has worn on, and only dedicated G & S societies will give it regular airings. This must be due, in part, to the lack of instantly recognisable songs and catchphrases. There is no policeman's lot, no "What, never," and tarantaras, not to mention tarantulas, are decidedly thin on the ground. Moreover, the second half of the opera is desperately disappointing for the male chorus. After a fairly busy first half, culminating in a splendidly uplifting and operatic finale, the men have to wait until the last two pages of the vocal score before being bidden to open their mouths again. With the interval, therefore, this represents at least an hour's idleness. The better-organised chorus men may take the opportunity to catch up with some office work,which their early departure from their desks that day has precluded them from doing sooner. The danger of course is that they will be so ensconced in their transactions with clients in such far-flung locations as Johannesburg, Wyoming and Arbroath that they will omit to return to the stage for the final sequence. In such cases they will have to trust that on stage at the end there will be at least a few gentlemen whose brain cells that evening will not have been taxed by anything more complex than the puzzle page in the *Daily Express*.

The plot revolves round Reginald Bunthorne (baritone), an aesthetic poet, who is being pursued by a score of rapturous maidens, among them Lady

Angela (mezzo-soprano), Lady Saphir (soprano), Lady Ella (soprano) and Lady Jane (contralto). They in turn heartily reject the noisy, brutish attentions of the 35th Dragoon Guards who are in the vicinity, and among whom are Colonel Calverley (bass), Major Murgatroyd (bass) and the Lieutenant the Duke of Dunstable (tenor). Bunthorne, who confesses to being an aesthetic sham, has eyes only for Patience, a lowly dairy maid (soprano). She initially rejects his advances, but, brought up to believe that love must be unselfish, reluctantly accepts him. Disillusioned, the maidens instead turn their attentions to another aesthetic poet, Archibald Grosvenor (baritone), whilst the dragoons attempt to win favour with the girls by attempting to adopt aestheticism for themselves. Bunthorne, upset at losing the girls' attentions, frightens Grosvenor into discarding aestheticism, only for the maidens to discard it also, and submit happily to the dragoons! Grosvenor's new image makes him quite acceptable to Patience, and in the end only Bunthorne is left single. The alternative title of the opera, *Bunthorne's Bride*, is therefore wholly ironic.

The curtain opens to reveal the exterior of Castle Bunthorne, and a cluster of young maidens dressed in aesthetic draperies and clearly captivated by aesthetic ideals. They play on lutes and mandolins as they sing the opening chorus, "Twenty lovesick maidens we." In the chorus they lament the hopelessness of their love for a certain man, although they do not say who he may be. There is a brief solo for Lady Angela, and also one for Lady Ella; it is her only solo input into the musical content of the show. *Patience* is not the only G & S opera in which the minor lead's one big moment occurs very early on in the proceedings; not only may the audience still be in a less than cordial "I've driven twenty miles to see this show I've had a hard day's work so come on entertain me" humour, but some of the audience may, as the soloist nervously clambers to the summit of her register, still be in the process of setting their car alarms in the multi-storey next door. By the time they are ensconced in their seats, the soloist will have merged back into obscurity with nothing more exciting to look forward to that evening than Mrs Prescott's interval coffee and delicious bilberry scones.

It is Angela who, in the following dialogue, reveals that it is one Reginald, an aesthetic poet, whom they adore, but who, according to Lady Saphir, remains icily insensible to their longings. Lady Jane enters and reveals that Reginald's attentions are directed towards Patience, the village milkmaid, who has never loved before. Saphir exclaims "Oh, he cannot be serious!" Spectators who recall the almost legendary outbursts by John McEnroe at Wimbledon in the 1980's may forgive Saphir the sudden adoption of an American accent (and perhaps an imitation of an angry tennis stroke!) at this point, although it is less certain whether the producer will. Some producers will pride themselves on rigorously following the script and the stage directions to every last detail, and will defend their principles by claiming that "we are the only society within a radius of 20 miles to be able to offer definitive G & S productions." Some will opt for a middle course, preserving the essential framework of the original production but introducing *soupcons* of topicality when occasion demands. Others will send a shudder through the ranks of the hardened, seen-it-all-before actors by announcing that they intend to offer a "novel interpretation" of the work in question. The saviour of any society that falls victim to this misplaced enthusiasm will be one of the committee members who will gently point out that the fireworks planned for the Act 1 finale will activate the smoke detectors, the descent from the flies by parachute will contravene the theatre's health and safety regulations, and the construction of an ocean liner on stage will require the whole performance hall to be extended sideways by a hundred feet, thus making not inconsiderable inroads into the Curl Power hairdressing salon on one side, and Mr Meaty's burger bar on the other.

Patience then appears; like Mabel before her, she is a caricature of Victorian innocence. In a recitative with contributions from Saphir, Angela and the chorus ("Still brooding on their mad infatuation"), and subsequent aria with chorus ("I cannot tell what this love may be"), she expresses her thanks that she has not been touched by the love that seems to make the maidens so miserable. In a welter of pretentious gobbledegook in the ensuing dialogue, Jane points out to Patience that the apparent discomfort that is visited on the allegedly truly happy is "a transcendentality of delirium....which...is aesthetic transfiguration." Patience tells the girls that the 35th Dragoon Guards, to whom they were engaged a year ago, are approaching, but the girls, their tastes now etherealised, scornfully dismiss the idea of waiting for them. Instead they exit into the castle, serenading their Reginald by way of a refrain of "Twenty lovesick maidens we." Immediately after they have left, the dragoons appear, led by Major Murgatroyd. In total contrast to the aesthetic ideal, these men are tough, unimaginative militarists, yet in their way they too are objects of Gilbert's satire, both for their mindless boastfulness and, like the aesthetic shams, their dependency on their costume to attract the fair. They begin by singing a splendid marching song of introduction, "The soldiers of our Queen." Colonel Calverley, another dragoon, then enters and in one of the great G & S patter songs ("If you want a receipt for that popular mystery") he sets out the ingredients for a heavy dragoon. By all accounts, the model heavy dragoon would seem to be a remarkable character, requiring – among other attributes – the "grace of an Odalisque on a divan" and "style of the Bishop of Sodor and Man." There is a vast catalogue of references to famous personages past and present, and the learned and enthusiastic programme contributor will enjoy spending an evening putting together an impressive glossary explaining each and every reference. The problem is, of course, that it will often be too dark to read the programme in the auditorium, and the interval, when a further opportunity for its perusal arises, may be given over to the consumption of much-needed refreshment. It is therefore quite possible that the programme will remain unread and, when conveyed homewards, will be left languishing on the back seat of the car amongst out-of-date road atlases, half-full packets of jelly babies, and 99p cassettes of the work of such musical luminaries as Joe Loss and Frank Ifield.

No sooner has the Colonel finished than the Duke of Dunstable arrives; he is a foppish, upper-class twit who is bored with flattery, adulation and deference and in dialogue explains that he has taken up the military life in the hope of being treated more disrespectfully. The ladies approach but instead of addressing the dragoons they ignore them, preferring to feast their eyes upon Reginald Bunthorne, the object of their affections, who appears at last. With his velvet jacket, knickerbockers, knee-stockings, long hair and eyeglass, he is Whistler, Swinburne and Wilde rolled into one, and is indisputably one of Gilbert's greatest comic creations. A stunning ensemble musical number commencing with female chorus ("In a doleful train") marks his entry with the girls. Although the chorus title may suggest a journey in some uncomfortable rolling stock, it is actually a masterpiece of construction. Firstly the maidens sing of their unrequited love, after which, in much faster tempo, the dragoons sing of the absurdity of being rejected. Angela and Saphir then sing solos of admiration for Bunthorne, Bunthorne sings in admiration for himself, and finally the two chorus tunes are put together in counterpoint. Bunthorne has, all this time, been composing a poem, pretending he has not seen and heard the display of maidenly devotion. In the dialogue following the musical number he makes a great show of searching desperately for the words he requires to complete his composition. Having done so, he makes equally great play of falling into the Colonel's arms, recovering in time to offer to read his poem to Patience who is now amongst those present. Patience, much frightened by his demeanour, gives him permission, and he then launches into the mock-heroic and absurdly pretentious "Oh Hollow! Hollow! Hollow!" Patience dismisses it as nonsense but the other maidens appear to be enchanted by it, and, to add insult to injury, they are scornful of the dragoons and their uniforms. In another display of aesthetic gobbledegook, Jane suggests that a "cobwebby grey velvet, with a tender bloom like cold gravy" might be the basis for an acceptable uniform. Bunthorne and the maidens then depart, to yet a further reprise of "Twenty lovesick maidens we." The dragoons remain, and in another rousing solo from the Colonel, with chorus ("When I first put this uniform on"), they extol the brass helmets, scarlet tunics and gold braid of their uniform, at the same time expressing incredulity that the maidens reject its glamour and charisma. The brief orchestral section which occurs at the beginning of the song, and also as the dragoons leave angrily at the end, offers some possibility for marching. The average collection of chorus dragoons will contain at least one self-styled expert whose knowledge of guardsmen's routine will prove to be a thorn in the side of the producer from the moment he begins to promote it, and sadly for both of them, there will also be at least one dragoon who is stubbornly content to confine his knowledge of drill to the little he remembers from watching the soldiers on duty at Pippin Fort, Camberwick Green.

The dragoons having marched off, Bunthorne makes a dramatic return, to music suggesting the appearance of an intruder. His stealth and slight apprehension are not without good reason; he at once confides in his audience that he is in fact an aesthetic sham, and that his "medievalism's affectation, born of a morbid love of admiration." After his recitative of confession ("Am I alone and unobserved?") he proceeds in an aria ("If you're anxious for to shine") to explain exactly how to become an aesthetic sham in one easy lesson. The song includes such tips as walking down Piccadilly "with a poppy or a lily in your medieval hand," the cult of the lily being well-established amongst the Pre-Raphaelites of the aesthetic movement. After the song Patience appears, and in dialogue Bunthorne confides in her that he is not as aesthetic as he might seem. He presumably hopes that this will make him more acceptable to her. Unfortunately, she remains unimpressed with him, notwithstanding his final attempt at softening her heart with a piece of poetry with the unlikely title *Heart Foam*. As he exits, Angela appears. Patience asks her how love is to be distinguished from insanity. Angela, adopting the aesthetic viewpoint, tells her that love, if it is true, must be totally unselfish. She seems surprised when Patience tells her she has never loved anyone, but, in a charming duet which follows ("Long years ago"), Patience sings of the love she had perhaps fourteen years ago for a little boy at least a year her senior. The words "He was a little boy" occur a number of times, the emphasis coming on a different word each time as the significance of the young love affair unfolds and Angela attempts to clarify the situation. Straight duets for two sopranos are extremely rare in the operas, and this particular item may therefore be a good choice for females of the higher vocal range wishing to collaborate in the course of a compilation evening. It may particularly boost the confidence of singers who have previously attempted to pick their way through Delibes' *Flower Duet* and lost each other by the end of the first page, the pianist by the end of the second, and their nerve a few bars further on.

No sooner has Patience resolved to embark on a course of unselfish love than Archibald Grosvenor appears. Named after the Grosvenor Gallery, an art gallery often visited by the Pre-Raphaelites, his version of aestheticism has been described by Geoffrey Smith as "blandly healthy and self-satisfied, modelled after the more earnest Pre-Raphaelites." Whilst Bunthorne exudes showiness, Grosvenor is languid, solitary and sorrowful; it has been suggested that his character is modelled on that of William Morris. Immediately he and Patience begin a duet, "Prithee, pretty maiden" – another favourite "compilation" item because of its easily-remembered tune and lack of contrapuntal complexity – in which Grosvenor, who confesses both his dolefulness and his wealth, actually proposes marriage! Quite reasonably Patience declines, on the basis that she does not yet know him. In the dialogue which follows, Patience gets to know him very quickly. She realises Grosvenor is her childhood love; furthermore, in an alliterative fever, he confesses that he has loved her with a "Florentine fourteenth-century frenzy for full fifteen years!" His beauty and belief in his own perfection and infallibility quickly weave their spell with Patience, who is ready to give him her heart – until, with horror, she realises that she cannot love him, because love for such a perfect being could never be unselfish. Whilst he may love her, she may not return this love, and in a sad reprise of their duet ("Though to marry you") the sad situation is confirmed and they exit despairingly in different directions. Grosvenor's line "Oh, fatal perfection, again you interpose between me and my happiness" is cited by Henry Lytton, the great D'Oyly Carte Opera Company actor, as an example of a ridiculous line which must be delivered with absolute seriousness in order to underline what he calls the "delightful drollery of the piece." This quotation is taken from his book *The Secrets of a Savoyard* which also makes reference to those who do not know what to do with their hands when on stage. Amateurs seeking an answer to this eternal problem will receive little comfort from Gilbert's advice to Lytton, which was to "cut them off at the wrists (and) forget you've got any!"

The Act 1 finale ensues, beginning with the entry of Bunthorne who is crowned with roses and hung about with garlands; he is led by Angela and Saphir and accompanied by maidens who play on a variety of archaic instruments and sing "Let the merry cymbals sound." Despite their attentions, Bunthorne is extremely miserable. In response to the dragoons' brisk entrance and demand to know what is going on, Bunthorne says that, heartbroken as he is by Patience's rejections, he is going to put himself up to be raffled for. He says he has done this on the advice of his Solicitor, whom he produces. While the maidens are delighted, the dragoons pronounce a curse on the lawyer in question. The Solicitor has no lines of dialogue or solo singing and is on stage for just a few moments. Because of this, it is quite possible for a member of the dragoons to don the Solicitor's costume for the Act 1 finale only. However, in order to attempt to preserve credibility, the more zealous producer may insist that the character playing the Solicitor should take no other performing role in the production. The role therefore may very well be suited to somebody whose business commitments prevent him attending all but the dress rehearsals, or to one who not only has no musical or acting ability, but has the highly unusual gift of recognising the fact and is happy to make an otherwise exclusively backstage contribution to the production. It may be less appealing to the aspiring principal who tries unsuccessfully for every lead role in the production, and who hoped that the part allotted to him would be rather more demanding of his thespian skills than his Sixth Villager was in last December's performance of *Mr Macaroni And The Exploding Pizza Pie*.

The dragoons make one final appeal to the maidens, first by the Colonel's desperate "Stay, we implore you" and then by the Duke's mini-aria "Your maiden hearts." This is a marvellous moment in the opera, where in order to impress the maidens with a show of deep emotion the Duke instructs the men to sigh, then kneel, then weep, and the dragoons respond by doing all these things strictly to order and with military precision. Bunthorne could not be less impressed, and with his impatient "Come, walk up and purchase with avidity" tries to hurry the girls into buying their tickets. In the meanwhile, the dragoons march round the stage, pretending not to mind that they have been rejected. Jane then enters and to Bunthorne's consternation informs him that she, too, will buy a ticket. Fearing the worst, he bids her draw the winning girl's name, but before she can do so, Patience enters and in a dramatic solo ("If there be pardon in your breast") agrees to marry him. Bunthorne is overjoyed, believing that her change of mind has been prompted by genuine affection. Patience responds immediately, "No, Mr Bunthorne, no – you're wrong again." In rehearsals this line is sure to attract some laughter if the character playing Bunthorne has indeed failed to sing his preceding recitative correctly. The danger is that a mischievous member of the cast will cotton on to the phrase and use it mercilessly the moment anybody is guilty of the slightest musical or dramatic error. Even worse, a producer may at 11.10 p.m. unthinkingly bellow "No, chorus, no, you're wrong again" after the players' seventh unsuccessful attempt to execute a dance, and find half of them singing the dreaded words back at him with a sadistic zeal that suggests intimate knowledge of either the Spanish Inquisition's principal torture manual, or the mystical force which causes the debit card machine at Tesco to malfunction whenever more than six trolley-laden customers are queuing up behind.

Patience goes on to explain the basis of her decision – that love for one so unappealing to her must indeed be unselfish. Bunthorne does not mind at all; he has Patience and that is all he cares about. The two of them leave the scene. For a moment, resigned to losing Bunthorne forever, the maidens return to the dragoons. In a sestette and chorus ("I hear the soft note") which has a distinctly sacred feel to it, they sing of their old love from which they will waver no more. The sestette section, involving principals only, is unaccompanied; if it remains in tune, it is truly one of the tenderest and most impressive musical moments of the opera. Unfortunately the dragoons' joy is short-lived, for after the chorus section Grosvenor appears on the scene and his entrance causes the maidens to withdraw from the embrace of the men. Worse still for the dragoons, Grosvenor announces that he is a "broken-hearted troubadour whose mind's aesthetic and whose tastes are pure." The word "aesthetic" is all that the maidens need to hear; at once they leave the dragoons and announce their love for Grosvenor. Grosvenor, whose heart is set on Patience, is now in an identical situation to that of Bunthorne at the start of the finale; the thought that the maidens love him fills him with dismay. In a most operatic and impressive ensemble finish to Act 1, the maidens sing of their love, Grosvenor of his woes, Patience (who has returned) of her unselfishness, Bunthorne (who has also returned) of his jealousy of this new rival, and the dragoons of their anger. The multi-part harmony, reaching its climax with a held top C for Patience, is one of the finest musical sections in the opera. This may perhaps heighten the sense of anticlimax subsequently felt by the chorus men as they queue up for Mrs Prescott's exquisite bilberry scones, knowing that their musical endeavours over the ensuing hour will be restricted either to humming snatches of the audition pieces for *Chu Chin Chow*, the society's next show, or rehearsing those Act 1 male choral sections of *Patience* the existence of which has only just been brought to their attention.

The maidens, however, are back in action the moment the interval has passed, singing an off-stage plea to Grosvenor ("On such eyes as maidens cherish let thy fond adorers gaze"). At the same time, and as the curtain opens, Jane is discovered leaning on a cello in a glade. She reflects that Bunthorne should hurry to claim her while she is still sufficiently good-looking; in a recitative ("Sad is that woman's lot") and aria ("Silvered is the raven hair") she sings of the diminishing attractions of women as they grow older. The song is one of the saddest in all the G & S operas, with its images of greying hair and declining sight. After her solo, Jane exits and the maidens appear with Grosvenor, imploring him in song to "turn, oh turn in this direction." Grosvenor, with some reluctance – for it is Patience after whom he still hankers – agrees in dialogue to read them some poetry, and produces two verses which he recites out loud. In contrast to Bunthorne's pretentious compositions, they are utterly prosaic, bearing more than a passing resemblance to Hilaire Belloc's cautionary tales for children. Despite their simplicity, the maidens are enraptured by the poems. Angela is particularly moved by the fate of Teasing Tom, the very bad boy who put live shrimps in his father's boots, who was consequently "lost to*tally* and married a girl in the *corps de bally!*" "Marked you," she exclaims, "how grandly – how relentlessly – the damning catalogue of crime strode on, till Retribution, like a poised hawk, came swooping down upon the wrongdoer?" Grosvenor, tired with the admiration, asks for "the usual half-holiday" and sings to the girls of the fable of the Magnet and the Churn ("A magnet hung in a hardware shop") in which the Magnet was able to wheedle everything but his beloved Silver Churn. As he recites and then sings to the maidens, who join in the end of each verse, he is directed to remain seated; Audrey Williamson suggests that he should sit on a tree stump. The rural, idyllic landscapes in which both this Act and also sizeable parts of *Iolanthe* and *Utopia Limited* are set suggests that any G & S society wishing to perform all the operas should have a tree stump on permanent standby. The producer may direct that a principal should sit on it either to facilitate a moment of calm reflection or soliloquy, or to add some extra movement into a scene, or indeed because in a standing position the performer's gaucheness and nervousness are reminiscent of the Fowler Road Sports Club Under 15 "B" team goalkeeper about to face a penalty kick from Brazil's top striker. Since prior to show week the tree stump will remain in the darker recesses of the props cupboard or stored away with other society paraphernalia in a farmhouse several miles from the society's meeting hall, some other object will have to be used by the producer to represent the stump during rehearsals. A chair is the obvious choice, although it will be a lucky producer who does not find that, within five minutes of the commencement of the evening's work, this item has been unwittingly appropriated by an ignorant chorus member who is taking advantage of a few moments of idleness to continue work on her great-nephew's woollen bootees.

The maidens, apparently resigned to failure in their quest for Grosvenor, leave the stage, and Patience appears. In dialogue she confesses to Grosvenor how unhappy she is in her unselfish love for Bunthorne, but despite her joy at knowing how much Grosvenor loves her she feels quite

78

unable to return that love. Grosvenor departs in sorrow, and immediately Bunthorne and Jane appear, the latter singing a solo reprise of "In a doleful train." Bunthorne is consumed with jealousy at the thought of Patience spending time with Grosvenor, while Jane is equally jealous of Patience and the love Bunthorne has for her. In some bitter spoken exchanges, Bunthorne accuses Patience of being unaware of what love is, thereby prompting Patience to sing a ballad, "Love is a plaintive song." Jane and Bunthorne exit as the song begins. Although it is a pleasant and not overdemanding number, the words are intensely sad, as the singer paints a picture of true love as an act of duty, with little or no reward and much heartache and suffering. Patience exits in tears, while Bunthorne and Jane re-enter and continue their heated dialogue. It is clear from the conversation that Bunthorne's jealousy makes him incapable of acknowledging Jane's affection for him. He only seems to mellow towards her when she promises to help him reduce Grosvenor's following amongst the female fraternity, and in a spirited duet ("So go to him and say to him") Jane encourages him to confront Grosvenor and use a mixture of insult and threat to frighten him off. The catchy tune and its liberal sprinklings of "Booh to you, pooh pooh to you, Bah to you, Ha ha to you," sung at not inconsiderable speed, makes it an obvious choice for an encore. The audience, however, is in for an even greater treat; no sooner have Bunthorne and Jane left together than the Duke, Colonel and Major appear dressed and made up in imitation of aesthetics. Their dragoon uniform has been discarded in favour of velvet coats with lilies or sunflowers attached, velvet knee-breeches, flowing ties and long hair. With suitable staccato accompaniment to suggest puppets on strings, they combine marionette-like dancing round the stage with stiff, constrained and angular attitudes – a deliberate exaggeration of those adopted by Bunthorne and his followers earlier on. As they dance, they sing a trio full of short, punchy staccato notes ("It's clear that medieval art"); this number, in which the dragoons try to justify their actions, should prove to be the highlight of the evening. During the dialogue that follows, all three strike an attitude which, although excruciatingly uncomfortable, seems to bring its reward as Angela and Saphir appear and in suitably picturesque language express their delight at the dragoons' new commitment to aestheticism. "How Botticellian!" Saphir exclaims, whilst Angela remarks "Oh, Saphir, are they not quite too all-but?" Saphir's reply "They are indeed jolly utter" has a touch of the Angela Brazil about it. The girls do not seem at all concerned that the only reason the dragoons have done this is to win back their affections, and are delighted at the fresh attitudes "expressive of aesthetic rapture" that are struck once the girls have suggested their hearts might return to the men once more. The only question is how the pairings will work; with three men and only two girls this might be problematic, but in a quintet with ample scope for dancing ("If Saphir I choose to marry") it is agreed that the odd male out will have to be contented with the heartfelt sympathy of the others. To the unbiased observer, a goodly helping of sympathy would appear to be preferable to a requirement to adopt cramp-inducing poses to order, or to use picturesque language to respond to a tax demand or communications from the municipal sewerage corporation.

With the five of them leaving the stage, the scene is set for the final showdown between Grosvenor and Bunthorne. Grosvenor enters first and reflects once more on his beauty, but he is soon interrupted by the appearance of his rival. In an animated conversation, Bunthorne wastes no time in expressing his displeasure that Grosvenor is so popular with the girls. Grosvenor is only too keen to shake them off, but he refuses to do as Bunthorne suggests, namely become matter-of-fact and – unthinkable for a Pre-Raphaelite – have a back parting in his hair. Bunthorne threatens a curse unless Grosvenor complies, and despite Grosvenor's pleas for mercy, he persists until Grosvenor gives in. Bunthorne is jubilant, and Grosvenor is after all relieved that he has a pretext for abandoning his current lifestyle. A duet ("When I go out of door") follows, in which Bunthorne looks forward to a glorious future as a champion of aestheticism and consequent object of female admiration. In the meantime Grosvenor considers with pleasure a life out of the aesthetic hothouse as "A very delectable, highly respectable, threepenny-bus young man." Inflation has of course taken its toll on the idea of a threepenny bus ride, but with so many words to fit into limited supplies of music it might be unreasonable to rechristen Grosvenor as the "One pound twenty bus young man" or for the even more economy-conscious the "London Transport One Day Travelcard (Not available before 10 a.m. Mondays to Fridays) young man."

Grosvenor exits and Bunthorne remains. Patience appears and, in dialogue, Bunthorne reveals that whilst still embracing aestheticism, his brand thereof will be more cheerful, amusing and pastoral. This is music to the ears of Patience, who fondly embraces him – until she realises that because Bunthorne is now perfect, there can be nothing unselfish about loving him! To compound Bunthorne's anguish, Grosvenor re-enters, followed by the maidens, all singing a musical reprise of the previous song. Not only has Grosvenor discarded aestheticism, but the girls have all discarded it too, and in the song proclaim themselves to be "prettily pattering, cheerily chattering, everyday young girls." The chorus dragoons are at last directed to reappear, and follow Grosvenor and the girls on to the stage. Grosvenor has had the quickest haircut on record, and has also changed into a suit with exactly matching waistcoat – a suit of loud checks will be most appropriate – and pot hat. As his subsequent spoken lines reveal, he may also have acquired a regional dialect, depending on the location of the show. His ordinariness is of course quite acceptable to Patience who fondly embraces him, much to Bunthorne's disgust. Only Jane seems to remain loyal to Bunthorne and when she says she will never leave him, he does not seek to argue! At this moment a flourish announces the reappearance of the Colonel, Duke and Major, each one in their dragoon uniform once more. The Duke has determined to select a bride and, on the basis that all the good-looking girls will be contented enough with their own beauty, he unselfishly chooses the one who "has the misfortune to be distinctly plain." It is, of course, Jane. Moments after vowing to Bunthorne that she would never desert him, she promptly hurries to the Duke, demonstrating that she is apparently now indifferent to the attractions of aestheticism and much keener on the Duke's uniform and his "thousand a day." A singularly disappointing Act 2 finale follows, led by the Duke ("After much debate internal"); in a musical reprise of the quintet the maidens and the dragoons unite happily, and the company agrees that Bunthorne will have to be contented with a tulip or li*ly*. Thus does another ephemeral craze bite the dust, as Donny Osmond, punk rock, flared jeans and Sinclair C5's were to do decades later. The message of the opera is clear, namely that there is a distinction between passing fads and things of truly timeless and enduring quality; such things might include love, friendship, humility, and, of course, the recipe for Mrs Prescott's mouthwatering bilberry scones.

"My Lord, I know no Courts of Chancery; I go by
Nature's Acts of Parliament"

After three operas in which the supernatural was entirely absent, the seventh G & S offering saw it return with interest. As soon as thoughts were directed to a successor to *Patience,* Gilbert decided that he wanted a story which involved interaction between fairies and prosaic mortals. Initially he thought that these mortals should be lawyers but, as with *Patience*, he changed his mind and the story evolved into a tale involving a confrontation between fairies and Parliament. This enabled him to indulge in his love for the nonsensical and fantastical, and take a dig at not only the legal profession, but also the Lower and Upper Houses. His most piercing satire was reserved for the House of Lords; the idea of birth being qualification for membership of an assembly which had the power to approve or veto legislation appealed very much to his sense of the ridiculous. At the time, this theme was particularly topical, as much of Gladstone's legislation was being blocked by the Lords. The inclusion of members of the peerage meant that Gilbert could create a colourful and grandiose spectacle, reflected in music by Sullivan that was instantly reminiscent of Wagner and Mendelssohn. As if to reflect the thespian and musical demands that this opera would pose, rehearsals for the new work, which the cast were told was to be called *Perola*, were correspondingly intense. As with all the operas, Gilbert had every last detail planned. As Hesketh Pearson points out, "nothing was left to chance, and the company had to go through its evolutions at the word of command, repeating them as on a parade ground, until the process became automatic. Knowing what he wanted, (Gilbert) took endless pains to get it, occasionally repeating a word 20 or 30 times before the actor could speak it rightly, often doing a scene over and over again until the performers were breaking under the strain." However, his wit was never far away; on one occasion he famously remarked to his chorus of peers "For heaven's sake wear your coronets as if you were used to them." His insistence that the peers shave off their moustaches – which were very fashionable in those days – caused one chorus member to resign; as George Grossmith remarked, "the moustache stayed on but he did not."

The real bombshell for the cast exploded just hours before the opening performance on 25th November 1882. Sullivan announced to them that the name *Perola* was to be replaced by *Iolanthe* whenever it was mentioned in the book. The composers had always intended to call the work *Iolanthe* but used the false name deliberately to mislead potential pirate performers (there is also a suggestion that Henry Irving, a contemporary of theirs, had used *Iolanthe* in a play of his own and *Perola* had thus been used pending resolution of any possible copyright problems). The change caused huge consternation until Sullivan reassured the company that it would not matter too much if they forgot the change since the only one who would notice would be Gilbert – and he would not be at the first night anyway!

Sullivan was right; Gilbert did not attend the first performance. Gilbert often did forgo the pleasure of seeing his own work from the auditorium; Hesketh Pearson remarks that he "felt sick of a work by the time it was ready for the public." He thus gave directors of subsequent productions the perfect precedent to absent themselves from the theatre on performance nights. News of such absences may be hailed as a godsend by those performers who feel able to reinstate any pieces of so-called comic business the producer has seen fit to expunge. These may be so innocuous that upon learning of them the producer may turn a benevolent blind eye; at worst, however, they may distort the composers' intentions to such an extent that audience members may be forgiven for wondering if they mistakenly turned left instead of right at the Hogs Head traffic lights and have blundered into the Old Wash House Festival of Alternative Comedy (Not Suitable For Children Or Those Of Sensitive Disposition).

Whilst *Patience*'s popularity has dwindled with the passing years, *Iolanthe* is still a favourite with all operatic societies, and not just those that specialise in G & S productions. With its combination of escapist nonsense, biting political satire (the opera still has a topical feel about it even today) and Sullivan's most impressive music, it remains one of the classics of the G & S operas. There are two aspects of the opera which are of particular historical significance; it was the first opera to be premiered simultaneously on both sides of the Atlantic, and was the first opera to receive its British premiere in the Savoy Theatre (the New York opening was at the Standard Theater). Its initial run at the Savoy was 398 performances. The opera received mixed reactions when it was first performed. The satire was found by some to be a little too pronounced, and indeed two numbers were subsequently removed from the production for that reason. However, there was great acclaim for the music, and five months after the premiere Sullivan was offered a knighthood. This must have been of great consolation to him, following not only the death of his mother earlier in 1882, but also the startling revelation – on the very day of the first performance – that his stockbrokers had become bankrupt and therefore he had lost his life savings. Sadly, financial matters will never be far from the thoughts of amateur societies that are devoted to the works of G & S, and members staring insolvency in the face will certainly not be helped by constant reminders that essential debts are overdue, to wit the current year's £30 subscription plus £20 costume levy, £5 show-week coffee and biscuit money, £4 contributions to gifts for the production team, down payments on the fish-and-chip supper to be provided after the Saturday matinee, and money for flowers for Mrs Harbottle who has just gone into hospital for removal of a troublesome verruca.

The opera – the alternative title of which is *The Peer And The Peri* – revolves around its title character Iolanthe (soprano), a fairy who has been ostracised from the other fairies including Celia (soprano), Fleta (soprano) and Leila (soprano) by marrying a mortal. Her son, Strephon (baritone), is of course half a fairy and in love with Phyllis (soprano), a ward in Chancery. Her choice of husband is within the gift of the Lord Chancellor (baritone), who, together with the Lords Mountararat (bass) and Tolloller (tenor) and the other members of the House of Lords is in love with her himself. Indeed the entire assembly of peers has come after her. Fearful that the peers will have their way, the Fairy Queen (contralto) decides to get revenge by sending Strephon into Parliament with a view to forcing through legislation that the peers are afraid will undermine them. Whilst Tolloller and Mountararat decide not to pursue Phyllis, the Lord Chancellor is still determined. Iolanthe then reveals that the Lord Chancellor is in fact her husband and Strephon's father. Aware that she risks death by doing so, she goes to the Lord Chancellor – who believes her to have died – and tells him she is still alive. By fairy law she should be put to death, but all the other fairies have fallen in love with the peers and the Fairy Queen herself cannot resist the charms of Private Willis, the Sentry (baritone). A simple change of law enables the full company to fly off to Fairyland together.

The opera opens in an Arcadian landscape. As with *Patience*, it is the girls who are given responsibility for opening the show; as fairies, they enter and trip round the stage, singing of their fairy qualities as they dance ("Tripping hither, tripping thither"). There is a lovely piece of (presumably) tongue-in-cheek writing where the fairies find themselves singing "We are dainty little fairies" double *forte* to a thumping orchestral accompaniment! The very first production of *Iolanthe* in the Savoy saw electric lights powered by invisible batteries twinkling in their hair. However, the fairies are not happy; in dialogue they recall how it is now twenty-five years since Iolanthe, the life and soul of Fairyland, was banished from their community because she married a mortal, and by fairy law she should have died. At this point the Fairy Queen (hereinafter the Queen) enters and points out that it was at her behest that the death sentence was commuted to one of penal servitude. The Queen is one of the more satisfying of the aged G & S alto roles; there is more than a hint of the Wagnerian heroine Brunnhilde in her, and extra gravitas will be imported to the role if she dons a winged helmet and armour after her Teutonic counterpart. Despite her quite formidable appearance, she admits that it was her love for Iolanthe that saved the latter from execution, and she seems dismayed when she learns that Iolanthe is working out her sentence "on her head" at the bottom of a stream. In this context "on her head" means "without difficulty" but some listeners might develop mischievous visions of a fairy with a cranium covered in unappetising pieces of sand and weed, and legs kicking vainly and impotently above the surface of the water.

The other fairies try to persuade the Queen to recall her from this watery incarceration; the Queen, who remembers how despite her not inconsiderable size Iolanthe taught her to "dive into a dewdrop" and "nestle in a nutshell," consents. A musical invocation follows ("Iolanthe, from thy dark exile thou art summoned") in which Iolanthe appears from the watery depths, the Queen officially pardons her, and the fairies welcome her back to fairy duties. This will be a difficult scene to portray realistically unless a trapdoor is built into the stage and Iolanthe can appear magically through the floor. Alternatively, dry ice can be pumped across the back of the stage, and out of the swirl of white Iolanthe can make a suitably atmospheric entrance. The dry-ice pumper has a heavy responsibility; whilst the release of an insufficient quantity will call into question the wisdom of a forty-mile round trip to obtain the necessary equipment, an excessive output may eliminate any thoughts of Arcadia and instead provoke images of the view from the Isle of Wight ferry during a severe sea fret.

In dialogue Iolanthe explains that the reason she chose the stream, rather than any other venue, for her confinement was to be near her son Strephon, who was born soon after her banishment. Leila expresses surprise that with her young features she could have a son of nearly 25 years. It is therefore important that if possible the character playing Iolanthe does *not* in fact look old enough to have children or indeed grandchildren approaching that age. However, even if the audience forgive an aged society membership for failure – or, more likely, inability – to cast a comparative youngster in the role, Leila may be guilty of stretching the imagination of the spectators a little too far, particularly in societies with a wide age range of members, when she announces that one of the advantages of being immortal is that "we never grow old!" Gilbert may well have smiled inwardly as he wrote these words, and modern-day audiences may also smile ruefully as they gaze upon a cluster of elderly troupers on whom even the most rigorous application of make-up cannot compensate for their appearance on the waiting list for the local hospital's next consignment of Zimmer frames.

Iolanthe tells the fairies that her son is an Arcadian shepherd, in love with Phyllis, and to reflect his parenthood, he is a fairy down to the waist but his legs are mortal. As if to satisfy the curiosity of the fairies, he enters at this point, accompanying his recitative of introduction, with chorus ("Good morrow, good mother"), on a flageolet. In the dialogue that follows, he tells the fairies the bad news; because his lover Phyllis is a ward in Chancery, and effectively therefore the Court of Chancery is her guardian, he needs the Lord Chancellor's consent to marry her, and this is not forthcoming. Moreover, the very fact of his being half a fairy is a perennial problem for him; as he says, it is no use being able to get his body through a keyhole if his legs are left kicking behind. Even the offer of a passport to Parliament – which through the vagaries of the parliamentary system the Queen can provide him – fills him with trepidation as his fairy and mortal halves have different political persuasions. The Queen suggests he might like to be returned as a "Liberal-Conservative" which over a century later would make little sense; even the most traditional G & S producer should consider substituting "Liberal Democrat" here.

Whilst singing a solo of farewell and offer of future assistance ("Fare thee well, attractive stranger") the Queen leaves him, and the fairies follow, singing a reprise of part of the opening chorus. Iolanthe gives her son a fond farewell and also leaves. As soon as she disappears, Phyllis arrives, also playing on a flageolet, greeting her beloved in song ("Good morrow, good lover") which with Strephon adding his voice at the end, is a straight reprise of the earlier number with similar title. The lovers embrace and in dialogue indulge in an exchange which says much about Gilbert's views on marriage: when Strephon says "We are to be made happy for ever" Phyllis responds drily "Well, we're to be married!"

Phyllis seems uneasy that Strephon is deliberately defying the law by going ahead with his marriage to her immediately rather than waiting two years until she is of age. However, one look at a pocket mirror convinces Phyllis that it would be unreasonable for Strephon to expect to wait two years, particularly as half the House of Lords are madly in love with her themselves. The couple confirm their devotion to one another in the delightful love duet "None shall part us." The semiquavers in the orchestral accompaniment give the impression of a rolling stream, as reflected by the words: "Thou the stream and I the willow; thou the sculptor; I the clay." The entrance of the peers is now imminent and there will be frenetic activity in the wings during this song as the male chorus prepare to enter in full pomp and splendour; one hopes that the pastoral charm of the young lovers' professions will not have to compete with less Arcadian sentiments such as

"Where the hell's Mick? He's supposed to be at the front!"... "Hey, Stan, your coronet's on the wrong way round..." "No, Ian changed that bit last night, we turn left when we get to the front and stop on the third 'Tantara'..." "No he didn't, that's only the first basses – we turn right and then bow on the first 'Tzing Boom'..." "If you'd ducked the spade lead on round 3 we'd have got them down..."

The lovers exit, leaving the way clear for the entrance and march of the peers of the realm, and peers' chorus. This is one of the great spectacles in all G & S opera; Geoffrey Smith describes it as one of the "stellar moments" in the series. A critic at the premiere of *Iolanthe* gave an idea of its grandeur: "Dark and light blue, crimson, pale green and rich purple mantles, embroidered with quaint devices and mottoes – ermine, velvet, pearls, strawberry leaves, enamel and glittering metal – all these and many other splendid emblematic gauds will meet the eye." The words of the peers' chorus of introduction ("Loudly let the trumpet bray") embody a sense of shameless superiority – "Bow, bow, ye lower middle classes, bow, bow, ye tradesmen, bow ye masses." It is traditional for the peers, each man a picture of lofty arrogance, to execute a well-drilled march round the stage before and during the chorus, but other less conventional business has proved popular in recent years, such as a cricket match in a 1991 D'Oyly Carte production!

As soon as the chorus has ended, the Lord Chancellor appears. This is one of the most delectable G & S comic roles, with three splendid songs including the most famous patter song in all of G & S opera. At the same time, the character is no buffoon, and indeed his scene with Iolanthe towards the end of the opera is arguably the most touching and tender ever given to a G & S comic lead. For the time being he enters to the strains of a mock-Baroque fugue which will be heard twice more to signal his entry on to the stage. According to stage directions, he should be assisted by a train-bearer, which like Hercules in *The Sorcerer* and the Midshipmite in *H.M.S. Pinafore* is eminently suitable for a child performer; the fact that the train-bearer has no name and does not appear in the list of *dramatis personae* may come as a disappointment to youngsters who dream of stardom. The Lord Chancellor sings a solo, with chorus, in praise of the Law ("The Law is the true embodiment") but goes on to complain that his own legal duties are frustrating, in that he spends all day giving away attractive Chancery wards but never seems to end up with one for himself. Lord Tolloller then enters and the Lord Chancellor explains to him in dialogue that he is singularly attracted by one of the wards, namely Phyllis. The other peers are similarly enamoured of her, and the Lord Chancellor will raise many hopes by saying to them "If I could reconcile it with my duty, I should unhesitatingly award her to…" before crushing them by adding "….myself!"

The Lord Chancellor goes on to elaborate upon the conflict of interest that would emerge if he married one of his own wards without his own consent! Lord Mountararat then appears and informs him that the lady in question has been persuaded to present herself to them. It will therefore be noted that neither Tolloller nor Mountararat, presumably selected for their roles because of their strong singing voices, are scheduled to be on stage for the march of the peers. This will not stop some producers requesting that they deign to participate in the number anyway, particularly if the male chorus line is limited to two tone-deaf tenors and three bumbling basses, two of whom are incapable of holding a line and one of whom has heard nothing out of his left ear since 1946.

Phyllis enters and begins a lengthy musical sequence with a short introductory recitative ("My well-loved Lord") whilst the peers react with delight at the vision of loveliness that stands before them. Tolloller sings a solo of admiration ("Of all the young ladies I know") which Mountararat and then the chorus enthusiastically endorse, but mixed with the gushing compliments is a note of snobbery, as Tolloller remarks "Her origin's lowly, it's true." Phyllis rejects the peers' advances and their suggestions of her inferiority; she even goes so far as to sing in the following recitative ("Nay, tempt me not") that virtue is not to be found amongst the country's elite. It is now Tolloller's turn to defend his corner, and in one of the most majestic and enjoyable tenor arias in the operas ("Spurn not the nobly born") he, supported by the chorus of peers, points out that his blue-blooded background is no bar to respectability or pure-heartedness. However, Phyllis remains unmoved, and causes further consternation by announcing that her heart is given to another. On enquiry from the Lord Chancellor as to the identity of the one who has stolen her heart from them, Strephon appears, and as Phyllis joyfully rushes to his arms he proclaims that he (Strephon) is indeed the man. In a musical section with a decidedly rustic flavour ("A shepherd I") Strephon proudly announces to the peers that he and Phyllis are betrothed and intend to get married that day. This is a massive shock to the peers, but their innate proudness gives them the necessary determination to depart in a dignified and stately manner, at the same time as the Lord Chancellor separates Phyllis from Strephon and sends her away. As the peers depart, their outward bearing as domineering as when they entered, they sing a reprise of the latter section of the peers' chorus; timing is important, since it would be most unfortunate if the exit was too quick and the only audience for the final "Tantara" was a harassed wardrobe assistant waiting to see what might be done to reshoe the young peer who has been loftily flaunting his sartorial elegance and refined superiority in a pair of ten-eyelet cherry Doc Martens.

The Lord Chancellor is left on stage with Strephon who in dialogue explains his disobedience to the laws of Chancery by reference to the commands of Nature. The Lord Chancellor fails to find any legal justification for Strephon's actions, and insists on applying strict rules of evidence to the situation. He sings of his own devotion to his legal duties in the second of his great trio of songs ("When I went to the Bar"). This song is perhaps Gilbert's most potent dig at the legal profession, in which barristers are impliedly accused of misleading juries, failing to read their case papers, failing to turn up when required, and routinely treating hostile witnesses as liars. The song is not only damning in its satire; it is extremely catchy with a busy, almost mischievous orchestral accompaniment, and only the most pedestrian Lord Chancellor will fail to mime the Army, the Navy, the Church and the Stage in the final verse. In turn the conductor should allow suitable pauses for him to complete each mime before directing the orchestra to pick up the tempo again. The Lord Chancellor leaves to what should hopefully be thunderous applause. Strephon, however, left alone on the stage, is not applauding and finds himself in tears. Iolanthe, his mother, enters and in dialogue comforts him, promising to take his case to the Fairy Queen herself. As Strephon is consoled by his attractive young mother, who of course never grows old, the peers creep on to the stage and look, aghast, at what appears to be an act of dastardly unfaithfulness by their rival for the affections of Phyllis. Music begins, and with Strephon reflecting in recitative ("When darkly looms the day") on his ability to confide in a sympathetic mother in times of difficulty, the Act 1 finale gets under way. In fact it is the longest finale in the G & S operas, running to 35 pages of vocal score. Those entrusted with making interval coffee may mistakenly believe, as the finale starts, that the time for refreshment is close at hand, and turn up the urn by a couple of notches. As the finale proceeds, they may have cause to regret their decision, particularly if the consequently generous accumulation of humid steaminess prompts a passer-by either to alert the local fire brigade or strip down to his boxer shorts in the honest belief that he has stumbled upon a Turkish bath.

It is most unfortunate that Iolanthe should look so demure and indeed so desirable. Not only the peers but also Phyllis mishear Iolanthe's motherly words to her son. Tolloller mistakenly believes her (Iolanthe) to have remarked that she would meet Strephon "inside St James's Park and give him one." Well might the Lords, and of course Phyllis, recoil in horror! The listening group bide their time, then pounce; Phyllis angrily commands Strephon "Oh, shameless one, tremble" and Strephon's response that the lady is his mother meets merely with a derisive uproar. The Lord Chancellor enters and demands to know what is going on, but when the situation is explained to him, he too refuses to believe Strephon's story. Further laughter comes from the peers; Sullivan actually wrote some notes for the peers to sing "Ha ha ha ha ha ha ha ha ha" to, although it is likely that the only people who will sing them will either be the purists who believe that every last note of Sullivan's should be sung precisely as it is written, or those whom the musical director cannot necessarily trust to emit laughs in time with his beat.

Strephon insists in a recitative that she "is, has been, my mother from my birth" and then sings a ballad ("In babyhood upon her lap I lay") in which he stresses his childhood dependence on his mother for shelter and sustenance. This rather sentimental solo prompts mock sobbing from the peers, closely followed – at Mountararat's bidding – by genuine tears of regret that Strephon is still alive. In giving a passable impression of weeping, each peer may be required by the producer to dry his tears with a handkerchief that is secreted somewhere in his robe. A society that prides itself on professional standards will no doubt boast an assiduous properties assistant who will check with each peer that the relevant item is in place; in more relaxed societies the members may have to remember such details for themselves, and it will be unfortunate but unsurprising if a hand that is dipped into the interior of a robe emerges with nothing more effective in wiping lachrymal deposit than a scrap of paper with a reminder to bring half a dozen vol-au-vents to the after-show party.

Iolanthe manages to escape as the mockery of Strephon continues, although what hurts the half-fairy most is Phyllis' announcement to the "traitorous one" that she and he must part for ever. She refuses to listen to his pleadings, and he is shamed into departing the stage. As he leaves, Phyllis decides to give her heart to one of the peers, but in a solo ("For riches or rank I do not long") she makes it clear that such a decision arises out of necessity rather than true love. Indeed in response to the peers' puzzled enquiry, she says she is not really bothered which peer she ends up with. Strephon returns, but this time he is not alone; he has summoned the fairies, including their Queen, and for the first time in the whole opera both the male and female chorus are on stage together. The fairies provide a reprise of "Tripping hither, tripping thither" before a brisk piece of patter singing in which each of the main protagonists sets out his or her point of view, with Strephon protesting his innocence, the Queen rallying to his support, and the peers maintaining their disbelief. They are particularly uncomprehending of the fact that Strephon claims to be 25 and his mother eight years younger. As the chorus confirm, "that's the kind of mother that is usually spurious!"

A piece of true grand opera now approaches, as the Lord Chancellor implores the Queen to "Go away, madam" and in a big concerted number, in the minor key, he and the peers insist on the brazen-faced Queen and her fairies taking their leave. Meanwhile, the Queen threatens "all the most terrific thunders in my armoury of wonders." The complex contrapuntal harmonies in the ensuing chorus reflect the divisions between the stubborn peers and the mischievous fairies; it is immensely dramatic music and requires considerable coaching from the musical director. Directors fortunate enough to be working with knowledgeable or experienced societies may have few problems, but for inexperienced performers some "note bashing" is inevitable. The one who will suffer the most, as each part is laboriously played and sung one line at a time, and then sung with random combinations of soprano and tenor, alto and tenor, soprano and bass, soprano, tenor and bass, will be the one person in the room who actually has sung it before and knows his or her part. Unable to sneak away from the rehearsal through being hemmed in by the fourteen-and-a-half stone Mrs Wilson-Pugh on one side, and the officious secretary with her immaculately-kept attendance register laid out on her knee on the other, profitable activity may be restricted either to attempting to read the first page of the minutes of the highly confidential executive committee meeting that can be seen resting beneath Mrs Fotherington's chair, or counting the number of bluebells in the pattern that has been revealed by the peeling wallpaper behind the piano.

The Queen and the Lord Chancellor continue to squabble, she protesting at his cavalier attitude and he admitting that he has underestimated the forces he is up against. As Leila points out, however, "they meet who underrate our calling doom appalling." The Queen then makes her pronouncement; inviting Strephon to "henceforth…cast away crooks and pipes and ribbons so gay" and directing him to go into Parliament. There then follows a list of examples of legislation that she expects Strephon to see enacted, each one gravely damaging to the peers' interests. Not all of them are comprehensible to an audience watching *Iolanthe* over a century later; "marriage with deceased wife's sister," for instance, which in any case became lawful in 1907, would not strike the modern audience as an issue that was likely to fire the peers with anger. As each proposal is announced, the peers react with cries of dismay and disbelief. The final suggestion is that "a Duke's exalted station be attainable by competitive examination;" a more topical substitution, which should bring a smile to the faces of any teachers in the audience, might be "attainable by comprehensive education!"

All this is too much for the Lord Chancellor, who may be directed to faint with horror before the now triumphant fairies. In a final ensemble section, bringing the Act 1 finale to an end ("With Strephon for your foe, no doubt"), the fairies look forward eagerly to the big changes Strephon will bring, while the peers march angrily round the stage swearing their defiance and determination to get their revenge. They are insistent that the exalted ranks of Parliament should not be diluted with "base *canaille*," "vulgar *plebs*" and "hoi polloi" (the vocal score and libretto both show the original Greek spelling of this expression), all synonymous with the riff-raff or rabble. The scene should end with the fairies glowering at the peers with their wands, and Phyllis, now cast away by Strephon, fainting into the arms of Mountararat and Tolloller. As soon as the curtain falls, the stage crew will chivvy the cast off the stage in order to tear away the Arcadian landscape and construct Palace Yard at Westminster. It may be that a longer interval than usual is required to effect this very considerable change. The precious soloist will be able to spend longer in the toilet endeavouring to impress those queuing up outside with some elaborate vocal exercises, and will still have time to complain at length to the conductor about her crucial entry being sabotaged by a wayward bassoon two bars before letter G. Other performers will sit down and relax, or find time to gossip with non-performing or erstwhile society members in the audience who have come backstage for some interval chat. With hordes of welcoming cast members offering them free tepid tea and ageing ginger biscuits, it would take a spectator of exceptionally thick skin not to say what a superb show he believes it to be, however much of the first half he has spent studying the discarded Kit Kat wrapper on the floor below him.

As has already been intimated, by the time Act 2 begins the action has moved from Arcadia to the metropolis – to be precise, Palace Yard, Westminster. Here, the Sentry, Private Willis, is to be found reflecting in song ("When all night long a chap remains") on what it is to be an M.P., and the fact that an M.P. having to vote as instructed by his party leaders is less disastrous for the country than an M.P. having to think for himself! Private Willis is always a popular role for which to audition, with just one solo and one quartet to learn, a handful of lines to remember, a Cockney accent which will hide any glaring inadequacies of diction, and the possibility of doubling up as a peer in the first Act and therefore the ability to enjoy some lusty choral singing as well as the glory of an important solo role. Moreover, there will be a fine guardsman's costume to wear, complete with a suitably convincing rifle. Experienced performers will not need to be coached in basic rifle-handling technique; however, the uninitiated may expect to be taken aside by one or more well-meaning former National Servicemen amongst the cast and be given a course of intensive instruction, using – assuming that the rifle is as yet unavailable – anything from a cricket stump to a broomhandle from the darker recesses of Mr Crump's store cupboard, preferably with the brush removed first.

The fairies trip back on stage, and announce in an exuberant chorus ("Strephon's a Member of Parliament") that their hero is reducing the rest of Parliament to submissive jelly. The peers then march on and confirm – also in chorus – that Strephon is managing to carry every bill he wishes. In the ensuing dialogue Celia explains that the fairies use their influence to ensure every M.P. votes as Strephon pleases. That evening, it is likely that legislation will be enacted which will throw the peerage open to competitive examination, which the peers agree will be disastrous for the country. In a line which was perhaps particularly topical during Margaret Thatcher's administration, they attribute the potential chaos to "women interfering in politics!" Mountararat then sings one of the great mock-patriotic songs of the operas, with chorus ("When Britain really ruled the waves"), in which he attributes the nation's illustrious past to the total inactivity of the Upper House, proclaiming that as Wellington was beating Napoleon, the House of Lords "did nothing in particular, and did it very well!"

Mountararat's stirring tribute to the action – or more appropriately inaction – of the Lords impresses the fairies deeply. The dialogue following the song sees them torn between anger towards the peers for their high-handedness, especially towards Strephon, and affection for the peers' regal magnificence and masculinity. In the ensuing chorus with solos for Ceila and Leila, the fairies alternate a series of sung rebukes ("In vain to us you plead") with a series of equally passionate entreaties ("Don't go!"). The Lords however do march off in suitably injured fashion. The tripping semiquavers in the accompaniment to this song have more than a hint of Mendelssohn about them, and will be a tricky test for the accompanist. Whereas Sullivan envisaged a full compliment of strings, woodwind, brass and percussion to do full justice to his fine orchestrations, he would undoubtedly be mortified to seeing them being reproduced on what may be tinpot uprights with squealing pedals, notes that continue to sound long after the key has been released, and lids with a disconcerting propensity to crash down on the player's fingers at irregular intervals. However, a defective piano is probably preferable to no piano at all; if the accompanist fails to turn up, then unless a suitable substitute can be found amongst the ranks of those present, musical assistance may be in the form of a cassette player hastily imported for the evening. Since it is unlikely that the cast will maintain the same tempo as the professionals who have made the recording, the rehearsal may soon disintegrate into cacophonous chaos. Even this scenario may be preferable to that which may ensue if a well-meaning society stalwart volunteers young Matthew from among the first basses to demonstrate his ivory-tinkling prowess following his pass at Grade III level, the cast member volunteering him clearly ignorant that that pass was ten years ago and young Matthew's intimacy with the world of the keyboard is still not such as to convince him that Bluthner is anything other than Germany's centre-half or that Rachmaninoff is not, after all, the house speciality in the King's Arms.

The fairies remain on stage together with their Queen for the dialogue that follows. The Queen deplores the fairies' weakness for the peers, but admits that she has a weakness of her own. The object of her affections is Private Willis, who has remained on sentry duty since the end of his song. Despite her fancy for him, she tells the fairies severely that she manages to keep her feelings under control. She then develops the theme in her big solo number, with chorus ("Oh, foolish fay"), in which she likens love to a fire, and wonders if Captain Shaw's brigade could quench it with their cold cascade. It might be prudent for there to be a programme note explaining that Captain Eyre Massey Shaw was chief of the Metropolitan Fire Brigade at the time the opera was written, and was actually sitting in the audience during the very first performance of the work!

The Fairies and the Queen leave the stage, and Phyllis enters, in low spirits. Aloud, she reflects that she still has not forgiven Strephon but her engagement to two of the Lords seems to give her no consolation. The two peers in question, Mountararat and Tolloller, then enter, and in the dialogue that follows it becomes clear that neither wishes to claim her at the expense of the other, if the result is the termination of a beautiful friendship; they both agree that that friendship, which has persisted since boyhood, is paramount and even the hand of Phyllis is not worth that sacrifice. A quartet ensues ("Though p'r'aps I may incur your blame") in which Phyllis, the two peers and Private Willis invite the name of Friendship to take precedence over a woman's hand in marriage. Those who know *Iolanthe* well will see this quartet as merely an appetiser to the two musical gems which are now imminent, but the harmonies have the subtlety and texture of a serious sacred work, and are most effective if the balance and tuning are accurate. After the song, all are directed to depart including Private Willis. His static sojourn on the stage, unless a benevolent producer has taken pity on him by allowing him off during the time the chorus of peers were on the stage earlier in Act 2, has certainly been a long one, although his smart Sentry uniform will have helped to decorate the surroundings. Perhaps the worst thing that could happen to him would be to commence a piece of drill which brings him into direct eye-contact with a fellow performer who, standing in the wings, promptly assumes a look of abject horror and points distractedly at his (the Sentry's) fly-buttons. The fact that later they are found to be properly fastened will be of little consolation to the Sentry if the action of his colleague has caused him to spend the next five pages of music gazing furtively but impotently towards his nether regions.

Now comes the moment that everyone has been waiting for. The Lord Chancellor enters and goes straight into a musical sequence in which he confesses how his unrequited love for Phyllis has affected his slumbers so much that sleeplessness go together with terrible dreams. It is the highlight of *Iolanthe* and one of the greatest moments in all the operas. After a brief recitative in which he states that "Love, unrequited, robs me of my rest" the patter singing begins with "When you're lying awake with a dismal headache." The musical material repeats itself, but the song rolls on and on; the words, like the nightmare, seem never-ending. The accompaniment is masterful; as the Lord Chancellor's nightmare takes him on to a cross-Channel steamer the orchestra imitate the tossing of the boat on the water, and when the action moves to bicycling on Salisbury Plain they give the impression of the turning of a bicycle wheel. The climax, when the Lord Chancellor sums up all the various aspects of one's nocturnal discomfiture, from a crick in the neck to pins and needles, places the greatest demands on the singer. The performer who gets most of it right can expect generous applause; the performer who gets all of it right is a star; the true genius, however, is one who loses it halfway through and still manages to pick it up again. As in the next musical number in the piece, even a straight "concert" performance of the work may see the soloist engaging in some amusing business to attempt to enliven the proceedings. Concert performances, or semi-staged performances, of G & S opera can be ideal means of bringing out the richness of Sullivan's music and Gilbert's words without the need for extensive rehearsal or large expenditure on sets and properties. The danger is that one or more of the soloists, who perhaps have broad experience of fully staged versions of G & S opera, will regard it as acceptable to import little comic touches of their own, in the mistaken belief that this will enhance the performance as a whole. The soloist will look pitifully upon the other performers who feel the need to bring their copies on stage with them, evidently less integrated into the world of G & S opera. Poetic justice will often be done when, carried away by the brilliance of his interpretation, the soloist suddenly realises that he has forgotten his words, and the conductor is forced to add his own musical contribution at minus five seconds' notice.

The Lord Chancellor's work, however, is far from done; Mountararat and Tolloller reappear and in dialogue persuade him that there is nothing legally improper about his pursuing Phyllis, providing, of course, that he wears the right hat. This leads to the exhausting but highly entertaining trio "If you go in." It usually receives at least one, possibly more, encores. As with "Things are seldom what they seem" from *H.M.S. Pinafore*, this is little more than a collection of proverbs, but the gist is that if the Lord Chancellor wants his girl he should not hesitate to go and claim her. The trio is a fast, catchy song in triple time, which demands some energetic dancing from the three Lords when they are not actually singing. Dancing is a word likely to instil foreboding into any amateur operatic performer, particularly if his acquaintance with it is limited to the final snatches of *Come Dancing* on BBC1 prior to the late film, or, more dauntingly still, a fragment of the Royal Ballet's impeccable rendition of *The Nutcracker* caught whilst trying to locate the right channel for *Only Fools And Horses* on Boxing Day. In fact there are a number of common steps and movements, the reasonable execution of which will guarantee lasting admiration from the majority of the assembled company. There is the slow march, where one foot goes forward and the other foot comes up to join it; it helps if the performers, particularly those at the front, remember which foot goes forward first. There is the sway, always popular in an Act 2 finale, where again it assists if each line decides to sway the same way at the same time. There may be a line dance; at its simplest, partners stand opposite each other, join right hands, advance two steps, retreat two steps, advance two steps and then the gentleman stands still while the lady pirouettes; the fun begins when couples walk up the dance and make arches for other couples, and nobody can remember whether one is supposed to be creating, or walking underneath, an arch at any given time. A dance may involve nothing more strenuous than to stand and alternately bring the right and left foot out and point them, and then execute a neat circle of three hundred and sixty degrees. A line of dancers may be invited to perform a figure of eight, where the key to success is remembering whether one begins by passing right shoulder to right shoulder or left shoulder to left shoulder. Despite the lack of expertise required to carry out these routines, and the enthusiasm with which they are tackled when their simplicity is demonstrated, the chances are that the week after they have been plotted, they will have been forgotten. The sensible producer will have noted down every last detail so that if a query arises as to the finer points, a confident and unequivocal answer will be supplied, and the questioner will retire to the ranks with a due sense of humility. Producers who are guided more by creative impulses than careful forward planning will, by contrast, be in some difficulty when such problems arise, particularly as they suddenly find that the whole dance has been rendered nonsensical by the absence of two nimble-footed girls from last week, and the presence, for the first time, of two men who have each contrived to acquire more than the single left foot God gave to both of them. The 20 minutes' drinking time that was sacrificed to perfect the dance last week turns to 40 minutes this week as further experiments are tried, conscientious cast members apply further crossings-out to the notes they have made in their libretti, and the chairman braces herself for another irate piece of correspondence from Mrs Winterbottom who has already threatened to resign after the producer likened her demeanour on stage to that of an overcooked suet sponge pudding.

The trio exit and Strephon now appears for the first time in Act 2, followed by Phyllis. Now that he and Phyllis are alone, he can, in dialogue, at last explain the truth to her about his fairy mother. Phyllis has never been particularly fond of the peers and is only too pleased to accept his explanation; indeed she philosophically reflects that whenever she sees him kissing a very young lady, she will know it is an elderly relative. Another of Gilbert's wry comments on marriage may be found in this sequence. When Strephon says "We might change our minds – we'll get married first" and is asked by Phyllis if they can change their minds afterwards, he replies that that is "the usual course." There is then a spirited love duet ("If we're weak enough to tarry") following which Iolanthe appears and, in dialogue, welcomes her daughter-in-law to be. All seems set for the happy ending, the Lord Chancellor's permission being the only prerequisite to the legal union between them. Despite the fact that Strephon has failed so miserably to gain the necessary consent, the couple assume he will not be able to resist the fairy eloquence of Iolanthe herself.

It is then that the plot develops an unexpected and – for the lovers – most unwelcome twist. Strephon and Phyllis learn that the Lord Chancellor, as cruel luck would have it, is Iolanthe's husband, and Strephon's father. He believes his wife to have died childless; if she reveals herself to him, the reprieve which was bestowed upon her for marrying a mortal will surely be rescinded and she will lose her life. At this moment of crisis, the Lord Chancellor himself appears, and as the lovers leave and Iolanthe veils herself, he inadvertently breaks the tension with a speech of pure Gilbertian nonsense. In it, he recounts how, in his capacity as lover of Phyllis, he made an application to himself, in his capacity as Lord Chancellor, for consent to marry her. As he states, "I then endeavoured to work upon my feelings. Conceive my joy when I distinctly perceived a tear glistening in my own eye!" The outcome was that his application to himself has been granted. Like all of Gilbert's libretto in *Iolanthe*, not one word seems to be wasted or out of place. There is therefore extra responsibility on the speaker to ensure its accuracy, particularly in any operatic society which prides itself on producing authentic G & S. A performer joining such a society having been accustomed to a more relaxed attitude to such matters may be surprised, after rendering what he believes to be a fairly commendable declamation of one of Gilbert's longer speeches, to see the prompt looking at him as though he had just taken a bath in a pool of raw sewage, and then to be curtly informed that he has inserted an extra "that" which does not appear in the libretto. The chastened performer will return to his seat and take a fresh look at his lines, and on hearing a loud bang from below the stage will nervously look up to ascertain whether it is the wardrobe mistress' grandson playing with empty potato-crisp packets, or the prompt's murderous reaction to a fellow performer missing out an exclamation mark.

As the Lord Chancellor ends his speech Iolanthe braces herself to make her appeal to him. Her recitative ("My lord, a suppliant at your feet") and subsequent ballad ("He loves! If in the bygone years") are two of the most emotionally-charged pieces of music in G & S opera. To begin with, she simply asks the Lord Chancellor to change his mind and consent to Strephon marrying Phyllis, inviting her husband to recall his own marriage and the sadness he felt when (as he believed) it came to an end. In recitative ("It may not be"), beginning a taut musical sequence, the Lord Chancellor then reveals to her that he cannot consent, for the very good reason that he intends to marry Phyllis himself. Iolanthe therefore has no choice; she now reveals, as she must, that she is still alive, and by doing so she will sacrifice her own life. The fairies, though not on stage, are fully aware of what is happening, and cry out "Forbear! Forbear!" The Lord Chancellor looks incredulously at his wife; his simple recitative "Iolanthe! Thou livest?" must encompass pathos, amazement, bewilderment, and profound happiness. The fairies then enter with the Queen. The Queen pronounces death on Iolanthe, while the fairies mournfully cry "Aiaiah! Aiaiah! Willahalah! Willalloo! Willahalah! Willalloo!" This is a take-off of the Wagnerian Rhinemaidens' wailings "Wallala weilala weia" and another instance of Sullivan drawing inspiration from grand opera. There is no significance in the words beyond that, even though it may assist a fairy performer, who has difficulty in committing them to memory, to reflect on the similarity between "Willalloo" and the name of the London terminus at which as a child she once boarded a train bound for a beach holiday in Bournemouth.

As the music finishes, the plot, which seems on course for a tragic ending, takes another twist. The peers (including Mountararat and Tolloller) and Sentry enter, and Leila announces in dialogue that during their recent absence from the stage, the fairies have paired up with the peers and have all turned into fairy duchesses, marchionesses, countesses, viscountesses and baronesses! The Queen realises she will have to slaughter the whole company if fairy law is to be complied with. It is the Lord Chancellor who solves the problem. Working from the scroll which somebody has hopefully remembered to bring on to the stage, he suggests the law be changed so that every fairy shall die who *doesn't* marry a mortal. The Queen readily agrees, but being left without a husband herself, her own life is in jeopardy. Accordingly, she invites Private Willis to become a fairy guardsman, and he is happy to, as he says, "ill-convenience" (or, as it is sometimes pronounced, "hillconwenience") himself to get her out of her difficulty. The Queen tells him he is a fairy from that moment, and wings should spring from his shoulders. This is guaranteed to bring some merriment from any supporters of Private Willis who may be in the audience, although spectators may be puzzled that as they are not yet married, the Queen is in fact breaking the newly-amended law herself!

The Queen also invites the peers to join the ranks of fairies with a view to departure to Fairyland. As she does so, Strephon and Phyllis enter, their union presumably now approved by the Lord Chancellor. Tolloller and Mountararat agree that with an Upper House full of intellectuals, they are no longer any use on earth, and on behalf of the peers they are glad to accept the Queen's invitation. As a result, wings are supposed to spring from the shoulders of the peers. The acquisition of wings for the peers and Sentry may present an interesting challenge to the properties department, which may not have the time or the ingenuity to assemble an elaborate wing-mechanism in the costumes concerned. A compromise might be to fit the wings on in advance of the reappearance of the performers on stage, and trust that nobody moves in such a way that the wings are prematurely revealed or that they do not fall off. Nothing is likely to harm a potential fairy husband's self-confidence more than the realisation that his passage to Fairyland has been blocked, not by the furies or the fates, but by a strip of temperamental Velcro.

With a reprise of the music for the "If you go in" trio to new words ("Soon as we may, off and away") the company then end the opera by looking forward to their new lives "up in the air, sky-high, sky-high." Producers who have run out of ideas for elaborate line dances by this time may resort to directing that the cast effect a simple sway from right to left during the brisk triple-time refrain. The supposedly eternally young fairies will then need to apply their ageing grey matter to remember whether their line starts to sway to the right or to the left first, and trust that any travel-sickness which results from seeing two lines lurching in opposite directions will not set in before they have even reached platform nine at Willaloo station.

"Is that second lorryload of costumes
still stuck at Junction 17?"

Princess Ida, the eighth opera in the series and earliest surviving G & S opera to be set outside Victorian England, is something of a contradiction. It contains some of the finest music Sullivan ever wrote, and a number of scenes that are as hilarious and enjoyable to play and watch as any in the operas. On the debit side, however, the satirical element was somewhat misplaced even when it was written, and is now hopelessly outdated. More irksome from a logistical point of view is that the opera is in three Acts. Even if they were of equal length, this might be of some consolation, but Act 2 is far longer than the other two Acts, and Act 3 is absurdly short. Discarding, therefore, the option of having the interval between Acts 2 and 3, there will be a choice between placing a single interval between Acts 1 and 2, which may test the attention span of even the most hardened G & S devotee, or having intervals between each Act. This may benefit the sales of strawberry ices, and boost bar takings, but makes it a very long evening indeed. Another unusual, and again not necessarily attractive, aspect of the opera is that the spoken lines are written in blank verse, with a strict ten syllables to each line, and therefore some of the dialogue seems both laboured and contrived. Gilbert had to work that much harder with his cast as a result, and Grossmith was once moved to grumble to him that he had rehearsed "this confounded business until I feel a perfect fool." Gilbert's reply was immediate: "Now we can talk on equal terms." Another actor, faced with Gilbert's stern quest for perfection, is said to have remarked to him "I will not be bullied. I know my lines" to which he received the reply "That may be so, but you don't know mine."

Princess Ida was premiered on 5th January 1884 at the Savoy Theatre. It was based on Gilbert's 1870 play, *The Princess*, which was itself a pastiche of a poem of Tennyson's – also called *The Princess* – written in 1847. Gilbert described the opera as a "Respectful Operatic Perversion" of Tennyson's work. Again, Sullivan had to rush to complete the work in time. The dress rehearsal ended at 2.30 a.m., and it is little wonder that, despite being charged with generous quantities of black coffee and morphine, Sullivan collapsed after conducting the first performance. The show was received with considerably less enthusiasm than its predecessor. Its opening run was just 246 performances, making one of the shortest opening runs of all the G & S operas. It had an even shorter opening run of 48 performances in the States. The blame lay with the show's subject matter, regarded by at least one critic as "desperately dull." Coming at a time when women's colleges were starting to open, it sought to satirise and at times ridicule simplistic feminist notions, as well as women's education and advancement in fields traditionally dominated by men. But even in 1884 the notion, as expressed in Act 3 of the opera, that women should "bind up... wounds but look the other way" was questionable; one only needed to recall the work of Florence Nightingale in Crimea thirty years before. Other themes alluded to in the opera include the boorishness of the male sex, and the Darwinian theory of evolution, with the suggestion in one song that men are synonymous with monkeys. It was quickly condemned as being unsuitable material for family entertainment, and following its opening run it was not revived until 1919. Its fortunes took a further downturn when the D'Oyly Carte scenery and costumes for the production were destroyed by bombs in the Second World War. It is not a great favourite with amateur operatic societies, despite its glorious music. Ironically, the most effusive recorded response to *Princess Ida* came from a Frenchman in the first night audience, who rushed to Gilbert and cried *"Savez-vous que vous avez un succes solide?"* (to which Gilbert replied stoically "It seems to be going very well.")

The plot has as its base the fact that twenty years ago Princess Ida (soprano), the daughter of King Gama (baritone), had been engaged in infancy to Prince Hilarion (tenor), the son of Gama's rival King Hildebrand (baritone). This very day Hilarion is due to meet his baby bride. Gama arrives with his warrior sons Arac, Guron and Scynthius (all basses) and tells Hildebrand that Ida has rejected male society and established a women's university called Castle Adamant (*Castle Adamant* is the show's alternative title), engaging Lady Psyche (soprano) and Lady Blanche (contralto) as lecturers. Blanche's daughter Melissa (soprano), as well as Chloe and Sacharissa (both sopranos), are among the students. Hilarion decides to break into Castle Adamant with his friends Cyril (tenor) and Florian (baritone) to claim Ida, whilst Gama and his sons are held hostage by Hildebrand. Hilarion's failure to make headway, despite his valiant impersonation of a new female student, results in the storming of Castle Adamant by Hildebrand's forces and a battle between Gama's sons and Hilarion and his friends. Gama's sons are beaten and Ida submits to Hilarion.

One look at the plot will demonstrate that there are a considerable number of lead roles, and therefore there is extra work for the auditioning committee. Principal auditions will rank amongst the most sensitive aspects of a society's preparation for a production. There is a strange coyness about applicants for solo parts; few performers will say directly that they intend to audition, as if afraid that potential rivals will slip something into their post-rehearsal tipple, but will use guarded remarks such as "I might possibly have a stab at something" or "I'll have to see how my work commitments are before I apply." Even the absence of the applicant on audition night means little, since there will always be some performers who use the vague excuse "I'll be away on audition night" as a pretext for auditioning at a different time when the tension, ever present and quite palpable on audition night, is negligible, and the atmosphere markedly less hostile and competitive. The auditions themselves will be conducted in circumstances which will vary according to the professionalism of the society as a whole. In some societies, the procedure will be carried out with scrupulous fairness. Procedures of other societies would give Genghis Khan's system of summary justice the appearance of a model of considered impartiality. Some societies will employ skilled members to read in pieces of dialogue that forms part of the audition, while other societies will use a single piece of dialogue to assess the merits of a number of auditioners at the same time. This may well provoke anger amongst unsuccessful applicants who will claim that the feeble performance of one of the other applicants put them off. The applicants themselves can be divided into three categories. There are those who have done the part many times before, and who, fairly certain they will get the part and having no reason to suppose there is anyone who will stop them, will cursorily glance at the relevant audition piece whilst queuing at Mr Fishey's takeaway half an hour before they are due at the hall. There are those in the middle category who feel they are capable of being awarded the part but who are aware of the strength of the competition; they will go to great lengths to impress the audition committee, such as learning the prescribed dialogue by heart, employing a prop or piece of costume within the audition, or attempting a piece of comic business that has been borrowed from a cursory viewing of a video of the neighbouring society's 1985 production. That leaves those who are clearly quite unsuited for the part, but who, egged on by supposed well-wishers, will blunder their way through the audition piece whilst onlookers intensify the study of the contents of their navels, the sense of discomfiture felt both by the auditioner and the witnesses being mightily increased when the aspiring principal gets off to a false start and has to beg the long-suffering audition committee to give him another chance. All three categories of applicant will assemble on audition night. The rules of some societies may in fact preclude them from witnessing any of the proceedings and force them to remain, perhaps indefinitely, in surroundings that exude the congeniality of the waiting room of a dentist who has never heard of local anaesthetics, and boast a temperature resembling either that of a kitchen in a Calcutta curry house during a heatwave, or a Reykjavik bus shelter during a blizzard. When the applicant is called in, he will find himself performing before a tribunal that comprises the producer, musical director and inevitably one or two complete strangers, invited to ensure fair play; these may include the formidable vice-president of a neighbouring operatic society, often an elderly lady dressed in severe tweeds, and with a disconcerting propensity for making angry jottings on her notepad whenever an error is made. Even the musical director, who last night was supping a pint of best with the nervous performer, will gaze at him with the same warmth with which a wine-grower might regard a brace of giant mealy bugs. Having performed as best he can, the applicant will then return from whence he came, and having waited for two more hours until 11.05 p.m. for the verdict, is told that the panel still has not reached its final decision and since Mr Crump, the janitor, is anxious to lock up, the discussions will continue at the chairman's home and the results will be announced at rehearsal in two days' time. When the results are announced, the unsuccessful but unfussy applicant will philosophically say "Oh, well, it's much more fun being in the chorus anyway – I never really wanted the part." The less gracious performer will take his medicine sulkily but quietly, finding consolation in gleefully gloating over every wrong note sung, or dance step misplaced, by the person who got the part he wanted. The more litigious performer will foolishly attempt to reverse the audition committee's decision by pointing to some gross irregularity in the proceedings. When that approach fails he will suddenly remember that he has an important business meeting on dress-rehearsal night which under Rule 78(3)(b)(iv) precludes his appearance in the show, leaving him free then to commence enquiry as to the audition pieces for the next show of one of six other operatic societies with which he has performed lead roles in the past two years and a quarter.

The action of *Princess Ida* begins beside a pavilion attached to King Hildebrand's palace, with soldiers and courtiers discovered looking out through opera glasses and telescopes at the distant horizon. Among them are Florian and Cyril, friends of Prince Hilarion, who is Hildebrand's son. The company sing of their need to "Search throughout the panorama for a sign of royal Gama" and, in a solo between sections of chorus, Florian threatens dire reprisals should King Gama fail to appear with his daughter Princess Ida. She is expected at the palace that day in order to honour her childhood vows. In the ensuing dialogue Hildebrand explains that she and Hilarion were betrothed twenty years ago, when Ida was just one year old, and states that if Ida fails to appear he will declare war on Gama. Apparently Gama is a most unattractive man; Hildebrand says that his sting lay in his tongue, and furthermore "His 'sting' is present, though his 'stung' is past." This is not the only appalling pun which Gilbert saw fit to introduce into the dialogue! Florian interrupts Hildebrand by announcing that he has seen Gama approaching over the brow of a mountain. Hildebrand asserts that if Gama has brought Ida with him, he should have a royal welcome, but if he has not, he will be thrown into prison with a diet of cold water and dry bread. The same sentiments are expressed in his ensuing solo with chorus ("Now hearken to my strict command"). The song demands a number of enthusiastic cries of "hip, hip, hurrah!" from the assembled company, and on one or more of the "hurrahs" the chorus may be directed to mime the waving of a handkerchief or engage in some similar gesture to denote general approval of their King's pronouncements. Assiduous chorus members will painstakingly note each "hurrah" on which such muscular exercise is called for, while those whom the producer has had the good sense to relegate to the very fringes of the stage, or better still concealed in the wings, will only remember to offer their waves when they see their more conscientious colleagues doing so. The resulting inadvertent Mexican wave may certainly be innovative, but it will be as welcome for the production team as the sudden news, five minutes before the opening performance, that no alcohol can be sold in the interval because the secretary, having filled out the drinks licence application three months ago, forgot to post it and has just found it hitched by a paper clip to an invitation to her daughter's school welly-whirling contest.

The chorus now leave the stage and Hilarion appears, confirming in a recitative his hope that "Today we meet, my baby bride and I." In an aria with words of stunning banality he then states what is already known, that "Ida was a twelvemonth old twenty years ago;" he points out that although she was then, of course, half his age, the gap in maturity between them is now negligible. His father returns and in dialogue breaks the sad news that there is no sign of her. Hilarion states that he has heard that Ida has shut herself away and devotes herself to academic pursuits, so he is not surprised about her failure to appear. He is, however, clearly distracted by it, and speaks at length about his profound thoughts which crossed his mind when he became betrothed to her – thoughts which he kept to himself "for at that age I had not learned to speak." The titters which this line will generate should quickly disperse as the chorus return and give a musical reprise of the opening chorus, but this time proclaiming that "From the distant panorama come the sons of royal Gama." There follows the entry of three of Gilbert's finest comic creations, namely the warrior sons of Gama named Arac, Guron and Scynthius. They lumber on to the stage in weighty armour and sing a trio, with chorus ("We are warriors three"), in which they introduce themselves as both bellicose and devoid of intelligence. The parts of Gama's sons may well be eminently suitable for older men whose lack of litheness or freedom of movement will, for a change, be of positive assistance to them. Unfortunately with the requisite thespian ineptitude may come a corresponding lack of competence in the musical department; the musical director can only despair when, after painstakingly going through their harmonies line by line, he sees them produce a sound not dissimilar to that generated at the time when his 78 r.p.m. gramophone reproduction of a Paul Robeson medley was foolish enough to obstruct the path of his three-year-old niece's wayward beaker of orange juice.

After the warriors have introduced themselves, Gama appears. Gama is one of the uglier G & S comic roles, both physically – he himself mentions his crooked leg and the hump on his shoulder – and temperamentally. Many commentators have seen in him traces of Gilbert himself, with a distinct air of petulance, irascibility, quick-wittedness and crushing repartee. In his opening song of introduction, with chorus ("If you give me your attention I will tell you what I am"), he admits that he is naturally nosy, suspicious of others' motives, knowledgeable of others' failings, and the proud owner of an "entertaining snigger" and a "celebrated sneer" – yet, he says with his tongue firmly in his cheek, he cannot think why people regard him as a disagreeable man! In the dialogue which follows, he and Hildebrand – the latter assisted by Cyril – trade a succession of insults. Relations between them are not improved when Gama states that his daughter has forsaken male society completely, to the extent that in her academy of one hundred girls she will "scarcely suffer Dr Watts' hymns – and all the animals she owns are 'hers'." Even the crowing which gets the girls up in the morning is carried out by an "accomplished hen." Gama, thoroughly enjoying himself, commences the Act 1 finale by singing that if Hildebrand and his company "address the lady most politely" she may deign to pay them some attention. The smile is wiped off his face when Hildebrand orders that he (Gama) and his sons will be taken prisoner, and states that should Hilarion come to any harm in his mission to win Ida round, the four of them will be hanged. The prisoners are marched off, and after a recitative ("Come, Cyril, Florian, our course is plain") in which Hilarion resolves to set off to Castle Adamant with his two friends next day, a charming trio with chorus follows ("Expressive glances") in which the three of them determine to win Ida with flowers, sparkling wine and love songs. However, this serene interlude is short-lived. Gama and his sons reappear in chains, and there follows a boisterous finale ("For a month to dwell") in which the sons regret, but Hildebrand gloats over, their military inactivity whilst in custody. An exhausting final chorus ("But till that time you'll here remain") confirms the punishment which Gama and his sons must suffer. The hostages are now marched off, and Act 1 comes to an end. The girls, who have hitherto decorated the stage as members of Hildebrand's court, must utilise the interval to change into their academic dress as they become students at Castle Adamant, and the set needs to change as well to reflect the fact that

Act 2 is set in the gardens of this strictly feminine establishment. The fact that, as with *Iolanthe*, a river is meant to run through the gardens across the back of the stage, crossed by a rustic bridge, will be an obvious challenge to even the most talented set designer. While some societies may simply ignore the stage direction, others may create a convincing-looking riverbank but without attempting even to simulate the effect of running water. The risk, of course, is that the length of bare polished floorboard between the green mounds will be clearly visible to spectators high up in the theatre, who may resent having their intelligence insulted by being asked to accept that this is the result of a period of prolonged drought or excessive abstraction by the local water authority.

As the Act commences, the entire female company are discovered on stage, save for Ida and Lady Blanche, Professor of Abstract Science. The girls start by singing a chorus with brief solos for the students Melissa and Sacharissa, and the lecturer Lady Psyche ("Towards the empyrean heights"), in which they declare their thirst for knowledge. Jane Stedman writes that the academic dress employed in the first production was particularly fine, consisting of "velvet brocades over plain undergowns in chocolate and salmon, purple and peach, primrose and black." Psyche, who is Professor of Humanities, is heard to extol the virtues of a number of famous writers and scholars such as Juvenal and Ovid, notwithstanding a high content of obscenity and eroticism in them! When asked by Sacharissa, however, "what's the thing that's known as Man?" Psyche is horrified and in a burst of rather facile feminism, reels off a list of singularly uncomplimentary adjectives for the male sex, such as "donkey" and "goose." After the song, Lady Blanche enters. She is another formidable G & S contralto, and does nothing to enhance her popularity by announcing, in dialogue, a list of punishments which have been incurred for such heinous offences as drawing a sketch of a double perambulator! In the course of this dialogue, Chloe, a minor principal and one of the offenders, has her only spoken word in the whole of Act 2 – the single word "Ah." This rather disappointing fragment of libretto may be overlooked altogether, but the studious Chloe could make life intolerable for the producer by pointing out the various inflections and degrees of expressiveness which this annoying little interjection might carry. If she is a woman of some influence, the producer will ignore her at his peril, knowing that to do so may result in a complaint to the committee. An enthusiastic thespian may well, at some stage in his amateur operatic career, be invited to serve on a committee of the G & S society to which he belongs. Those seeking to engage him will cheerfully stress to him the benefits that such an office confers, and leave him to find out for himself the less glamorous side of committee membership, from the forty-five minutes spent debating whether the accompanist should be allowed a five per cent increase in her travelling expenses, to discussion at 12.20 a.m. as to how the society could most meaningfully contribute to the festivities to mark the restoration of the town's ornamental horse trough.

Having given her list of punishments, Blanche then announces the arrival of Ida herself. The chorus welcome her in song ("Mighty maiden with a mission"), during which she appears and begins a terrifying sequence, beginning with a recitative ("Minerva") in which she asks the goddess Minerva to hear her, continuing with an aria ("Oh, goddess wise") in which she appeals to Minerva to enable her to provide enlightenment to her students, and culminating in a vast speech. In her speech she extols women's virtues, derides the failings of men, and looks forward to a new age in which women are dominant, and when adding two and two can result in any figure that one chooses to name. The consequence of failure, she tells the girls, is that clothes will misfit, hairpins will lose their virtue, and buttons will fail to slip into buttonholes. No sooner has her long speech finished than Blanche launches into a pompous discourse of her own concerning the Is, the Might Be, and the Must. Gilbert's aim, through all of this, is to make the listener laugh at the absurdity of feminine logic and sense of priorities. Laughable though it may be, Ida's speech presents a massive challenge for the actor cast in that role, and the song which precedes it is also technically most demanding. Audrey Williamson goes so far as to state that the part of Ida should be tackled "only by a singer with a voice of dramatic soprano quality and volume, and a first class musical training." This may not stop societies with a dearth of readily tappable amateur talent fielding an Ida whose musical training consists of a single singing lesson, her teacher then suddenly remembering he had an important appointment in New South Wales. Many aspiring amateur G & S performers will avail themselves of singing lessons which can boost both their performing abilities and confidence, as well as the bank balance of the tutor. If the tutee then subsequently takes a principal role in a production or concert, the pen-portrait that goes to the local paper or into the programme can grandly proclaim that he or she has "studied under Orlando Soriano," at the same time carefully omitting to mention that her tutor's real name is Stanley Gubbins whose own solo work is confined to karaoke nights at the Pig and Whistle.

Everybody save Blanche then exits, the girls singing a reprise of the Act 2 opening chorus but to slightly different words ("And thus to empyrean heights") in which they again reflect on their search for enlightenment. Blanche, who is left on her own on stage, delivers another long speech to the audience, explaining that her chief aim is to take over as principal of Castle Adamant. She then sings what Ian Bradley delightfully describes as a "burlesque of the rather over-blown Victorian drawing-room ballad" entitled "Come, mighty Must" in which she suggests, again pompously and melodramatically, that she is predestined to become leader of the university. It could not be described as the most enjoyable piece in the opera; Audrey Williamson writes that although the music in *Princess Ida* was raised to a level that its libretto hardly deserved, even Sullivan was defeated by the words supplied for this aria! However, better things are to follow; as Blanche leaves to dutiful applause, Hilarion creeps on stage with his friends Cyril and Florian. They immediately sing a trio ("Gently, gently") in which they sing of their difficulties in penetrating the walls of Castle Adamant. Both Hilarion and Cyril then sing of the outlandish things they believe Ida and the feminist revolutionaries are planning to do, such as sending wires to the moon and teaching pigs to fly. Despite the fact that they are intruders, the trio and the dialogue that follows suggest that they are revelling in the situation, so much so that on spotting three academic robes lying nearby they decide to try them on. They then sing an exhausting and wonderfully catchy trio ("I am a maiden, cold and stately"), in which they fantasize about what being a young lady must be like. There is considerable scope for dancing and suitable gestures with the hands on the words "Haughty, humble, coy, or free" which crop up four times in the song. It is splendid entertainment, which will surely bring to life any audience member reduced to restful slumber by the philosophical ramblings of Ida and Blanche. The biggest problem will be the donning of the academic dress immediately prior to the trio. It is to be hoped that a thoughtful properties manager will have remembered to leave the robes in place before Act 2 commences; failure to do so may land him with an extensive drinks bill in the bar afterwards. The trio must then find their way into the robes, always running the risk of putting them on either back to front or upside down, and must endeavour to fill the awkward silence that will accompany the robing process in the absence of any prescribed dialogue. Some dialogue may be added by the producer in advance, but it may not be enough to tide the trio over any extra time spent unravelling themselves from states of entrapment which may result from donning the garment incorrectly in the first place. It is this situation that will test the professionalism of the actors to the full. Seasoned thespians will ad-lib effortlessly and comically, delighting the audience and the producer. Inexperienced perfomers will be reduced to deafening silence and a face the colour of the beetroot in Mrs Prescott's interval sandwiches.

The trio's revelries are brought to an abrupt halt almost immediately the applause for their song has died down, as Ida herself is seen approaching! In

111

dialogue, Hilarion decides that there is no alternative but for the pretence of womanhood to be maintained, so, clinging to his falsetto voice, he introduces himself and his friends as three new female students. Ida is completely fooled and joins with the men in a quartet bemoaning the decadence of the world outside ("The world is but a broken toy"). Given the absurdity of the situation, Sullivan might well have written a jolly tune to give the song a humorous slant, but instead he chose to write some of the most exquisite harmonies to be found in any of the operas, resulting in a quartet of haunting beauty. The audience may be left somewhat puzzled as to how Ida suspects nothing, notwithstanding that she is accompanied obligingly by two tenor voices and a baritone voice!

As she leaves the stage, however, she appears to be none the wiser, and the trio collapse into laughter; in the dialogue that follows they realise that they now have no choice but to keep up the pretence. Moments later, however, their collective nerve is tested again as Psyche approaches. Florian realises that this is his sister and she will be bound to recognise him. Hilarion decides the best course is to entrust their secret to her, and indeed once the initial shock has passed she seems more than happy to laugh and joke with them about happy times past. She then, however, feels constrained to tell them a story in a song, with ensemble refrain at the end ("A Lady fair, of lineage high"), about an ape who despite his best endeavours could never make himself attractive to the lady he loved, even though he tried to call himself "Darwinian Man." Effectively, she says, man is simply a monkey who has shaved. The song, popularly known as "The Ape and the Lady," is not only a reminder of the Darwinian theory of evolution which had been formulated only a few years before; it also satirises the feminist's simplistic view of man as a graceless oaf, although such a view may perhaps be given some credence by the demeanour of Gama's sons, and totally vindicated by the beer-bellied bloody-mindedness of Mr Crump the janitor.

Melissa, who is actually Blanche's daughter, has entered unobserved during Psyche's song. Psyche, who is evidently aware that she (Melissa) has seen through the disguise, is horrified, but in dialogue Melissa assures them that she will not tell anyone else of the deception. In fact, she finds the novelty of male company not only stimulating but pleasurable, particularly the cheeks which do not have "that pulpy softness one gets so weary of in womankind." This is cue for yet another fine song, this time a quintet ("A woman of the wisest wit"), in which the three men and Psyche join in Melissa's exultations about this new exciting discovery. The succession of splendid musical numbers in Act 2 is known as Sullivan's "string of pearls" and the quintet, with its infectious gaiety, is as exuberant and frolicsome as the "broken toy" quartet is moving and powerful. The three men and Psyche dance boisterously off the stage, just before Blanche makes her entrance and speaks severely to her daughter. She (Blanche) has worked out that the harmony she has just heard included male voices, and having discovered cigars in an etui which one of the men has hopefully remembered to drop at some point during his sojourn on the stage, she quickly realises the true gender of the alleged new students. Melissa manages to procure her mother's silence by promising to help her attain the headship of Castle Adamant. A duet follows, in which they both look forward to this event and Blanche reflects bitterly on her enforced subservience to Ida. Known colloquially as the "hoity, toity" duet, as this expression is used in the refrain, the duet is entitled "Now wouldn't you like to rule the roast." The current Chappell edition of the musical score substituted the expression "rule the roost;" this is in fact a more recent corruption but probably makes more sense to modern listeners than the original and its images of a harassed cook slaving over the Sunday joint whilst inclining half an ear to the omnibus edition of *The Archers*.

Satisfied, Blanche leaves, and Florian enters alone. In dialogue Melissa has to tell him that her mother knows their secret. She recounts how her mother exclaimed "'Why these'..." then proceeds "'*Are men*,' she would have added, but '*Are men*' stuck in her throat!" This particularly laboured pun is a reference to the famous line in *Macbeth*, "'Amen' stuck in my throat." Students of Shakespeare amongst the audience will chuckle knowingly, their laughter mingled with the satisfaction that in understanding the joke they are on a higher intellectual plane than the majority of the audience whose knowledge of the Bard is limited to the two expressions "To be or not to be" and "Friends, Romans, countrymen" and who, when asked what images are conjured by Stratford-upon-Avon, will respond with reference to coachloads of Japanese tourists being served overpriced cream teas.

Melissa pleads with Florian to leave and take her with him; their plans are however placed on hold by the sounding of a bell which signals the arrival of lunch. Immediately the girls appear, Ida escorted by Hilarion and Psyche by Cyril, with Blanche proceeding unescorted. As they sing a chorus in anticipation of the feast, with solos from Blanche and Cyril ("Merrily ring the luncheon bell"), luncheon is served by the Daughters of the Plough. These are huge strong weatherbeaten females and therefore not necessarily the most sought-after chorus roles within the opera. In the song Blanche warns the girls to subdue their appetites, which Cyril, also in the song, interprets as a licence to tuck into cold roast lamb. As with *The Sorcerer,* the properties section is faced with the not inconsiderable logistical challenge of providing a convincing-looking luncheon for the party. Conscientious souls will prepare a generous spread which will eagerly be gobbled up by the female company. Less gastronomically-minded societies will make do with token offerings of three-day-old pies and rolls culled from the back room of the bakery where a cast member works; after a couple of mouthfuls of barely edible fare the prudent soprano or alto may feel it best to forsake this refreshment and console herself with the thought of tucking into the pack of Hula Hoops and Bounty bar purchased in anticipation of another interval. This snack will be all the more necessary in view of the fact that not only is Act 3 still to come, but also the chairman's interminable speeches of thanks at the end, encompassing everybody from the stage manager down to the herd of cattle that supplied the milk for the audience's interval coffee.

Cyril's hymn to cold meat fails to arouse Ida's suspicions; after the song she talks pleasantly to Hilarion about Hildebrand's court, and even asks after Hilarion himself. Hilarion, having to keep up his womanly voice, speaks emotionally of his twenty-year-old love for her. Ida still suspects nothing, until Cyril – who has been enjoying a drink or two – begins to talk tipsily and somewhat carelessly about the love that he and his two "lady" friends have for Hilarion. To begin with, Ida is merely perplexed, but Cyril compounds his indiscretion with a solo ("Would you know the kind of maid") in which he sings drunkenly of the type of woman that sets his heart aflame. Additional hilarity can be imported into this song by suitably amorous gestures towards a horrified Blanche. Ida is now enraged, her fury reaching its climax when in the ensuing dialogue, to the accompaniment of orchestral music, Cyril calls Hilarion – who has unsuccessfully been trying to restrain him – by his proper name. Ida, now fully aware of what has been going on, runs to the bridge to direct the girls' evacuation from the scene, but in her excitement she falls into the stream. Music from the orchestra continues whilst the girls give a running commentary of Hilarion's (ultimately successful) attempts to save her. This scene will be difficult to portray convincingly, particularly if the lead soprano is by nature unusually fastidious or particularly precious. Gallery audiences at an early production obtained a perfect view of Ida, not plunging into icy depths, but floundering on a feather mattress thoughtfully arranged by the properties department. It is moreover unlikely that any Ida will be particularly partial to crawling, unseen, off stage, and having a bucket of water thrown over her at the same time as being smeared with wet leaves, bird droppings and fragments of frogs' legs.

Far from thanking Hilarion for his trouble, Ida is furious with the trio for their deception, and as soon as the girls have expressed their approval in a brief choral section which introduces the Act 2 finale ("Oh joy, our chief is saved") she pronounces a sentence of death upon Hilarion and his friends. Hilarion, seemingly resigned to his fate, sings philosophically that "if dead to me my heart's desire, why should I wish to live?" The final few bars of his brief solo contain a top B flat, the highest solo note that any male has in the operas (although Ralph and Frederic have top B flats in *H.M.S. Pinafore* and *The Pirates of Penzance*, they are optional, with alternative notes written underneath, and Captain Fitzbattleaxe's top C in *Utopia Limited* is intended to be mishit!). The Daughters of the Plough lead the three gentlemen away, to play no further part in Act 2. However, Ida's troubles, far from ending with the trio's imprisonment, are only just beginning. Melissa announces that an armed deputation has gathered outside the walls to procure Hildebrand's entrance to the castle, and a few moments later, despite Ida's protestations, Hildebrand's soldiers, together with the three handcuffed warriors, sweep on to the stage. The soldiers triumphantly pronounce that "Walls are unavailing, we have entered here!" The girls respond with a lament for the storming of the walls of their fortress, and a moment later both tunes are placed together to provide a piece of splendid operatic writing. Hildebrand himself then enters, and reminds Ida of her promise and the dire consequences of breaking it, not being afraid to admit that he is a "peppery kind of King, who's indisposed for parleying to fit the wit of a bit of a chit." These last few words require particularly careful enunciation for obvious reasons. It is usual, before the start of each of the two verses of Hildebrand's mini-solo, for him to walk menacingly around the stage and for the girls to draw back with screams of horror as he wields his sword at them. In performance, this will work effectively enough, but is less likely to be so successful in rehearsal. Few amateur performers, especially if they know they will have to run through the relevant section of the finale half a dozen times during the course of an evening, will be in the mood for manufacturing fear that they patently do not feel, and even the most demanding producer would be guilty of gross over-optimism to expect them to simulate the fear on the faces of the velociraptor's intended victims in *Jurassic Park* when Hildebrand's rehearsal weapon is a discarded toilet brush and the only audience is Boppit, Mr Crump's cocker spaniel.

The three warriors sing a trio ("We may remark, though nothing can dismay us") in which they look ahead anxiously to their seemingly inevitable demise and inform Ida that Hildebrand's threats are genuine. Ida maintains he is bluffing, but Hildebrand, in a dramatic recitative, confirms that if she fails to release and marry Hilarion she will effectively be causing the death of her three brothers. This ushers in the final, climactic section of the finale, in which the determination of Hildebrand and his henchmen contrasts with the

115

defiance of Ida and her colleagues. This is one of the most stirring passages in any of the operas; early on, Ida must sustain a top B flat for a number of beats, while the full ensemble sing underneath her. After a few bars of block harmony in distinctly martial flavour, there comes some dramatic counterpoint and then another top B flat from Ida before a brisk orchestral playout in a dotted rhythm which again has a strong military ring. A nice touch is to end the Act with a tableau showing Ida and Hildebrand in the centre of the stage, their swords raised against each other as though in preparation for the conflict that is to take place. The curtain then falls for the second time that evening. A short interval, at the very least, is necessary, since there is another scene change whereby the action transfers from the garden to the courtyard of Castle Adamant, and the girls are required to arm themselves with battleaxes or don some apparel suggestive of imminent conflict. Audience members who are not the least interested in the plot may actually believe that with the ending of Act 2 the opera has itself come to an end. Others who are fully aware that there is more to come may depart anyway, lured by the temptation of Mr Langley's home-brewed scrumpy at the Half Moon, or *One Million Years B.C.* on the satellite movie channel. The front-of-house staff may have omitted to raise the house lights, assuming that during the brief pause everyone would remain glued to their seats in eager anticipation of the result of the coming conflict. Too late will they realise the folly of their inaction as a procession of audience members blunder their way towards the exit, the Reebok trainers of the conductor's next-door neighbour's teenage son crashing down hard on the bunioned feet of life member Mrs Fothergill (gold medal and three bars) in row B, and the stiletto heel of Florian's secretary grinding to pulp the packet of lozenges that have slipped from the lap of life member Mrs Rigby (silver medal and two bars) thus condemning those sitting nearby to an unmitigated fusillade of coughing and spluttering through the remainder of the performance.

Act 3 begins with the lady students lustily singing a chorus ("Death to the invader") in which they confirm their determination to stand up to the intruders, but, as Melissa's intervening solo makes clear, they are anxious not to get hurt. At the end of the chorus Ida enters, attended by Blanche and Psyche. Ida knows nothing of the girls' misgivings, and in dialogue sets about preparing them for battle, interrupted only by another meaningless discourse from the tiresome Blanche. It soon turns out, however, that the girls, far from relishing the prospect of battle, are quite unprepared for it. Sacharissa confesses that she does not wish to be involved in amputating injured limbs; Chloe says that the rifles have been left in the armoury; and Ada, who has precisely one two-line speech in the entire opera (it would indeed be a cruel irony for an applicant for the part of <u>Ida</u> being cast in the

116

role of <u>Ada</u>!) says that the band do not feel well enough to play. For Ida, perhaps the most cruel blow comes from Psyche, her trusted colleague, who confesses that she favours flashing eyes and savage tongues rather than physical weapons. Ida addresses her as the one who superintends the "lab'ratory;" the "o" was left out to preserve the blank verse, but those unfamiliar with the American pronunciation of the scientist's workplace, or not expecting to find it in an English opera, may be forgiven for wondering why the Professor of Humanities has suddenly been demoted to cleaning out the college latrines.

It seems, therefore, that Ida is left on her own. The producer now has a choice; some editions of the libretto direct her to sing her big Act 3 solo here, whilst other editions, and the current musical score, interpose the entrance of Gama, and *his* big Act 3 solo, at this point. The advantage of the latter is that it brings the comic lead back into action at an earlier stage in the proceedings, and may help to assuage the doubts that certain audience members are feeling about remaining for the final Act. It also provides a better balance as between male and female solo material. Assuming Gama does enter at this point, he informs his daughter that Hildebrand, loath to go to war with women, has proposed that Ida's brothers should go to battle against Hilarion's friends, and that Ida's fate should depend on the outcome of this fight. Ida at first is minded to refuse, but she is won over when she hears of the terrible tortures her father is undergoing. Hildebrand has found a way – perhaps the only way – to make him suffer: he has given him so many wonderful things that he has nothing to grumble at! He amplifies this in his solo with chorus ("Whene'er I spoke sarcastic joke"). The plight of the permanent "whinger" who is reduced to infuriated silence by having nothing to whinge about might not only give the listener an insight into Gilbert's own often irascible character but into the type of individual who populates every operatic society. Despite the fact that he is not obliged to be there at all, he is to be found condemning every aspect of the production at any possible opportunity. An early finish to the evening will be considered a waste of good rehearsal time, and a late finish a gross intrusion into valuable drinking time. A dance step which has been used before will be contemptuously described as "stock D'Oyly Carte move number 426," and a new dance step will be condemned as unworkable and clearly inconsistent with Gilbert's avowed intentions. A piece of familiar stage business will be written off as "just a rehash of the last eleven times we've done this," but a novel and original approach to the piece of the action will be deemed to be "too risky and not what the town expects of this society." When the conductor draws attention to a musical inaccuracy, this will be blamed on the fact that "we didn't have nearly enough musical rehearsals;" but when a vocal solecism goes unnoticed by the M.D., the complaint will be that "we're just not getting the harmonies right at all and the M.D. doesn't take a blind bit of notice." The perennial grumbler will be at his best, or worst, when costumes and properties begin to appear, and each item of dress or article for use on stage is in turn dismissed as lacking any conceivable authenticity. Naturally, when at the A.G.M. consideration is given to raising the subscription to help finance more appropriate costume, he will, amongst his many other submissions to the long-suffering committee, point out that the annual subscription already outstrips by forty per cent every other society that uses the rehearsal hall, from Egg Painters' World to the Buster Keaton Appreciation Society.

Assuming the producer has followed the order in the vocal score, all exit except for Ida. In a short speech followed by a sad solo which might have been lifted straight from grand opera ("I built upon a rock") she reflects on the failure of her grand hopes and plans. At the end of her solo the gates are opened and the soldiers, accompanied by Gama's sons, then enter. Immediately they sing of their keen anticipation for battle in another splendidly bellicose chorus ("When anger spreads his wing") containing a few lines of patter singing on which is eventually superimposed a simpler, broader melody for the girls, who have reappeared with the soldiers and mounted the battlements. There then follows what is arguably the most famous song in the opera, sung by Arac with chorus ("This helmet, I suppose"). It is pure Handel from start to finish, and but for the words might have come from one of his sacred oratorios. By contrast with the majestic music, the words paint an absurd situation, as the warriors, who have been parading sweatily and cumbersomely in their armour throughout the opera without actually fighting, now sing about their intentions to remove the armour because it will actually impede their performance in battle! Indeed by the end of their song the three warriors are attired only in shape suits (long pants and pullover tunics). The greatest worry in this song is not the technical difficulty of the melody itself – it is one of the most splendid and singable tunes in the opera – but the need to remove the armour from the warriors' bodies, as indicated by the stage directions. It is self-evident that however great an impediment the wearing of armour is to success in battle, an even greater handicap is a trailing leg-piece that defies all efforts at separation from the warrior's Marks & Sparks thermal underwear.

Gama appears, and so do Hilarion and his friends, still bound and still wearing the college robes. Some spoken sparring takes place, including Arac's sole (two-line) contribution to the dialogue. After this, then assuming the robes are now removed, the battle takes place accompanied by a chorus

("This is our duty plain"). In the course of this number the bystanders agree that they ought, among other things, to "piously ejaculate," which sounds an intriguing way of passing the time when hostilities are in progress. In fact the ejaculation refers to their cries of "Oh, Hungary, oh, doughty sons of Hungary!" This is the first indication that the opera takes place, or at any rate that the protagonists hail from, anywhere other than in England; one reviewer suggested that Gilbert simply used the word "Hungary" to rhyme with the word "ironmongery" which shortly follows!

Wherever the action takes place, it appears to be going badly awry for Ida, as her brothers are subdued in battle and lie, wounded, on the ground. As though drained of any further courage or resolve, she instructs the girls in the ensuing dialogue to bind up the wounds "but look the other way" – as though conceding that women cannot cope when confronted by the grim realities of the battlefield. She asks Blanche if she will replace her as head of Castle Adamant in the event of her resigning with dignity; Blanche of course is only too pleased to accept. Ida shares her sadness at her failure with Hildebrand, but, as he points out, if all women were to embrace her philosophy there would be no subsequent generations to thank her for what she had done!

Hilarion, pressing home his advantage, pleads with Ida to give men a chance, suggesting that they, rather than women, might serve as more suitable guinea pigs for any other theories she may have. Certainly Psyche and Melissa, besotted as they are now with Cyril and Florian respectively, indicate that they do not readily intend to return to Castle Adamant once they have left with their new partners. Gama delivers the final blow to Ida's feminist ideals by speculating on what would have become of her had her mother thought as she did. With a deep breath, Ida yields herself to Hilarion and the opera ends, rather tamely, with an ensemble number including solos for Ida and Hilarion ("With joy abiding"), in which the singers reflect on the power of love, regardless of the situation. The music is a straight refrain of the music for "Expressive glances" back in Act 1, and provides a reflective, rather than exuberant, end to this long opera. At last the action is over, and the message firmly established in the audience's mind that the woman's place is in the home, cooking, washing and cleaning, and well clear of any male-dominated pursuits. There are, however, some compensations that womanhood brings; whilst female cast members are able to depart fairly soon after changing out of their normal clothes, it is the men that are conscripted to remain and shift furniture ready for the Sunshine Club Coffee

Morning under the scowling eye of Mr Crump, the janitor, as he endeavours to dislodge the congealed mass of crushed lozenge from under Mrs Rigby's chair.

"Technical rehearsal tonight then, is it?"

8 CHOP IT OFF, CHOP IT OFF

The Mikado, set in Japan, is the one G & S opera of which even the newest convert to the series is likely to have heard. From the ecstatic reception at its first night at the Savoy Theatre on 14th March 1885, and its initial run of 672 performances (the longest opening run of any of the operas) its popularity has never waned, and is the one most likely to spring to mind were a researcher ever to probe the man on the Clapham omnibus or the woman in the queue at the Londis cigarette counter.

The poor returns at the box office for the last G & S offering had threatened to bring the partnership to an end. Carte was not unnaturally anxious that the two composers should conceive a new work quickly in order to make up for *Princess Ida*'s comparative failure. However, Gilbert's suggestion that the plot be based on a magic lozenge was emphatically rejected by Sullivan, who yearned for a believable story of human interest. Legend has it that the event which broke the deadlock, and which inspired the Japanese subject matter that was to lead to the partnership's greatest success, was the falling to the floor of an ornamental sword from the wall of Gilbert's home. It is likely that Gilbert was influenced to a greater extent by the craze for things Japanese at that time; not only were Oriental prints and ceramics highly popular, but a Japanese village had been established in Knightsbridge. He therefore had the idea of an opera set in Japan. Within this colourful Eastern setting he managed to concoct not only a splendid (if quite absurd) story with generous doses of pantomime, comedy and romance, but also elements of wit and satire that would immediately be seen to be targeted at English institutions and traits. Indeed, although the satirical element was not as obvious as in *H.M.S. Pinafore, Patience* or *Iolanthe*, there were clear digs at hypocrisy, pluralism, "jobs for the boys," corruption, bureaucracy, the English fascination with brutality, and – as with *H.M.S. Pinafore* – the conflict between the demands of society for conformity, and the wishes and needs of the individual. Much of the hilarity in the opera is derived from constant references to painful and tortuous deaths; the potential performer or spectator of nervous disposition might be reassured to learn that in fact no such deaths ever take place!

Sullivan, when he heard about Gilbert's proposals, seemed delighted on being led to understand that he intended to construct a plot with no "supernatural or improbable elements." It would perhaps have been asking too much of Gilbert not to include any improbable elements, but nonetheless Sullivan readily agreed to set it. With the exception of the music for the Mikado's entrance, the score itself, like the libretto, was to be thoroughly

English in flavour. Rehearsals for the new work seemed especially stressful. As Hesketh Pearson points out, Gilbert drilled his company until they were exhausted – and then drilled them again: "Every step, every gesture, every expression, every inflection was rehearsed and rehearsed until the players achieved automatic exactitude." A geisha girl gave the chorus lessons in Japanese deportment; rumour has it that her English was limited to the two words "Sixpence please!" The effect of Gilbert's perfectionism was disastrous on Grossmith, who suffered a crisis of self-belief. Even when he did acquire the confidence to introduce some comic business of his own, this did not escape the director's disapproval; when he (Grossmith) replied that he got a big laugh by it, Gilbert retorted testily, "So you would if you sat on a pork pie."

Once again it was a struggle to complete the work on time. Sullivan recalled how with barely a fortnight to go before the show opened, he spent the whole of one night on the Act 1 finale, finishing at 5 a.m. having completed 63 pages of scoring at one sitting. It is said that immediately before the first performance Gilbert rushed round the Savoy dressing rooms, begging each player to do their best, and according to bystanders, making a general nuisance of himself. Sullivan seemed more confident, asking the cast to "sing the music with the same ease on the first night as you'll sing it after 100 nights." Gloomily, Gilbert responded "You're presuming of course that the opera will run for 100 nights." He then left the theatre, unable to bear the strain of watching the show, and only returned to take a bow with Sullivan at the end of the evening.

The audience and critics were unanimous that the show, enhanced by traditional Japanese costumes with fabric ordered specially from Liberty's, was a triumph. Other commentators would be singing its praises over a century later. Geoffrey Smith writes "The whole thing is like a glass of champagne...a sparkling mixture of pantomime, satire, fairytale, romance and oriental spectacle." It also enjoyed massive success across the Atlantic. Pirate performances abounded and Carte was not always successful in having them stopped. At one time in the U.S.A. it was not regarded as socially acceptable to take a young lady to see the opera without sending her a Japanese curio as a souvenir of the evening.

The original opera has inspired numerous unorthodox versions, such as a 1920's interpretation in Berlin which included an automobile, a Charleston and nude bathing! Over a century after its first performance, *The Mikkerdoo*, as hardened amateur opera buffs are wont to call it, is still the best-known and best-loved of the G & S operas. In amateur operatic circles, a production of the opera can almost be guaranteed to wipe out the deficit generated by whatever disastrous venture a society has just completed, be it a production of one of the lesser G & S operas or the producer's own creation, *Blood and Mud*, a searing indictment of Russian peasant life in the early 1700's.

The action of *The Mikado* takes place in Titipu (*The Town of Titipu* is the opera's alternative title) in Japan. Nanki-Poo (tenor), the son of the Mikado (bass), disguises himself as a strolling musician to flee the attentions of Katisha (contralto), an elderly lady of his father's court. He is in love with a schoolgirl, Yum-Yum (soprano), but rivalling him for her affections is Ko-Ko (baritone), the Lord High Executioner. Ko-Ko and his townsfolk, including Lord High Everything Else Pooh-Bah (baritone) and a Noble Lord Pish-Tush (baritone) are threatened with ruin because no execution has taken place in Titipu lately. Nanki-Poo, who realises he stands no chance against Ko-Ko for Yum-Yum's hand, plans to kill himself, but instead offers himself to be executed if he can marry Yum-Yum and have a month with her before being beheaded. Ko-Ko agrees, but as Yum-Yum, together with her fellow school chums Pitti-Sing (soprano) and Peep-Bo (soprano), prepares for the wedding, she is informed that when Nanki-Poo is beheaded, she will have to be buried alive. As a result she is unwilling to continue with the plan! Ko-Ko therefore agrees that in return for Nanki-Poo marrying Yum-Yum and going off with her for good, he will sign an affidavit to the effect that Nanki-Poo has been executed. He does not realise Nanki-Poo's true identity until the heartbroken Katisha tells him. He saves his bacon only by persuading Katisha to become his partner, and then, when Nanki-Poo returns to prove he is still alive, using some convoluted logic to avoid punishment at the hands of the bloodthirsty Mikado.

The action of the opera begins in the courtyard of Ko-Ko's palace in Titipu, where Japanese nobles, traditionally attired in kimonos and equipped, of course, with fans are discovered standing and sitting in attitudes suggested by native drawings. *The Mikado* is one of only three G & S operas, *H.M.S. Pinafore* and *The Pirates Of Penzance* being the others, where the male chorus only are on stage at the start of the show. (The girls do rather better; there are five G & S operas in which they alone are on stage at the start.) They sing an opening chorus of introduction ("If you want to know who we are") and, sniggers at their refutation of the suggestion that "this throng can't keep it up all day long" having passed, Nanki-Poo appears. In no other G & S opera is the lead tenor obliged to display his musical skills so early. After his recitative in which he inquires as to the whereabouts of Ko-Ko's ward Yum-Yum ("Gentlemen, I pray you tell me") he then introduces himself to the nobles in one of the most celebrated of all the tenor arias ("A wandering minstrel") in which, with the help of the chorus, he demonstrates his versatility as a performer of songs romantic, martial and nautical. It is unfortunate that this gem of a number comes so early in the opera, when the audience members are still settling back in their seats regarding the soloist in the same way as a class of twelve-year-old school pupils regards a new teacher. The only crumb of reassurance the performer can seize upon is the knowledge that, generally speaking, any suspicion of nerves or fallibility on his part will not result, as it might in the classroom, in chitchat, the throwing of paper darts, or overt ingestation of anything from cannabis to Curly-Wurlies.

Pish-Tush, one of the nobles, asks Nanki-Poo the nature of his business with Yum-Yum, and he replies that he is in love with her and has heard that his rival in love, Ko-Ko, a cheap tailor, has been condemned to death for flirting. Another dreadful pun is heard, as Nanki-Poo states that Yum-Yum's engagement to this tailor meant that "my suit was hopeless." Pish-Tush shocks Nanki-Poo by singing in a solo, with chorus ("Our great Mikado, virtuous man"), that Ko-Ko has been elevated to the rank of Lord High Executioner on the basis that, as he is next in the queue for the chop, he would need to cut his own head off before any further executions could take place. At the end of the song, the nobles (save Pish-Tush) exit and Pooh-Bah makes his entrance. In dialogue he announces himself as a "particularly haughty and exclusive person" who is able to trace his ancestry to a "protoplasmal primordial atomic globule." Since Darwin had suggested that all mankind had originated in this manner, this was Gilbert's way, as Ian Bradley states, of "reversing the anti-evolutionists' cry that such a descent greatly demeaned the dignity of man."

Pooh-Bah, who ideally should have an amply-built, indeed corpulent figure, exudes self-satisfaction, pomposity and self-importance, stating the various offices that he now holds as a result of the former office-holders' refusal to serve under an ex-tailor. These include Archbishop of Titipu (it is common for this title to be chanted rather than spoken) and there is no reason why he should not add a few titles of contemporary topical interest as well. Geoffrey Smith writes that "it is as this one-man governing body that Pooh-Bah passed into Victorian slang, carrying the concept of 'jobs for the boys' and centralised government to unimagined heights." His tendency to pluralism is equalled only by his winking at corruption, as shown when he accepts money from Nanki-Poo in order to reveal the whereabouts of Yum-Yum. The passing of money from one actor to another can result in embarrassment if forgetful recipients do not return the proferred coins. Such business may of course be mimed quite convincingly, and indeed that may be the preferred option if the actor playing Pooh-Bah, through many months of work on the show, has a tendency to amnesia and wonders why he can afford so many more lottery tickets while the actor playing Nanki-Poo is left without sufficient coinage to finance his bus ride home.

Pooh-Bah, his palm now greased, sings a solo with refrain echoed by the other two men on stage ("Young man, despair") in which he informs Nanki-Poo that the wedding of Yum-Yum and Ko-Ko is imminent. The trumpets in the orchestra provide suitable accompaniment to the words "The brass will crash and the trumpets bray" as Pooh-Bah pictures the wedding scene. Pish-Tush exits at the end of the song. In recitative ("And have I journeyed") a stunned Nanki-Poo demands confirmation of the worst, which Pooh-Bah readily gives before heralding Ko-Ko, the Lord High Executioner himself. As Pooh-Bah and Nanki-Poo exit, the nobles process grandly back on to the stage, singing a song of acclamation ("Behold the Lord High Executioner"). In fact the audience will soon see that this effusive welcome is wholly ironic. When Ko-Ko enters, and introduces himself within the same song ("Taken from the county jail"), it will be observed that in stature and appearance he is anything but grand or lordly; in build he should ideally present a contrast to the bulky Pooh-Bah. He is described by Audrey Williamson as a "blithe Charlie Chaplin," and the nearest to a clown of all Gilbert's comic lead roles. It is certainly one of the biggest roles in any of the operas. When the nobles have finished acclaiming him, he then begins one of the most looked-forward-to songs in the opera, with chorus ("As some day it may happen that a victim must be found, I've got a little list"). In the song he lists a number of people who by virtue of their antisocial activities are deserving of the executioner's block, including autograph hunters, clever children and the "idiot who praises with enthusiastic tone all centuries but this and every country but his own." It is, however, customary for contemporary performers to substitute more modern victims, thereby investing the song with a dash of topicality and originality which is comfortably within the spirit of Gilbert's writing. Indeed to adhere slavishly to the original words will baffle some audience members, having no idea why anybody should take exception to a "*Nisi Prius* nuisance," and infuriate others, who have seen *The Mikado* more times than any other opera and look forward to having the soloist share with them their own current objects of hatred, from telephone purveyors of double glazing to over-exuberant game show presenters. Chairmen and secretaries of operatic societies may during the preparations for the opera incite their members to murder by constantly announcing the establishment of a "little list" of one or more bands of reprobates, perhaps because they have not yet provided a raffle prize for the annual dinner dance, have failed to return their vocal score from the previous show, or have omitted to hand in sponsor money due to society stalwart Lionel Pratt who to raise funds for the new stage extension sat in a bath of cold tinned spaghetti for five hours.

After the song the nobles exit, leaving Ko-Ko on his own, but Pooh-Bah promptly reappears and dialogue recommences. In another burst of pluralistic fervour, Pooh-Bah places several different hats on his head in telling Ko-Ko how his wedding celebration should be organised; thus is advice provided by the Chancellor of the Exchequer, Private Secretary, Solicitor, Lord Chief Justice, and others, each with their own discrete opinion. Much of the amusement is provided by Ko-Ko insisting that each official should "come over here" where the previous official cannot hear them! As Pooh-Bah informs Ko-Ko that there is a price on his displaying deference to Ko-Ko's bride to be, the female chorus enter the arena, and the two men then exit. The girls have just completed their schooling and in their chorus of introduction ("Comes a train of little ladies") express their apprehension but at the same time fascination for the adult world they are entering. They all claim to be "eighteen and under" which in operatic societies with more than its share of mature ladies may lead to a certain scepticism amongst the audience if not proceedings under the Trade Descriptions Act.

The procession of girls is merely a prelude to the next gem in the opera, as Yum-Yum, Pitti-Sing and Peep-Bo enter and sing their celebrated and much-encored trio, in which they introduce themselves as "Three little maids from school." In this song they demonstrate a touching innocence as well as a sparkling and, one hopes, infectious *joie de vivre*; they are directed to giggle girlishly at a number of points in the song. Sullivan saves his *piece de resistance* to the end; after the chorus have joined in and sung "Freed from its genius tutelary" there is a delicious sequence of semiquavers from the bassoon, as though in imitation of the youthful chuckling. Ko-Ko and Pooh-Bah then re-enter, and in dialogue Ko-Ko introduces Yum-Yum as his prospective bride. Yum-Yum seems somewhat dubious about being embraced and kissed by him in public, but since the Lord Chamberlain (an office held, surprisingly enough, by Pooh-Bah) knows of a precedent for it, Ko-Ko proceeds to do it. Yum-Yum's subsequent "Thank goodness that's over!" certainly seems to be a less than ideal basis for a lifetime's married happiness to come.

Nanki-Poo then appears; the three little maids all rush to him and each delivers their own excited welcome speech to him at once. Ko-Ko is more amused than annoyed by the appearance of this rival for her hand, but wastes little time in calling Pish-Tush on to come and remove him. This having been done, the girls turn to the portly Pooh-Bah, regarding him with fascination. There follows one of the most endearing sequences of dialogue in the opera, as Ko-Ko tries to persuade him to show them some affection and it is only with a huge effort, and amid much hilarity from the girls, that he does so. He does state that he is not in the habit of saying "How de do, little girls" to anybody under the rank of a Stockbroker, a statement which in the hearer's mind may form a delightful vision of this kimono-clad dignitary pacing the station platforms of Virginia Water or Tunbridge Wells on a Monday morning and delivering inane pleasantries to those awaiting the arrival of the 8.06.

Ko-Ko leaves, and a joyous quartet, with chorus, follows ("So, please you, sir, we much regret") in which the three little maids ask Pooh-Bah to forgive them for their ebullience, and he asks their forgiveness for his stuffiness. Amidst much tra-la-la-ing and dancing, the girls (save Yum-Yum) disappear, as does Pooh-Bah. Nanki-Poo reappears and dialogue begins. He ascertains that although Yum-Yum is to marry Ko-Ko that day, she does not love him; this prompts Nanki-Poo to exclaim "Modified rapture!" This line had its origin in an exchange between Gilbert and Durward Lely, the first Nanki-Poo; when Lely exclaimed "Rapture!" too enthusiastically at this point, Gilbert responded "Modified rapture" and it stuck. It may earn an even bigger laugh from the audience if spoken in a matter-of-fact, throwaway fashion.

Nanki-Poo then reveals that he is no lowly musician but the son of the Mikado, and he has fled his father's court to escape firstly the attentions of an elderly lady Katisha, and secondly the scaffold that awaits him if he does not marry her. As he explains this, he comes towards Yum-Yum, but instead of responding eagerly to his amorous overtures, she feels compelled to warn him about the penalties for flirting. Nanki-Poo will then hopefully earn a laugh by looking out and saying "But we are quite alone, and nobody can see us." The larger the audience, the more amusing this line will be; when the audience, perhaps at a summer matinee with the temperature outside in the 80's and the thermometer inside the theatre registering an even higher reading, is restricted to just a handful of spectators, including a high proportion of inattentive children, the line may seem like a personal insult to the society treasurer who has still not cleared all the bills from the February production of *Miss Hook Of Holland*.

Although Yum-Yum feels constrained to try and keep her distance from Nanki-Poo at first, stating that to flirt is capital (Nanki-Poo, in another play on words, agrees that it IS capital!!), they are soon both locked in a heavy embrace and agree that but for the law, there would be no obstacle to their togetherness. A passionate love-duet follows ("Were you not to Ko-Ko plighted") in which they agree that it is, in the circumstances, wrong to kiss each other, but they still go ahead and do so anyway. The interspersing of kissing between lines of singing – and in a long pause before the last line of all – is one of the funniest aspects of the duet, particularly if done skilfully. It will of course be for the producer to decide whether the lips of one singer actually touch the lips or cheeks of the other, but much audience laughter may be generated by the couple administering the last, lingering kiss to each other behind a diplomatically-placed fan. As well as delighting the audience, such business may work to the advantage of the performers themselves. They may be only too happy, particularly if they are by nature tactile and easy-going in real life, to indulge freely in the most intimate meeting of lips and perhaps more besides. However, they may choose to avoid the meeting of any parts of the anatomy at all. This may be the desired option of the diffident performer whose level of confidence in such a situation compares unfavourably with that of the Christian in the Colosseum upon learning that the lion about to feed upon him has for the past month been restricted to a diet of raw cabbage.

The couple both exit sadly, and Ko-Ko re-enters. He gazes longingly after Yum-Yum, and expresses his admiration for her in a brief soliloquy, following which Pooh-Bah and Pish-Tush reappear. In dialogue Pooh-Bah says he has some bad news; the Mikado has decreed that unless there is an execution by beheading in one month the town of Titipu will be reduced to the rank of a village, which would spell irretrievable ruin for the officials. Pooh-Bah points out that Ko-Ko is most deserving of being executed, being under sentence of death, but he is of course incapable of cutting his own head off, and Pooh-Bah is not keen on being appointed "Lord High Substitute" in order to carry out the executioner's duties! The three men sing of the dilemma in a superbly-constructed trio ("I am so proud"). Each first sings a solo; Ko-Ko (distractedly) of the need for solidarity amongst his fellow citizens, Pooh-Bah (pompously) about the conflict within himself, and Pish-Tush (airily) about the painlessness of being executed. Each soloist has a different tune, and all three tunes are then sung at once. The trio finishes with some straight block harmony with a distinctly pattering flavour to the music, as Ko-Ko objects, Pooh-Bah declines, and Pish-Tush does not care, to sit solemnly and silently "awaiting the sensation of a short sharp shock from a cheap and chippy chopper on a big black block." In the early

1980's the concept of the "short sharp shock" was favoured by some politicians as a means of providing suitable corrective treatment for juvenile delinquents, and has frequently been quoted by both proponents and opponents of tough punishments for young offenders. Nobody would be more amused than Gilbert to discover that this simple three-word alliterative expression would have been seized upon and hymned so exultantly by right-wing politicians, blimpish reactionaries and any hack journalist anxious to fill gaps in his paper between stories of bed-hopping film-stars and rodent-eating comedians.

Pooh-Bah and Pish-Tush exit, and whilst Ko-Ko bemoans his fearful dilemma Nanki-Poo re-enters, armed with a length of rope. He announces that he is about to hang himself because of Ko-Ko's engagement to the girl he adores. Ko-Ko's instinct is to try to stop him, until he suddenly realises that Nanki-Poo, as a result of his decision to die, is an obvious candidate for the necessary beheading. Ko-Ko offers Nanki-Poo the chance to live "like a fighting cock" at his expense, and tells him that when the day of execution comes "you'll be the central figure – no one will attempt to deprive you of that distinction." Nanki-Poo is dubious at first, wondering if he might perhaps forget Yum-Yum in the course of time. Ko-Ko's assertion that he could not forget her so easily prompts Nanki-Poo to offer his own proposal; namely that he be allowed to wed her the next day and then be executed in a month, thereby enabling Ko-Ko to marry her once he has died. Barely has Ko-Ko agreed to the proposal than the nobles and the ex-schoolgirls enter together to start the Act 1 finale demanding, in a chorus ("With aspect stern"), to know what Ko-Ko has decided. When Ko-Ko announces he has found a volunteer, the chorus cry "The Japanese equivalent for Hear, hear, hear!" The fact that they sing these words, rather than actual Japanese words, is typically Gilbertian humour.

The chorus are delighted that Nanki-Poo has volunteered himself; after singing of his own passion for Yum-Yum, Ko-Ko invites him to take her (it is traditional for Pitti-Sing to try to grab Nanki-Poo at this point and for Ko-Ko to respond in speech "Not you, silly"). Ko-Ko exits, and Nanki-Poo is now able to be united with his beloved Yum-Yum. How much physical contact takes place between the couple both here and in the earlier duet may of course depend on the personalities of those involved. In the happy event of the couple having a passion for each other in real life, there are no risks of difficulty. If, however, one dislikes or distrusts the other, there is the potential for considerable embarrassment, particularly if the dislike is not mutual. It could be, therefore, that without suitably robust intervention by the producer, Nanki-Poo unleashes a succession of passionate kisses on to the lips of his stage beloved, believing this to be the highlight of his life so far, whilst Yum-Yum is during the interval complaining bitterly to her fellow schoolgirls about a close encounter with a bad case of garlic-flavoured halitosis.

The uniting of the two lovers is the cue for a joyous ensemble number ("The threatened cloud has passed away") which acknowledges that while the marriage will only be a brief one, the company may still celebrate "with laughing song and merry dance." It is an exhausting number to sing, particularly if dancing is incorporated into it, but the hard work is broken up slightly by a splendid recitative for Pooh-Bah in which he voices his own good wishes. The words "Long life to you" are sung four times, with one absurdly exaggerated melisma on the first "life" in which the chorus traditionally display all the symptoms of serious loss of interest such as muffled yawns. The yawning may be all too genuine, particularly if the technical and dress rehearsals have lasted into the small hours, and the entire cast were ordered to stay on after the second night performance to replot three big ensemble numbers owing to the untimely outbreak of food poisoning amongst those Japanese nobles who partook of a dodgy tandoori after the opening performance.

As Pooh-Bah finishes, the chorus add their good wishes, the happiness of the company apparently unrestrained – until the party is suddenly rudely interrupted by the arrival of Katisha. Of all the elderly G & S contralto roles, this is certainly the most formidable. The dress that the very first Katisha wore on the night of the opening performance was thought to be about 200 years old, and indeed there is nothing youthful or refreshing about her personality either. Described in the list of *dramatis personae* and also by Nanki-Poo as an "elderly lady" she has none of the glamour and mystique of the Fairy Queen in *Iolanthe*, and with her fierce countenance and singularly unattractive features she casts a far greater shadow over the happiness of the lovers than Ruth in *The Pirates Of Penzance*. Jane Stedman suggests that her character was used by Gilbert to satirise the premium placed by Victorians on youthful beauty as the most desirable quality in marriage!

Whether or not Jane Stedman is accurate in her assertion, any natural beauties possessed by the actress playing this role will almost certainly need to be smothered by suitably unflattering make-up. The job of the make-up team is a thankless one. Pressured by the producer to spend quite a considerable time with the principals before each performance in order to create a severe elderly face out of a benign middle-aged one, or vice versa, the make-up artist and her assistants will also have to face a noisy gaggle of half-dressed men, each waiting for their allocation of base, rouge, lipstick and eyeliner. Some men, particularly of a lonelier disposition, will enjoy the feeling of being mothered, and will regard it as very much an integral part of the evening to stand for possibly fifteen minutes in a smelly overcrowded dressing room, queuing for the privilege of having their faces and neck regions lovingly attended to at no emotional or financial cost. For others, however, standing in the make-up queue is a tedious chore, made bearable only by indulgence in banal chit-chat with bystanders or singing desultory snatches of the opera that is about to be performed. Overstressed make-up assistants may indulge in a piece of unwise time management by suggesting the men might wish to apply their own base whilst waiting their turn in the queue. They will then wish they had not, as they are bombarded with queries as to whether it should be number 24 base, number 26 base or number 27.5 base, and, when the answer is revealed, they realise that that is the one base of which supplies are the most scarce. When the time comes for the more specialist and intricate applications, some men will place their hirsute and sweaty frames into the chair with irregular streaks of dark brown smeared randomly across various areas of skin between forehead and nipples inclusive, whilst there is always at least one who will present himself for inspection having daubed such generous quantities of greasepaint across his cheeks that only a squeeze of lemon and a sprinkling of sugar is required before serving it up on Shrove Tuesday.

Katisha announces that she has arrived to claim Nanki-Poo. The chorus try and shoo her away, but Katisha has other ideas. In a grim solo in the minor key ("Oh fool, that fleest") she pleads with Nanki-Poo to return to her and "Give me my place, oh rash, oh base." She then unleashes her fury on Yum-Yum, telling her that "thy doom is nigh, pink cheek, bright eye." Pitti-Sing breaks the tension by singing, in one of the catchiest little songs in the opera, that Nanki-Poo "is going to marry Yum-Yum." The chorus gladly join in, isolating Katisha completely. For a moment she seems defeated, and as she sings a pathetic solo, "The hour of gladness is dead and gone," one might almost feel some sympathy for her. The producer may want to maximise the contrast between the gaiety of Pitti-Sing's solo and Katisha's lament, by lowering the stage lights and getting each chorus member to turn their back on the centre of the stage, possibly in a "freeze" position. The effect of such a "freeze" can be most impressive providing, of course, that no troublesome itches take it upon themselves to visit the noses, ears, or other particularly sensitive body areas of the performers in question.

Katisha, however, is far from finished. As the lights come up again and the chorus focus on her once more, she threatens to Nanki-Poo that she will "tear the mask from your disguising." Exposure as the Mikado's son seems inevitable, but her announcement as to his true identity is drowned by the chorus, led by Yum-Yum and Nanki-Poo, singing *"O ni! Bikkuri shakkuri to!"* six times in succession. It may seem strange that the assembled members of the public, presumably with no notion of what Katisha might have been going to say, should suddenly wish to interrupt her in this way. In some ways it would be more logical to copy the early performances and invite Nanki-Poo and Yum-Yum to drown her voice initially and for the chorus to add their weight on subsequent declamations of this Japanese phrase. The choral interruptions are extremely hard to sing correctly, and the musical director may well be prepared to settle for accuracy in pitch and timing, at the expense of a certain Anglicisation of the original Japanese. As a result, the subsequent announcement of "Bickery Shackery Toe" may be suggestive not so much of Japanese expressions of surprise and shock – which is what the original words mean – as a country folk dance, an obscure Scottish mountain in the Cuillin Range, or a firm of provincial solicitors specialising in litigation arising from matrimonial breakdown and domestic violence.

Katisha's inability to make herself heard infuriates her, and with equally furious orchestral accompaniment she sings that she will go back to the Mikado and exact revenge on Nanki-Poo, Yum-Yum and the remainder of the company. In response, the chorus are both defiant and undaunted by the threats, determined that "to joy we soar despite your scowl." Despite the already heavy musical demands on Nanki-Poo and Yum-Yum during the finale, this last ensemble number requires Nanki-Poo to hit a clean top A as he sings "For joy reigns everywhere around." Katisha, however, will have none of it; furiously she rushes up stage, clearing the crowd away right and left, finishing on the steps at the back. A dramatic way of ending Act 1 is for the curtains to close and then part again, leaving a final picture of Katisha, her fan open, glowering down at the supposedly carefree revellers. Incidentally, the correct pronunciation of this name is "Catty-shar" but some variations are inevitable, usually involving the erroneous stressing of the second syllable to produce "Cur-TEE-sher"or alternatively "Cur-TISH-er," with the latter pronunciation prompting cries of "Bless you" from anyone within earshot.

Act 2 takes place in Ko-Ko's garden, and begins with the girls' chorus fussing around Yum-Yum as she makes her wedding preparations. They sing lovingly of the prospective bride ("Braid the raven hair") and only Pitti-Sing, in a solo in the middle of the number, seems to suggest that some modesty might be called for. After the girls have departed, Yum-Yum, left alone, reflects on her great beauty, first in speech and then in song ("The sun, whose rays") in which she likens herself to both the sun and the moon. Pitti-Sing and Peep-Bo then reappear and in dialogue remind Yum-Yum that although she may be the happiest girl in Japan, she is still faced with the beheading of her husband in a month. As Peep-Bo cruelly points out, "It does seem to take the top off it, you know!"

Nanki-Poo then arrives with Pish-Tush. Certain libretti direct that another noble, Go-To, rather than Pish-Tush, should accompany him on at this point; this reflects the introduction of the character of Go-To by Gilbert during the opera's initial run because of the problems encountered by the gentleman playing Pish-Tush in reaching the low notes in the ensuing madrigal. Although in many productions of the opera Go-To will not be used and Pish-Tush will actually return to the fray at this point, some producers may welcome the chance to utilise another solo singer. In fact they may be glad of any opportunity to create extra principal roles and/or resurrect some of those which Gilbert discarded, of which the pirate James in *The Pirates Of Penzance* is one example. Sometimes "extra" principals may be called upon, without fear of falling foul of copyright laws, to sing solo sections assigned to other principals or even to sections of the chorus. The advantages are obvious; budding major principals can be given a taste of the limelight and a chance to establish themselves amongst the hierarchy, even if their presence in the principals' dressing-room is treated with disdainful frowns by the elite-in-residence. Photographs in the foyer, a name in bold capitals in the programme, and a line in the local newspaper review will all combine to increase the performer's sense of self-esteem and accomplishment. New principals will however discover that the soloist's life can be a tough one. The first round of post-rehearsal drinks will be regularly delayed as the star-in-the-making is requested to remain behind for additional tuition; the soloist whose existing contribution is curtailed as a result of the new appointment will sit glowering at the performer and pounce vengefully and gleefully on the slightest error that is made; and the new soloist will be expected, along with the other principals, to feature in the cast picture for the *Daily Echo*. At its worst, this will involve the soloist having to be available at 8.30 a.m. on a wet Sunday morning in February beside the town's remaining fragment of castle ruin or other suitably historic edifice, clad only in a length of faded curtain material and a pair of oversized flip-flops.

Nanki-Poo finds all the girls in tears at the thought of his forthcoming decapitation, and endeavours, rather unconvincingly to soften the blow by encouraging them to think of each day as a year, thereby notionally giving

134

the two of them thirty years of married happiness. Peep-Bo exits while the other four try hard to be cheerful. In order to assist the process, they launch into a madrigal, "Brightly dawns our wedding day." In it they acknowledge that "solemn shadows fall – over one and over all" but still endeavour to "sing a merry madrigal." For lovers of English early music, or those who enjoy a chance to hear voices in harmony, this is the highlight of the opera, somehow even lovelier and more potent because of the un-English surroundings. For a few precious moments, comedy and pantomime are forsaken, and the performers must concentrate on being melodious, harmonious and above all tuneful. If the correct effect is achieved, and the madrigal is skilfully performed, the audience will afford the singers the courtesy of a few seconds' precious silence before breaking into thunderous applause. It is a classic favourite for G & S compilation evenings, and would not be out of place in any concert for unaccompanied singers. Indeed the four performers executing the madrigal in the course of a stage production may look nostalgically back on their rendition of the piece at a charity function at the plush home of the town's M.P. a few weeks before the show, where afterwards there awaited them a sumptuous finger buffet and ice-cool Pimms in fruit-filled glasses. It will certainly compare favourably with tonight's less palatable prospect of a ten-deep queue at the washbasins for removal of make-up and then a ten-minute walk to the Fisherman's Kitchen for a portion of soggy chips and mushy peas.

Pish-Tush (or Go-To) and Pitti-Sing leave the scene, and Ko-Ko enters to witness Nanki-Poo and Yum-Yum in an embrace. In the dialogue which follows he accepts he must get used to this over the coming month, but this is not the most important thing on his mind. He has found out from his solicitor (Pooh-Bah, of course) that when a married man is beheaded, his wife is buried alive. All the senior lawyers from whom he has sought legal opinion – the Attorney General, the Lord Chief Justice and the Lord Chancellor, among others (no prizes for guessing who they are!) – confirm this view. Nanki-Poo claims this law has never been put into force, and Ko-Ko responds with the statement "flirting is the only crime punishable with decapitation, and married men never flirt." Although pedants might wonder why Ko-Ko does not therefore select another means of execution, it should be remembered that the Mikado had insisted on a beheading, and it gives Gilbert the opportunity to make a somewhat ironic comment on marital fidelity. It also provides a few laughs for the bloodthirsty audience as they contemplate the wretched and quite unjust fate that awaits innocent widows of flirtatious husbands!

Yum-Yum suddenly becomes somewhat less keen on the idea of marriage to Nanki-Poo – but if she does not go through with it, not only will Nanki-Poo lose her to Ko-Ko but Ko-Ko himself will not get the execution he wants. They sing of their dilemma in the much-encored trio "Here's a how-de-do." The song gives ample opportunity for comic business, such as that employed by Martyn Green, the famous D'Oyly Carte soloist who pulled out a different fan from his sleeve at every encore, each smaller than the previous one. Henry Lytton, another celebrated D'Oyly Carte veteran, would at the end of the trio snap open a fan which split in two. Many hardened audiences of amateur productions will see nothing new in this, recalling the many occasions on which props have come apart on stage. The words of Nanki-Poo in the second verse of the trio, "Here's a pretty mess," may be especially apt! The truly skilful actor will by his demeanour convince the punters that anything that has broken was meant to do so, and will wait until afterwards to work out how to break the news to the donor of the prop in question that his cherished family heirloom, recently priced at £1100 by The Old Post Office Antique Shop in a neighbouring village, has suffered an unforeseen reduction in value.

Nanki-Poo, realising that Yum-Yum will never consent to marry him now, informs Ko-Ko in the ensuing dialogue that his immediate suicide is back on the agenda. As if this were not bad enough for Ko-Ko, Pooh-Bah enters and informs him that the Mikado is on his way to the city, and due to arrive in ten minutes, doubtless to find whether his orders have been carried out. Ko-Ko's own execution suddenly looms large. Nanki-Poo proposes a solution that would appear to please everybody; he invites Ko-Ko to behead him immediately. Pooh-Bah, conscious of the limited time available, implores Ko-Ko to "Chop it off! Chop it off!" It is to be presumed that it is indeed the head which Pooh-Bah is anxious to see removed, and not some other part (or parts) of the anatomy which *double-entendre* collectors might visualize falling victim to Ko-Ko's axe.

Again, however, the bloodthirsty must wait. Ko-Ko suddenly confesses that he is no expert in the field of capital punishment. In fact he states that, ignorant of how it is done, he is going to take lessons. By the time he discloses that "I can't kill anything! I can't kill anybody!" he is in tears. However, he then has an idea. He will draft an affidavit that Nanki-Poo has been killed, asking the Commander-in-Chief, Lord Chief Justice, Lord High Admiral and many others, to act as witnesses. The holder of these offices (guess who!) realises that all these personages will be guilty of perjury if they do, but Ko-Ko invites them to be "grossly insulted" – in other words, to accept another financial inducement. Pooh-Bah's next question "Will the insult be cash down, or at a date?" and Ko-Ko's reply, "It will be a ready money transaction" must be among the most neglected of all Gilbert's dialogue in the operas; even the most traditionally-minded producer will, as in the scene in *The Sorcerer* when Alexis purchases the potion from Mr Wells, permit payment by plastic together with the inevitable "That'll do nicely."

Nanki-Poo is still preoccupied with the thought of losing Yum-Yum; Ko-Ko, seeing that his (Nanki-Poo's) co-operation is essential to the scheme, has a solution. He orders Pooh-Bah, in his capacity as Commissionaire, to fetch Yum-Yum – which he does – and then allows her and Nanki-Poo to go off and get married providing they never come back. How convenient that the Archbishop of Titipu should be on hand and available to marry them. Ko-Ko just manages to dismiss the lovers (plus Archbishop) and exit himself before the Mikado (the Emperor) arrives. None of the other major G & S principal characters enter the fray as late in an opera as the Mikado does (the Prince and Princess of Monte Carlo in *The Grand Duke* enter even later, but their roles, though important, are small). Consequently the character cast as the Mikado can afford to set off for the theatre at a comfortably late hour, and may not need to set the video for *Coronation Street*; he will arrive at the theatre and find no queue for application of make-up and, if the chorus is occupied on stage, plenty of room to sit and change at leisure. He may not always be so fortunate; the producer may ask him to double up as a chorus member in Act 1 to swell the woefully weak first bass line, or he may suffer the same fate as a well-known D'Oyly Carte principal some years ago. Travelling by train into London one evening for his nightly stage appearance, his train came to an unscheduled stop and remained stationary for a very long time. A man sitting opposite him looked at his watch and said "This is very annoying; I'm supposed to be seeing *The Mikado* at the ****** theatre tonight" to which the singer was able to reply "I AM the Mikado!!"

The entrance of the Mikado is one of the most impressive of all stage entrances in the G & S operas, involving a full procession of all the chorus as they herald his arrival. The real Japanese words which the chorus sing, ("*Miya sama, miya sama, on n'm-ma no maye ni*") were lifted from a war song of the Japanese Imperial Army. As the Mikado begins to sing his introductory song, with chorus ("From every kind of man"), his subjects bow down in homage to him, but even he is upstaged by Katisha who has entered with him and, much to his annoyance, keeps interrupting his solo by referring to her own superior qualities as "his daughter-in-law elect." The Mikado, having subdued her with a withering glance, sings one of the most famous songs in all the G & S musical repertoire ("A more humane Mikado"). It is astonishing, but true, that Gilbert had intended to cut this song and it was only his cast who persuaded him to keep it in. In it, the Mikado – supported by the chorus – states the original and grisly punishments awaiting those who offend against society, with every transgressor receiving a punishment appropriate to his or her own particular misdemeanour. As each verse ends, it is traditional – following the example of the famous D'Oyly Carte performer Darrel Fancourt – to break into a thunderous sadistic laugh which strikes terror into the chorus and possibly the audience as well. Like the "short sharp shock," the very expression "letting the punishment fit the crime" which the Mikado states to be his "object all sublime" has passed into everyday criminological language. It is similar to Ko-Ko's "little list" song in singling out particular classes of offender, although it is also fair to say that the original words of the Mikado's song tend to be heard more frequently than the original words of Ko-Ko's, with perhaps less ad-libbing. The line referring to the "vocal villainies" of the much-maligned amateur tenor will usually remain, and although Nanki-Poo is not on stage at this point, there should be sufficient chorus tenors to assume expressions of fear and terror as their particular fate, to perform to Madame Tussaud's waxwork, is pronounced. Perhaps the most puzzling reference is to the fate of the billiard cheat, who is doomed to dwell in a dungeon cell "on a spot that's always barred." (The spot being a place on a billiard table where a ball is placed.) However there is nothing mysterious about his being condemned to play a match with "elliptical billiard balls." In performance the word "balls" will be followed by another blood-curdling laugh; a pause between the words "billiard" and "balls" and a particular emphasis on the "balls" will heighten the effect even more and take the thoughts of the less well-bred audience members well away from the billiard room. Some changes from the original have been suggested for the sake of clarity or political correctness; a reference to "nigger" was removed (as was a similar reference in the "little list" song) by A.P. Herbert at the request of Rupert D'Oyly Carte in 1948, and references to "parliamentary" trains – very slow trains with cheap fares instigated by an Act of Parliament in 1844 – will often be replaced by reference to a particular route near to the place of performance which is notorious for its poor or slow service. "Southend to Fenchurch Street" for instance happens to fit neatly with the music, but the performer may have more problem decrying the lines linking Coulsdon South with Kings Cross Thameslink or Barton-on-Humber with Cleethorpes.

As the Mikado's song comes to an end, Pooh-Bah, Ko-Ko and Pitti-Sing come and at once prostrate themselves before him. In dialogue, they proudly announce that an execution has taken place, witnessed by an assortment of dignitaries (there seems no limit to Pooh-Bah's versatility) including, this time, the splendidly-named Groom of the Second Floor Front. The Mikado asks them to describe the execution, and in the ensuing trio, with chorus ("The criminal cried"), a graphic and extremely painful description of the deed – in which all three played a part – is described. The chorus then leave the stage and there ensues one of the longest, but also one of the funniest, pieces of dialogue in the opera. The Mikado tells the trio that he is seeking his son, who disappeared from his Imperial Court a year ago. Katisha adds that she was going to marry him but he still fled nonetheless. She acknowledges – and Pooh-Bah agrees – that she is not physically attractive, but she claims to have other equally important attributes, such as a lovely left shoulder-blade and fascinating right elbow.

The Mikado's next words, however, bring a distinct chill to the proceedings, as he reveals that his son is disguised as a Second Trombone. The sudden ghastly realisation dawns on the three conspirators that they have purported to execute the heir to the Japanese throne! In desperation, they claim that he has gone abroad and is now living in Knightsbridge. Knightsbridge is, of course, the part of London in which the Japanese village had been situated which helped to inspire the opera in the first place. When the opera was first performed outside London, however, Gilbert gave instructions that Nanki-Poo's address should be a place that was close to the location of the production, and that tradition has continued to this day. Despite Gilbert's instruction, performers may wish to branch out even further and choose any place in Great Britain with a reputation for being less than exciting, or simply a place with a bizarre name, regardless of its proximity to the performance location. It would be a pity if, for instance, an operatic society felt that it had to take its production of The Mikado to Caernarfon or Holyhead in order to claim that Nanki-Poo had fled to Llanfairpwllgwyngyllgogerychwyrndrobwllllantysiliogogogoch.

Any further deception is however rendered useless when Katisha discovers Nanki-Poo's name on the death certificate. Whilst she is heartbroken, the Mikado seems more amused than annoyed. To begin with he appears quite sympathetic, suggesting that his son, by disguising himself in that way, thoroughly deserved all he got. Soon all three conspirators are laughing along with him, until he freezes the blood in their veins by airily announcing that he has forgotten the punishment for encompassing the death of the Heir Apparent. This causes the trio to drop to their knees. Their discomfiture is not relieved when the Mikado, still apparently jovially, states that the punishment due is, he fancies, "something lingering, with boiling oil in it."

Paradoxically, he states that he is "not a bit angry." It is extraordinary that the Mikado should be so nonchalant about what sounds a very unpleasant fate indeed. Jane Stedman writes: "The pantomime monarch's brutal disregard of human life is refined to a detachment which expresses itself not as despotic abuse but as utter non-humanity, embodied, however, in terms of perfect etiquette."

The three conspirators plead with him for mercy on the basis that they had no idea of Nanki-Poo's identity. The Mikado seems to raise their hopes by saying that there should be a suitable let-out clause in the Act prescribing the punishment for their crime, but then goes on to say that there isn't. The Mikado then says he will have it altered – but after a pregnant pause announces it will be "next session." With each raising and lowering of hope it is customary for the three unfortunates to lift their heads with relief and then drop them in despair, all in perfect unison. Mercy seems to be in short supply, but again in obedience to etiquette the Mikado asks them if it would suit them to wait until after lunch for their execution. Pooh-Bah, not surprisingly, says he does not want any lunch!

There follows a very English glee for the five performers ("See how the fates their gifts allot") in which a contrast is drawn between "happy undeserving A" and "wretched meritorious B." The Mikado and Katisha then exit and the recriminations begin. In dialogue all three conspirators blame each other for being so convincing in their account of their own part in supposedly executing Nanki-Poo. Ko-Ko realises that only Nanki-Poo's immediate reappearance can save them in the short term. As luck would have it, the newly-married Nanki-Poo appears with Yum-Yum, both ready for their honeymoon. Nanki-Poo is aghast to be told that his father and Katisha are in the district; if Katisha learns that he is married, she will insist on his being executed and on Yum-Yum being buried alive. By way of a solution, Nanki-Poo suggests that Ko-Ko should persuade Katisha to marry him (Ko-Ko) instead. Not surprisingly, this suggestion meets with some resistance, notwithstanding Pooh-Bah's assertion that Katisha's right heel is greatly admired by connoisseurs.

Nevertheless, there seems no other course. Nanki-Poo's relief and Ko-Ko's despondency are both vividly displayed in yet another wonderful song for all five singers ("The flowers that bloom in the spring, Tra la") which in its rhythm and exuberance has a distinct flavour of an Irish jig. It is recorded that Sullivan started writing the music for this after tea, and finished it before dinner the same evening! The song is certainly a popular one; much of the enjoyment comes from the contrast between Nanki-Poo's "Tra la's," being innocent expressions of joy which are echoed by Pooh-Bah, Pitti-Sing and Yum-Yum, and Ko-Ko's wholly ironic "Tra la's," being expressions of resignation to his joyless fate. His last solo words are "Oh, bother the flowers of spring." It may be tempting to follow the example of Eric Idle, who played Ko-Ko in Jonathan Miller's highly acclaimed production of *The Mikado* in the late 1980's, and substitute a different word for "bother" albeit with the same first and final letter and the same number of letters in between. A performer who is so tempted may want to check with the producer first before he does so, notwithstanding that this song will usually be sung after the 9 p.m. watershed. The producer's response may depend on the nature and sensibilities of the audience; what may be acceptable in a university production for the benefit of students may be less well-received when the show is being performed to a wider community, particularly if in the audience is the full complement of the Just Six Of Us Ladies Singers (Or JUST SOULS for short) among whom is the wife of the vicar of St Radigund's, the local Mother's Union president, and an elder of the Norwood Street Baptist Church.

All five of the singers depart, and the mood of frivolity, which the previous quintet and preceding dialogue has created, changes to one of sadness as Katisha enters. She immediately sings a bitter recitative ("Alone, and yet alive") and a brief aria ("Hearts do not break") in which she laments the hopelessness of her position. Again the audience will see the dichotomy between the vengeful amazon that swept on to the scene in Act 1 and the vulnerable, heartbroken soul who now freely shares her plight with her listeners. However, Ko-Ko's timid entrance is a cue for her more fiery nature to show itself. The ensuing dialogue sees Ko-Ko summoning all the eloquence at his command to convince Katisha (and indeed himself!) of the greatness of his love for her. His wooing takes the form of a passionate speech which is very lengthy; a producer who despairs of Ko-Ko's ability to memorise it successfully may legitimately direct him to read it – or at least refresh his memory from notes – on the basis that it would be entirely in character to do so.

Katisha, unsurprisingly, remains unmoved and dismissive. Ko-Ko therefore sings her a song full of pathos ("On a tree by a river") in which he tells the story of the little tom-tit who drowned himself as a result of unreturned affection, and makes it clear to Katisha that if she rejects him, he will do the same. Like so many numbers in *The Mikado*, this song with its "Tit willow" refrain has passed into G & S folklore as one of the all-time greats. The beauty of the song is not only in its familiarity to all G & S fans, but in its simplicity; the three verses are all identical, and there are no particular vocal

141

challenges for the performer, other than the necessity for absolute clarity in diction. It is therefore a good choice for anybody wishing to enter the G & S class in an amateur music festival, or the Male Solo class in a G & S festival, for the first time. These classes are in some ways more terrifying than auditions. The first-time entrant will find himself facing competition not only from fellow members of his own society, but veteran competitors from other societies who add to the newcomer's discomfiture by chatting matily and knowledgeably together over coffee (30p, biscuits 15p extra) about past triumphs and successes. These competitors, when called upon, may exchange sycophantic pleasantries with the adjudicators – whom of course they know well – and then, seemingly from nowhere, will produce a piece of costume and a prop before singing the chosen solo impeccably from memory. The most nerve-racking aspect for the new entrant will be the long wait until his turn comes as Competitor No. 23; the ultimate torture is when, after Competitor No.22 has finished, the adjudicators announce a 20-minute break and are presented with a tray containing steaming pots of hot beverage and liberal platefuls of ginger creams. When the singer has finally blundered his incompetent way through the chosen song – his only prop being his Chappell vocal score – and sympathetic applause has petered out, another long wait follows before the chief adjudicator stands and offers a public appraisal of each performance. The performer may of course be halfway through his second pint in the Frog & Toad and never get to hear what the appraiser thought about his inept rendition. The public will hear the adjudicator, anxious to avoid any libellous accusation, state "This was an adventurous choice of piece which demands first-rate vocal control. Your interpretation of it was wholly sincere and your courage in attempting it was unmistakeable. There is much potential for development under the tutelage of an experienced musician." The message, of course, is clear: "You were a waste of space."

Katisha has been greatly affected by Ko-Ko's song, and is close to tears. Ko-Ko confirms in the subsequent dialogue that he will go the way of the little tom-tit if she refuses him. She is finally won round, and indeed checks with Ko-Ko himself that he will not hate her because of her bloodthirstiness. He responds that there is indeed beauty to be found in this aspect of her character, and in the energetic duet that follows ("There is beauty in the bellow of the blast") both warm to this theme; whilst Katisha says "earthquakes only terrify the dolts," Ko-Ko responds that "if I have a little weakness it's a passion for a flight of thunderbolts." At the end, Ko-Ko and Katisha dance off together, the diminutive Ko-Ko looking anything but masculine alongside his far more formidable partner. A flourish heralds the arrival of the Mikado, together with the chorus led by Pish-Tush. Lunch is over, and all is ready for the executions. To everyone's surprise, however, Katisha appears with the three condemned prisoners, and begs the Mikado to show them mercy. Pooh-Bah, in his capacity as Registrar, has officiated at her wedding to Ko-Ko. The Mikado points out that this still does not alter the fact that they have slain the Heir Apparent. As if on cue, Nanki-Poo appears with Yum-Yum; as he says, the Heir Apparent is not slain! Katisha, when she learns of his survival and his marriage to Yum-Yum, is furious with the treacherous Ko-Ko, and sets about tearing him to pieces. The Mikado restrains her and waits for Ko-Ko's explanation which will need to be a good one; the promised execution has not taken place, and the irretrievable ruin of which Pish-Tush spoke in Act 1 appears to be a very real possibility. Grim consequences will also surely follow the creation of an affidavit which has proved to be manifestly false. However, as in so many other G & S operas, things are resolved, albeit in an absurdly contrived fashion. Ko-Ko persuades the Mikado that since his will is law, any command of his that something be done means that it is as good as done, and practically is done. In this case, then, the very fact that the Mikado has ordered an execution within a month means that the execution is as good as accomplished, and practically is accomplished. The company anxiously listens for the Mikado's reaction, and it is with considerable relief that he replies "Nothing could possibly be more satisfactory." A certain degree of suspense could be added by placing a lengthy gap between the words "more" and "satisfactory," whilst the rest of the company waits, with bated breath, for the Mikado's verdict on Ko-Ko's half-baked and ridiculous logic. Of course, many people in the audience will be fully aware of the outcome of the story, but will enjoy this touch of originality all the same; members of the cast, particularly for whom this may be the eighth or ninth time they have taken part in a production of this opera, may be rather less tolerant or sympathetic, and will be sustained only by the hope that during this pregnant pause the Mikado will actually genuinely forget what he is supposed to say next.

A joyful reprise of two of the songs from the Act 1 finale provides the final music of the opera, begun by Pitti-Sing announcing "For he's gone and married Yum-Yum." Nanki-Poo and his new wife look forward to "years and years of afternoon" while the chorus acclaim them "with joyous shout and ringing cheer." The Mikado's benign response to Ko-Ko's interesting logic has saved the city from ruin, the perjurers from boiling oil and melted lead, and Ko-Ko from Katisha's breakfast bowl. Nonetheless, it might be regarded as somewhat unjust that Ko-Ko's reward for ensuring the future married happiness of Nanki-Poo and Yum-Yum, saving the townsfolk from bankruptcy, and learning more lines than anyone else on stage, should consist of spending the long winter evenings admiring his wife's lovely left shoulder-blade and fascinating right elbow.

"Well, she did warn us if the producer
went on a minute after midnight..."

Ruddigore, like *Patience* and *Princess Ida* before it, tends to be left to the specialist G & S societies for regular airings. Yet whilst *Patience* shines because of its dazzling libretto, and *Princess Ida* abounds with beautiful music, Ruddigore never quite excels in either aspect. In fairness, it would have been almost impossible to surpass the phenomenal success of *The Mikado*, which made way for *Ruddigore* at the Savoy in January 1887. When a new opera to succeed *The Mikado* was discussed, Gilbert had again tried to interest Sullivan in the lozenge plot. Sullivan rejected it, and Gilbert was forced to look elsewhere for a suitable theme. He found it in his earlier work *Ages Ago*. In this piece, pictures of family ancestors came to life, with those depicted in the portraits temporarily forsaking their passive poses and rashly stepping down from their frames. Gilbert decided to work this idea into his new opera, with several generations of one family being reunited on a darkened stage in front of an enthralled, if perhaps not entirely credulous, assembly of spectators.

Using the walking picture frames as his basis, Gilbert decided to use his new opera to satirise the blood-and-thunder melodrama with its black-and-white morality. This kind of drama was very popular amongst Victorian audiences. There would be a shy likeable young farmer in love with a pure and virtuous maiden; by contrast there would be a debauched villain, a crazed woman, a reckless but noble sailor, a menacing ghost from the past, a collection of equally ghostly ancestors, and a chorus of cooing bridesmaids and dashing Regency dandies. The settings – a picturesque fishing village and a castle picture gallery – would match the colour and flavour of the characters. Through the opera, however, it would also be possible to see the recurrence of the themes that prevailed in other operas involving quite different settings such as *H.M.S. Pinafore*, *The Pirates Of Penzance* and *The Mikado;* the pursuance of individual self-interest, and recognition by the individual of an obligation to act in a certain way. It was certainly an ambitious work, and would cost more to stage than any of the previous G & S operas. Gilbert intended to burlesque the traditional melodrama by not only exaggerating its usual features, but actually by turning the stereotypes on their heads so that the villain and the crazed woman would attempt to reform themselves, the sailor and the maiden would be exposed as selfish and greedy, and the shy farmer would be made – against his will – to live the life of the criminal, and feel thoroughly uncomfortable about doing so!

As early rehearsals proceeded, *The Mikado* was still in full swing, and indeed it did not finish until 19th January 1887. This left just three days for rehearsals in the Savoy before *Ruddigore*'s first night, and it is not surprising that at least one of those rehearsals lasted until 5 a.m.! Gilbert upset Rutland Barrington, one of his principal soloists, by allowing friends to witness later rehearsals, and on objection from Barrington Gilbert relented somewhat. However, Gilbert had to have the last word; when a bystander sought to view a later rehearsal from the stalls, Gilbert told him "You mustn't sit here. Barrington won't like it."

The queue for unreserved seats for the first performance began building up several hours before the show began. At that time the title of the opera, to be called *Ruddygore*, was still a secret. The reaction to the name when it was discovered was not wholly favourable; one objector said it was no different from *Bloodygore*, prompting Gilbert to make the famous remark that "I suppose you'll take it that if I say I admire your ruddy countenance I mean I like your bloody cheek." He toyed with renaming it *Kensington Gore, Or Robin And Richard Were Two Pretty Men*. Perhaps it was in recognition of the fact that it would have been virtually impossible to follow the success of the previous opera, that he mischievously suggested a further alternative, namely *Kensington Gore, Or Not So Good As The Mikado*.

Eventually, however, he settled for one small change to the original, substituting an I for the Y, although it still entailed the printing of a new libretto. It was not only the name to which some of the first-night audience on 22nd January 1887 took exception. There was a very long delay between Acts as the set was changed from fishing village to picture gallery, and the wait could hardly have made the customers feel more conciliatory towards the new work. The most adverse reaction, however, was reserved for the finale of the piece, in which the ghostly ancestors returned to life for the second time in the opera; such was the hostility that some spectators were even provoked to booing.

Clearly affected by the unfavourable reaction from the audience, Gilbert and Sullivan undertook certain amendments to the work. It would be fair to say that in its revised form it found greater favour amongst subsequent spectators. The opening run was 288 performances (the opening run in New York was 53) which although paltry by comparison with *The Mikado* still exceeded that of *Princess Ida*. Gilbert, who regarded *Ruddigore* as one of his finest books, was pleased with the financial return it yielded. Arguably the happiest aspect of the new production was the emergence of Henry Lytton as a comic lead, replacing Grossmith who was indisposed. Gilbert however showed Lytton no mercy, and coached him rigorously; as he said to

147

him following one evidently imperfect rendition of some dialogue, "Every word I could I removed until it was of the length you find it today. Each word that is left serves some purpose; there is not one word too many. So when you know that it took me three months to perfect that one speech, I am sure you will not hurry it."

In true melodramatic style, the plot of *Ruddigore*, alternatively titled *The Witch's Curse*, has many twists and turns. It opens in the Cornish fishing village of Rederring. A young farmer, Robin Oakapple (baritone), is in love with Rose Maybud (soprano), a village maiden. His shyness prevents him declaring his love, so he enlists the help of his foster-brother Richard Dauntless (tenor), a dashing sailor who promptly falls in love with Rose himself. Torn between the two, Rose opts for Robin. As a result, Richard betrays Robin's secret; his true identity is Sir Ruthven Murgatroyd, one of the line of bad baronets of Ruddigore who under the terms of an ancient curse must commit a crime each day or die in agony. Robin had sought to escape the curse by fleeing, adopting an assumed name, and giving the world the impression that Sir Ruthven had died, thus passing the curse on to Sir Despard Murgatroyd (baritone), loved by Mad Margaret (soprano). Despard is happy to pass the curse back to Robin and begin to lead a reformed life with Margaret, while Rose promptly rejects Robin for Richard. Robin, far from comfortable in his new position, receives a visit from his ghostly ancestors, among them Sir Roderic, the twenty-first baronet (baritone) and is given a reminder about his responsibilities. Assisted by his valet Old Adam Goodheart (bass), he seeks to obey them by carrying off Rose's aunt, Dame Hannah (contralto). However, Sir Roderic again intervenes in order to protect Hannah who, it is discovered, is his old love. Robin is spared the wrath of Sir Roderic or indeed further obligations under the curse by pointing out that refusal to commit a daily crime would amount to suicide. Because suicide is itself a crime, Sir Roderic should never have died at all and the curse should not have passed on. Thus exonerated, Robin once more becomes acceptable to Rose while Richard contents himself with a bridesmaid named Zorah (soprano).

The curtain opens on Rederring to reveal an assembly of professional bridesmaids singing the praises of Rose Maybud ("Fair is Rose as bright May-day") although in a solo between sections of chorus the bridesmaid Zorah points out that Rose remains unmarried. At the end of the song Dame Hannah, Rose's aunt, enters. In dialogue the bridesmaids make it clear that in seeking to have Rose married they are not motivated so much by feelings for her as a desire to give them some work to do, and thereby justify their existence. The only other conceivable candidate for wedlock appears to be

148

Hannah herself, but she has pledged herself to undying spinsterhood after being in love with a man who turned out to be one of the bad baronets of Ruddigore. In a song with a distinctly gloomy feel ("Sir Rupert Murgatroyd") she explains how Sir Rupert Murgatroyd's act of burning a witch resulted in the whole line of Murgatroyds being cursed with the responsibility of committing a crime each day, or dying in torture. The chorus of bridesmaids listen and then in awestruck tones end the number by acknowledging the fate of each subsequent and future Murgatroyd. Meanwhile, the male chorus members remain idly in the dressing room; in no other G & S opera is their entrance so long delayed. The thoughtful producer, when beginning floor rehearsals, will have recognised this, and assuming that he is working through the show chronologically will have given the chorus men a couple of nights off before summoning them in order to set their first entry. He may even have reduced his intentions to writing by means of a formal rehearsal schedule. The most impressive schedules read like a complex army training exercise ("Tuesday, October 14th – 7.45 p.m. Richard and Rose, 8.05 p.m. Robin, 8.20 p.m. Mad Margaret, 8.55 p.m. Sir Despard, 9.28 p.m. Sir Roderic") and are compiled with the best of intentions – to prevent unnecessary waiting by those who are not needed. Nobody will however be surprised that when October 14th is reached the producer begins work with Mad Margaret at 7.59 (the accompanist's bus having broken down), Richard at 8.28, Rose at 8.43 and Sir Roderic at 9.01, Robin is on a hiking holiday in Sierra Leone, and at 10.13 Sir Despard is sitting drinking a can of beer having made no contribution whatever to the rehearsal thus far.

The chorus of bridesmaids exit and Rose comes on stage to join her aunt. Rose is one of the starkest caricatures in the opera; in her opening dialogue she reveals herself as the virtuous village maiden of humble origin, living in strict obedience to her book of etiquette. Her absurdly flowery speech in which she discloses her lowly background and her obedience to the precepts of her book, is the first obvious example of melodramatic burlesque in the piece. No less absurd are the examples of conduct she abhors, including pea-eating with a knife or biting bread!

Hannah inquires anxiously as to the reasons behind her unattached state, telling her of the affection one young upstanding gentleman named Robin has for her. Rose however points out that although he just as eligible as any other gentleman in the locality he is too shy to confess his love; moreover, in her song ("If somebody there chanced to be") with its subtle change from minor to major key, she declares it contrary to her book of etiquette for the girl to make the first move.Hannah now exits and almost immediately Robin

Oakapple appears. A nervous and stilted conversation takes place in which neither can bring themselves to declare their love for each other, but each pretend that the love is felt by a friend of theirs. In a pretty duet ("I know a youth who loves a little maid") they warm to this somewhat contrived technique of expressing their feelings, and each agree that their respective friends should make some sort of move. At the end, however, neither is any the wiser about their true feelings for the other. The innocence of the couple is one of the most touching aspects of the song. However, their wooing technique is unlikely to be adopted by agony aunts, and it is reasonably certain that Gavin Green, the gawky teenage chorus bass, will have to employ a rather more robust stance if he wishes to tempt Vicky van Dooyen, the vivacious make-up assistant, to share with him the delights of a post-show chicken korma at the Rising Sun Tandoori in Oliphant Road.

As Rose exits, Old Adam Goodheart, Robin's faithful servant, appears; this role is a skit on a character in Shakespeare's *As You Like It* with the same Christian name. In dialogue he addresses Robin as Sir Ruthven Murgatroyd, and it becomes clear that Robin is one of the line of Murgatroyds that inherited the dreaded curse; aware of the grisly consequences, he fled and assumed another name, leaving his younger brother, Despard, to assume that he (Ruthven) had died. Consequently, Despard has now shouldered the curse instead. Adam informs Robin that his foster-brother Richard Dauntless has returned from sea. Adam and Robin exit and the bridesmaids enter joyfully to proclaim in song ("From the briny sea") the arrival of this valiant sailor. Richard himself appears and sings a solo, with chorus, of one of his nautical adventures ("I shipped, d'ye see"). In the song he recalls how his boat came into confrontation with a French frigate but he and his crew heroically "allowed" the Frenchmen to proceed without engaging in battle. Amazingly, the correspondent of the French newspaper *Le Figaro* understood this to be an attack on French cowardliness, and objected accordingly, whereas of course it satirised the cowardice and patriotic fervour of the British!

Whatever the French may have thought of the number at the time – or indeed may think of it now – the singer of this solo has arguably the best tenor role in all the operas. Whereas many of the tenor principals, most notably Hilarion and Nanki-Poo, are comparatively static with little opportunity to demonstrate humour, character or mobility, Richard has plenty of scope for all three – no more so than at the end of his solo when a hornpipe follows. It was at the suggestion of the first Richard, Durward Lely, that this was introduced; after Gilbert had satisfied himself that Lely was capable of coping with it, Sullivan was asked to write a hornpipe, and it proved to be one of the highlights of the opening night. As Geoffrey Smith writes, "the sight of a tenor not only moving his limbs but using them to dance caused a sensation, earning a double encore." Subsequent Richards, forced to go through the same routine, will have felt that Lely has a lot to answer for. Unaccustomed to being asked to demonstrate his dancing skills in public, a contemporary Richard can only hope that the producer or choreographer will have sufficient compassion to spare him the humiliation of showing his ineptitude in front of a posse of female chorus members until some private tuition has taken place. Tutors will vary, from those who rely on their pupils to follow and memorise a sequence of steps which they demonstrate themselves, to those who thrust into their tutees' hands a series of diagrams which resemble something between a complex algebraic calculation and the legend accompanying a Texas Homecare self-assembly kit. As the would-be dancer pauses to disentangle his legs, he may indeed wonder if he has confused the material provided to him by the society choreographer with printed advice on how to construct a melamine-topped occasional table.

As the bridesmaids exit, Robin reappears. The ensuing dialogue between him and Richard makes it clear that the latter, like Adam, is fully aware of Robin's true identity. Robin confesses to Richard that his lack of self-confidence is hindering his attempts at wooing Rose. Richard, acting as he always does according to the dictates of his heart just as Rose relies on her book of etiquette, kindly offers to go to Rose and speak up on Robin's behalf. The most entertaining aspect of the dialogue between the two men is the nautical language of Richard; the reckless adventurer from the High Seas fits splendidly into the world of melodramatic burlesque, and here he is at his most eloquent in his employment of expressions more familiar to the ocean-going fraternity than delicate landlubbers. Indeed a phrase book would be helpful in translating "But vast heavin', messmate, what's brought you all a-cockbill" into "Good friend, please refrain from sighing and tell me why you are not your usual self" and "Just you lay me alongside, and when she's becalmed under my lee, I'll spin her a yarn that shall sarve to fish you two together for life" into "Kindly introduce me to her and when I have her confidence I will talk her into agreeing to marry you."

Robin expresses his admiration for Richard and longs for but a tenth of his self-assurance; in a solo ("My boy, you may take it from me") he (Robin) points out that his many and varied qualities, including intelligence, wit and creativity, are tainted by his being "diffident, modest and shy." Richard joins in the refrain in which it is conceded that to advance in the world it is necessary to blow one's own trumpet. After the song, Robin exits and Rose enters. At once Richard is deeply affected by this stunning-looking maiden, and he pronounces her fit to marry Lord Nelson. Rose notices that he is agitated, and Richard confides to the audience that "this here heart of mine's a-dictatin' to me like anythink." The truth is that he is falling in love with her himself. In the ensuing dialogue Rose expresses a willing acceptance of his string of compliments, aware that truthfulness is much approved of in her book of etiquette. She is not sure how to react when Richard effectively proposes marriage to her; one of the funniest moments in the opera comes next as she consults her book in order to formulate the precise, exceedingly formal, wording of her response, and in deciding how many kisses she is permitted to receive!

Eventually she accepts him and a rather sickly love duet follows ("The battle's roar is over"). It is not the most riveting musical number in the opera and it is hardly surprising that some of the D'Oyly Carte revivals omitted it from an already long first Act. However, since its words can be appreciated and understood out of the context of the story, and it is not too technically difficult, its romantic charm may make it a good choice for a G & S compilation programme. Compilation programmes are always in demand, but the success of them will depend greatly on the circumstances. Society members who had flown the nest many years before will suddenly and mysteriously reappear when soloists from the D'Oyly Carte Opera Company request an amateur choral backing in the town's Theatre Royal, with coverage on local television. By contrast, an invitation from the warden of Sunnybank Twilight Home for a few singers to provide an hour's entertainment will prompt most members suddenly to remember other pressing engagements as they recall last year's visit in which by the end of the *Mikado* medley four of the five audience members were asleep and the other was into her tenth refrain of "Knees Up Mother Brown."

The bridesmaids seem to have got wind of what is happening, for accompanied by Robin they hurry on to the stage and, in song, seek confirmation of the position ("If well his suit has sped"). Robin is delighted in the subsequent dialogue to hear Rose has accepted marriage, but his joy turns to anger when he hears that her new fiance is in fact Richard. All the while the girls continue to burst in with snatches of song, singing "Hail the Bridegroom, hail the Bride" until Robin shuts them up and orders them off, leaving just himself, Richard and Rose on stage to talk the matter over. It is only now that Rose realises that Robin is in love with her, and having found this out, she begins to have second thoughts about her liaison with Richard and inclines more towards Robin. Robin now finds himself in the position of defending his foster-brother from Rose's criticism! Much of the humour of this dialogue arises from the language used by Rose. In keeping with her virtuous character and upbringing, it might have come straight from the pages of the King James version of the Old Testament – "but it may be that he drinketh strong waters which do bemuse a man, and make him even as the wild beasts of the desert!"

A trio then follows ("In sailing o'er life's ocean wide") in which the three singers lament the awkwardness of having "a heart that does not know its mind." More significantly, Rose formally transfers her romantic attentions to Robin and away from Richard. Now it is Richard who is disconsolate and leaves the stage weeping, whilst Rose and Robin exit in the opposite direction. This will have been the ninth musical number, excluding the overture, but still the male chorus have yet to appear; Miss Glynis Dobbs, Personal Assistant to second tenor Mr Slidewell, will have to continue to wait for the appearance of her boss who persuaded her to buy a ticket for the show. However aggressively a show is marketed, ticket sales will make the major difference between a successful show and a disastrous one. An operatic society with a large following will be in the lucky position of only having to do a single mailshot, and half the seats will have sold within the week; members will simply need to be reminded to keep selling tickets in order to ensure the usual full house. Less fortunate societies may find responses to mailshots less productive, and bullying tactics will have to be used by the ticket manager to boost sales and thus prevent the society's drift towards insolvency. Each week the consciences of members will be sorely nagged by statements such as "This time last year we'd sold fifty per cent more," "we're still five hundred tickets short of breaking even," or, as has been heard twelve days before opening night and following a disastrous rehearsal, "You have a first-night audience of seven."

Mad Margaret now enters the action. She is, to quote Gilbert's directions, "wildly dressed in picturesque tatters, and is an obvious caricature of theatrical madness." Although many commentators have likened her to Ophelia in Shakespeare's *Hamlet*, Jane Stedman contends that Gilbert drew her from Madge Wildfire in Walter Scott's *Heart Of Midlothian*. As Madge had a penchant, to quote Stedman, for "wandering lovelorn in dishevelled Scottish peasant dress, (singing) wild snatches of song...racked by jealousy" so is Margaret reduced to her state of frenzy by her unreturned love. Moreover, Margaret's opening recitative is just such a sequence of "wild snatches of song" as she observes how "Cheerfully carols the lark over the cot....merrily whistles the clerk scratching a blot....over the ripening peach buzzes the bee." The music has a sense of incoherence and chaos which is quite frightening, and it is only when Margaret begins her song ("To a garden full of posies") that things appear to settle and she tells, in intensely

153

sad and poetic language, of how she is apparently rejected by the one she loves. When she finishes her song and bursts into tears, Rose appears and dialogue begins between them. Having refused Rose's offer of an apple, Margaret discloses that she loves Sir Despard Murgatroyd, the bad baronet of Ruddigore. Rose is alarmed by this, and even more so when Mad Margaret tells her that she has come to inflict retribution on her, being the one Margaret believes Despard loves instead. Rose is explaining that she is pledged to another, when Despard and his crew are heard to be approaching. Throughout this dialogue Margaret displays plenteous symptoms of an unbalanced mind, with snatches of manic laughter, song, melodramatic whisper, and expansive rhetoric. However, she hits the nail squarely on the head by saying that the approaching throng are quite mad because "they sing choruses in public."

These sentiments will be felt no more keenly than by the men waiting in the wings who only now are about to enter the fray. At last, with Rose and Margaret having tiptoed off, they come in the guise of Bucks and Blades. The first performances of *Ruddigore* saw them dressed in exact replicas of uniforms worn in 1815 by twenty different Army regiments, although more recent productions have seen the men dressed as Regency dandies in the style of Beau Brummel. The bridesmaids enter and herald them in song ("Welcome, gentry"); their welcome is enthusiastically acknowledged by the men with a different tune, and then both tunes are sung together to bring the chorus to a rousing conclusion. The sense of exuberance, however, is quickly extinguished as Despard enters. He is described by Ian Bradley as "the perfect caricature of the stage villain." His opening solo with chorus ("Oh, why am I moody and sad?"), in which he reflects on his appalling situation, has the bridesmaids cowering in terror and even the Bucks and Blades looking on in pity. The orchestral playout contains a number of percussive chords suggestive of the cracking of a whip. There is no reason why Despard should not actually have a whip, assuming that one can be found for him easily. It is to be hoped that perhaps a society member's connections with the horse-racing or hunting fraternity will provide the necessary prop, or that a reputable theatrical supply company can assist; the standing of the society and/or the proclivities of its members might be called into question by a programme note proclaiming that Despard's whip was loaned by The Pleasure House, the well-known local suppliers of all types of adults-only merchandise.

The terror-stricken girls together with the men flee from Despard, leaving him alone on stage. In a long speech he then explains to the audience that despite the curse with which he is saddled, he still manages to do much good in the community, and he catalogues not only a selection of his daily crimes but also some of his charitable activities. As he soliloquises, Richard appears and in dialogue informs him that his brother, who should have inherited the title and the curse, is not dead as Despard thought, but very much alive. Despard is delighted at the news, and determines to share it with his elder brother. A spirited duet follows ("You understand? I think I do") in which both Richard and Despard agree that however painful it may be, duty – which in this case will mean spoiling the wedding party – must be done. The song has an energetic, bouncy feel to it which may tempt the producer to set a further dance for Richard to perform. Thus it is that whilst the producer calls the chorus together to rehearse the first entrance of the Bucks and Blades, Richard and Despard may earn themselves some extra good-conduct marks by finding a side room to practise their dance in. In many rehearsal halls these side rooms may double up as committee rooms or general repositories, and as the two conscientious performers seek out a suitable venue there may be no knowing whether they will blunder their way into a heated and bitter discussion concerning the exact positioning of the new waste-paper bin in Henry Crescent, or be confronted with the remnants of St Polycarp's school lunch and a surplus of soggy mashed potato swimming in a stagnant onion gravy.

For the time being, the bridesmaids and their Regency male friends know nothing of Robin's dastardliness. As Richard and Despard leave, the chorus enter, and get the Act 1 finale under way by joyfully heralding Rose and Robin in song ("Hail the bride of seventeen summers"). Robin appears, attended by Adam and Richard; although Richard knows Robin's secret, he seems happy to bide his time. Robin embraces Rose, who in turn is embraced by Hannah and Zorah, and a delightful madrigal follows for the soloists and chorus ("When the buds are blossoming"), praising the qualities of the various seasons of the year. After the madrigal there is a stately gavotte (with more dancing for Richard!) but this is rudely interrupted by the entrance of Despard. Without beating about the bush, he proclaims Robin as his elder brother. The reaction of the chorus is one of amazement. Rose implores Robin to deny what she sees as a falsehood, but Robin cannot deny it. In a recitative ("As pure and blameless peasant") and a rapid patter song with chorus ("When I'm a bad Bart") he seems to accept immediately his new responsibilities, apparently without resentment. Zorah, however, demands in recitative to know which "wretch" betrayed him, and the chorus, presumably upset at being denied the wedding which they were promised, react angrily when Richard owns up. In a brief solo section ("Within this breast") Richard justifies his actions on the basis of the pricking of conscience, although of course there is so much at stake for him. The chorus appear satisfied with his explanation, as does Rose who informs Robin that he is utterly unacceptable to her, now that he is exposed both as a deceiver and a bad baronet. Instead she turns to Despard with a suitably melodramatic cry of "Take me! I am thy bride!" The bridesmaids, sensing that there may yet be a wedding, launch into another reprise of "Hail the Bridegroom, hail the Bride." Despard, however, has other ideas; he informs Rose that, now he is a virtuous person, he would prefer to pursue a relationship with Margaret instead. Margaret has entered just in time to hear this, and is overjoyed. Her embrace with Despard brings a further impulsive chorus of "Hail the Bridegroom, hail the Bride!" This leaves Rose and Richard to embrace each other, and the bridesmaids, who appear now to be on autopilot, react accordingly.

The closing ensemble number in the finale of Act 1 ("Oh, happy the lily when kissed by the bee") sees the two couples celebrating their togetherness, and all the onlookers, save Robin of course, reflecting on the happiness of "a lover when he embraces his bride." The singing is followed by another dance – as if the hornpipe and the gavotte earlier in the Act were not enough – but by contrast with the gavotte the music for this dance is more exuberant and rustic in style. Robin, of course, is the new villain, condemned to begin a life of crime, and now rejected by everybody. In some productions it has been known for him, after his brief vocal contribution to the closing ensemble number, to assume the same menacing appearance as Despard earlier. A flowing cape and whip, for example, will be quite in keeping with his new character, of which much more will be seen later. With the rest of the cast shrinking from him in abject terror, he will cut a lonely figure, contemplating whether – unused as he is to a life of crime – he will be able to appease his ancestors, to begin with at least, by nothing more than wilfully permitting his horse to foul the church path, or whether, assuming he has a whip, things will be expected of him that even the Rederring branch of The Pleasure House would reject as unacceptably adventurous.

After what has been one of the longest Acts in all the G & S operas, there is then a complicated scene change as the action moves from the fishing village of Rederring to the picture gallery of Ruddigore Castle. Pictures of the former bad baronets of Ruddigore are seen decorating the walls. Into this uncompromising arena steps Robin, or more properly Sir Ruthven (Riven) Murgatroyd, accompanied by faithful Adam. In a duet that has a distinctly ghostly feel about it ("I once was as meek as a new-born lamb"), Robin confirms his new identity, and Adam confirms he will stay loyal to him. He describes himself as Robin's former faithful *valley-de-sham*," this title being a corruption of *valet-de-chambre*, or gentleman's gentleman, and not,

156

as the name might suggest, a snug hollow beneath the nearby cliffs with shops specialising in the sale of cheap souvenirs manufactured three hundred miles away.

In the dialogue that follows, Adam asks Robin what crime he intends to commit that day. Robin has no idea, and Adam suggests poisoning the beer of Richard and Rose who are on their way to seek Robin's consent to their marriage. Robin does not feel up to such a dastardly deed, and instead suggests a rather feeble compromise, namely to tie Richard to a post and make hideous faces at him. Adam is unimpressed, despite the melodramatic way in which Robin expresses his suggestion. Audrey Williamson has no doubt that the actor playing the part of Robin has a harder task in Act 2; she states that what is required is a "command of melodramatic satire and depraved expression and make-up which can usually only be produced by an actor with a first-class technique and force of presentation." Adam, too, needs to have assumed the appearance of a wicked steward and undoubted accessory to at least some of Robin's criminal activity. Gilbert originally gave Adam the name Gideon Crawle but later changed his mind. Until comparatively recently, one edition of the libretto, whilst referring to Adam virtually throughout, preserved one intriguing reference to the old name in Robin's second-Act line, "Gideon Crawle, it won't do." One is tempted to ask how many producers, ignorant of the error, have allowed the line to remain unaltered, leaving the audience to speculate on whether the said Gideon Crawle is a Jacobean oath with obscene overtones, Robin's wire-haired Dachshund who has slumbered his way noiselessly through the preceding action, or perhaps just another Irish juryman who got on the wrong train at Birmingham New Street.

As Adam and Robin exit, Richard and Rose appear, accompanied by the bridesmaids. A duet follows, with chorus ("Happily coupled are we"), in which Richard sings joyfully of his future married happiness with Rose, whilst Rose sings anxiously about Richard's return to the High Seas and the girls he will meet and flirt with on his travels. She can hardly feel flattered by Richard's description of her (and taken up in the choral refrain) as, among other things, a "bright little, tight little, slight little, light little, trim little, prim little craft!"

Robin reappears and in dialogue tries to frighten Rose by threatening her with imprisonment. Richard responds by flourishing a Union Jack and promising deadly retribution for anyone who molests his bride-to-be. Rose further disarms Robin by inviting him to prove that his love for her was unselfish by agreeing to her marrying Richard – who, she points out, is his

157

dearest friend. She underlines her appeal in a ballad, with chorus ("In bygone days I had thy love"), and, faced with such emotional blackmail, Robin is forced to yield. The bridesmaids are delighted, and after proclaiming "Away to the parson we go" they deliver a reprise of the refrain of the previous duet, with Rose once more being likened to a small boat. With the exception of the very last chorus, this concludes the bridesmaids' involvement in the proceedings. A glance at the libretto will show that the undoubted highlight of the opera is just about to take place. At dress rehearsal – providing there is no invited audience – the girls may wish to adjourn to the auditorium to seize perhaps their only chance to watch this section with proper lighting and effects. Chorus members who decide to watch longer sections of dress rehearsals from the front may find that their lack of familiarity with the rest of the show will backfire on them badly. They may reassemble in the wings long before they are needed, and in any case find their entrance delayed as the producer decides to rerun the preceding number four times, despite his faithful assurances that this would be an uninterrupted runthrough. Alternatively, without any warning, they will find themselves sitting in the audience watching a number they are supposed to be taking part in. This will be particularly noticeable when the full chorus is supposed to enter, and, instead of a well-disciplined influx of bodies entering from the wings, a few conscientious chorus members will make their way hesitantly and bashfully on to the set. Despite their best endeavours, the absence of their colleagues and the utter hatred on the face of the producer will soon give them the same air of discomfiture as a non-English-speaking Croatian tourist in the Bankrupt Electrical Store attempting to obtain a refund for a faulty personal stereo.

As the happy couple and the girls disappear, Robin is left alone with his pictures, and makes a spoken appeal to his ancestors to be satisfied with his feeble attempts at evil-doing. As if in response to this, the stage darkens and there ensues one of the most spectacular, as well as one of the most logistically challenging, scenes in the whole of G & S opera. In it, the pictures, just as they did in Gilbert's earlier work *Ages Ago*, become animated and the characters they represent – the ghostly baronet ancestors – step down from their picture frames and join Robin in the gallery. As they do so they sing a doleful chorus of introduction ("Painted emblems of a race") which becomes very much more formidable as the ghosts hurl insults at Robin and command him to fall to the floor. As if the chorus of ghosts were not sufficiently intimidating, the even more frightening spectre of the late Sir Roderic Murgatroyd descends from his frame and introduces himself. With appropriate costume and make-up, he should present an awesome sight. However, until the full set of stage effects, including some suitably sombre lighting, is available, there will be precious little to terrify the chorus, short of the reaction of Mr Crump, the janitor, upon being publicly informed by the producer that because of the need for the cast to assemble early for Thursday's costume try-on, he will have thirty minutes less time to clear up after the Over 70's Ladies Crossword Club's Strawberry Tea.

Roderic's interaction with Robin begins in the form of musical recitative, which is a mixture of the macabre and the menacing. Having presented his credentials, Roderic sings, with help from the ghosts, what is unquestionably the finest and most dramatic song in the opera ("When the night wind howls") in which Gilbert's evocative writing is matched by some of Sullivan's most brilliant music. In the song, supported by his fellow ancestors, Roderic paints vivid pictures of the ghosts coming out to play, rejoicing at "our next high holiday – the dead of the night's high-noon." The frenetic orchestral accompaniment paints equally vivid pictures of ghostly activity. When the song finishes, dialogue begins which involves not only Roderic and Robin but also some of the ghosts. Although the libretto simply gives lines to First Ghost, Second Ghost, and so on, the list of *dramatis personae* includes seven of them by name and baronet number, including Sir Rupert, Sir Jasper, Sir Lionel and Sir Gilbert. Because it is by no means certain that these baronets will be individually cast or named in the programme, they are not amongst the most noteworthy characters in G & S opera. Their names and numbers will therefore provide ideal material for a G & S quiz night, and may flummox even the most expert competitors whose knowledge of totally useless G & S information knows no bounds, from the number of operas in which the principal contralto is on stage at the start of Act 2, to those operas which finish with the chorus sopranos singing a word of more than one syllable.

The ensuing dialogue begins with Robin speaking in somewhat derogatory fashion concerning Roderic's picture, but he is put very quickly in his place as Roderic informs him that he is not discharging his duties as he should be. Robin protests that he has been committing a daily crime for the week that the curse has been upon him. However, his catalogue is remarkably feeble; with the exception of shooting a fox, he has done nothing that is sufficiently evil in Roderic's eyes, and both Roderic and his fellow ancestors tell him so. Roderic proposes an ultimatum; unless he carries off (i.e. abducts) a lady of his choice, he will perish in inconceivable agonies. The only objector to the proposal amongst the ghosts is a bishop – the third and last cleric in the operas. Roderic summarily dismisses the objection, and the ultimatum is duly put. Robin flatly refuses, but when all the ghosts "make passes," as the direction puts it, his resultant agony causes him to change his mind and he agrees to obey Roderic at once. The ghosts are delighted, and celebrate Robin's capitulation in song ("He yields") before a reprise of a brief section of "Painted emblems" in which they return to their frames. A modern producer of the opera may devise a rather more imaginative way for the ghosts to induce Robin's agony. This might consist of anything from a medieval instrument of torture that has been borrowed from the town's history museum to the far more fearsome ordeal of specially selected extracts from Jimmy Osmond's *Long Haired Lover From Liverpool*, or a medley of Norwegian entries for the Eurovision Song Contest between 1975 and 1984.

As soon as the ghosts have gone, Adam appears. In brief dialogue Robin commands him to go and carry off a lady, then both men exit. It is worth noting that some editions of the libretto contain a recitative ("Away Remorse! Compunction, hence!") followed by a patter song ("Henceforth all the crimes") for Robin at this point, in which he reflects on his new criminal career and the misplaced desire that squires and M.P.'s have for a baronetcy. Assuming that is dispensed with or finished, and the stage is empty, Despard and Margaret enter. They now wear sober black clothes – it is also common for Despard to have an umbrella – and are the very model of strait-laced conformism. They sing a duet ("I once was a very abandoned person") in which they contrast their previously chaotic lives with their new well-ordered existences. Their movement must be very deliberate, stiff and starchy but, at the same time, precise. Geoffrey Smith writes that it should have the effect of "a sedate country dance…gone ever so slightly awry." This of course "takes a deal of training" as the two singers point out at the end of the duet! A society that is anxious to improve the quality of the dancing within the membership may well consider it worth its while to engage the services of an experienced choreographer for a full-day Saturday or Sunday dance workshop session. The difficulty may be that the attenders for such a session will be those who already enjoy dancing and move about the stage with a reasonable degree of skill. All too often it is the thespian who prefers to remain ensconced in his armchair in front of the televised Saturday afternoon rugby international who demonstrates, by his cavalier ineptitude at the next evening rehearsal, that it matters little to him whether in the course of a dance his second left foot lands on a piece of vacant stage or on to the bare toes of the besandalled Mrs Golightly, his hapless stage partner.

In the dialogue following their duet, Despard and Margaret announce that they have been happily married for a week. Whilst Despard is now entirely decorous, Margaret is still prone to fits of excitement and demonstrates this with a wild display of gratitude to her husband. In between bouts of hysteria, however, she states what is needed to bring her to her senses. This is not some extravagant melodramatic cure but the utterance of a single word "Basingstoke." The sight of Margaret relapsing, and Despard crying "Basingstoke, I beg!" is one of the classic instances of melodramatic burlesque in the opera, and indeed the name of this very ordinary Hampshire commuter town will be uttered many more times before the dialogue is over. Margaret's rehabilitation is not assisted by the arrival of Robin, whose actions have of course resulted in Despard being saddled with the curse. Margaret initially wishes to tear him limb from limb, but Despard dissuades her. He proceeds to speak of the crimes which Robin has vicariously committed during the past ten years – all the time, in fact, that he should have shouldered the curse but did not. Margaret begins sobbing, and Robin tries to bring her to her senses with the word "Birmingham" but in practice perhaps more hilarity will be generated by substituting – rather as with the new address of Nanki-Poo in *The Mikado* – a place with an unglamorous reputation that is near to the location of the performance. Greater verisimilitude will be achieved if the place that is selected has three syllables and begins with the letter B; whilst Bellingham, Brislington or Bridlington might be said to be easily confused with Basingstoke, it is less probable that the same could be said of Chipping Sodbury, Stansted Mountfitchet or Harlow New Town.

Margaret's outburst and Despard's history lesson fire Robin with the determination to defy Roderic and his fellow ancestors. There follows the most breathless musical number in all the operas, the patter trio "My eyes are fully open," notable for the constant repetition of the word "matter" throughout the song. Robin expresses his determined defiance despite his doom that will inevitably result, Margaret laments that her madness prevents her assisting him, and Despard laments the lack of a level-headed adviser. However, towards the end of the song, which goes at breakneck speed, Despard sums up the trio perfectly as he sings "This particularly rapid unintelligible patter isn't generally heard and if it is it doesn't matter." Nowhere in the operas is there a more damning indictment on the well-meaning musical director who insists on good diction!

After the trio, Despard and Margaret exit and Adam enters with the spoken announcement that, after a struggle, he has carried off a lady, in accordance with instructions. He produces none other than Hannah. Hannah is justifiably furious, and in a splendidly melodramatic scene, with speech above suitably suspenseful background music, she challenges Robin to a duel. She first produces a very small dagger, which she throws to Robin, and then from one of the armed figures in the gallery she produces a much bigger dagger for her own use! Obtaining properties is one of the most thankless tasks for the production team; often the task may fall to a single individual who raises the producer's blood pressure above E.E.C.-recommended levels by spending several precious minutes of a rehearsal going through three pages of props, asking who in the society can provide them, and meeting with responses which range from a suggestion that Dave Smith in the Drama Club used one of the missing items in his panto just before he emigrated to New Zealand, to a suggestion that the properties manager visit Portobello Market where an article answering to the given description was last positively sighted in August 1974.

Hannah's bearing is so formidable that Robin is forced to appeal to Roderic for assistance. He duly obliges, stepping once more from his frame, and is amazed to find himself face to face with his old love whom he describes as "Little Nannikin." He is very angry with Robin and, saving him from Hannah's further aggression, orders him to leave the scene. Robin exits, and the two old lovers sing in duet ("There grew a little flower") of the sadness of the flower and her love for the great oak tree. As Hannah sings of the flower's constant love for the oak tree, she is really singing of her enduring love for Roderic. Robin reappears at the end of the song with the entire cast, and in dialogue tells the couple that an idea has just occurred to him. His idea is yet another example of Gilbertian logic resolving an otherwise hopelessly entangled situation. He points out that to fail to commit one's daily crime, which is to invite certain death, is tantamount to suicide; and because suicide itself is a crime (or at least it was in those days) Roderic need never have died at all. Roderic is delighted to think that he is "practically alive" and fondly embraces both Robin's logic and his beloved Hannah. Robin, delighted to have effectively freed himself of his obligation to commit a daily crime, becomes acceptable to Rose once more. She wastes no time in returning to him and forsaking Richard, who instead goes to the bridesmaid Zorah. A joyful finale ("When a man has been a naughty baronet") sees Rose still obsessed with her book of etiquette, Richard anticipating the supping of bread and cheese with Zorah, and Robin again contemplating a simple farmer's life. It is left to Despard and Margaret to announce the most bizarre choice of future lifestyle, as they vow to "toddle off tomorrow...for to settle in the town of Basingstoke." Although Basingstoke was not then the town of vast concrete monoliths, complex ring-road systems and sprawling estates it has now become, it seems incomprehensible to want to abandon the fresh Rederring air for the doubtful pleasures of living there permanently, even allowing for walking picture galleries, old women with daggers, able seamen unable to communicate in conventional English, and chaste maidens who need to consult their pocket books for instructions on how to eat a poached egg.

The Yeomen Of The Guard, the tenth surviving G & S work, is the nearest Gilbert and Sullivan came to writing a serious grand opera. It is true that, as with every other G & S work, the plot is heavily contrived and highly improbable and there is plenty of humour to be found throughout the piece. Nonetheless, there is neither the burlesque nor the tilting at English institutions which is to be found in most of the other works. Moreover, the story itself, set in the austere surroundings of the Tower of London, is far from being a frivolous romp or absurd journey into topsy-turvydom – as many of the other G & S operas might be described – but a grim and ultimately tragic tale from which none of the principal characters appear to emerge entirely unscathed. The opera also differs from the other G & S works in that it is the only one of the series which has a solo, rather than chorus, immediately following the overture. As an aside, it is more likely than in the case of any of the other operas that its title will be misspelt on posters, publicity material or internal operatic society communications, with the word *Yeomen* being represented all too frequently as *Yeoman*!

Ruddigore's first run had come to an end in November 1887, and, as had happened after *Princess Ida*, Gilbert and Sullivan appeared to have run out of ideas that were mutually acceptable. The lozenge plot was again proposed and rejected, and once more an impasse had apparently been reached. However, fate took a hand. Gilbert, waiting on Uxbridge station platform, saw a poster advertising the Tower Furnishing Company. It bore the picture of a Yeoman warder of the Tower of London, or Beefeater, and it is said that this inspired him to write a work which centred round the Tower. Other commentators have suggested that the idea for an opera based around the Tower could already have been in Gilbert's mind even without the help of the Tower Furnishing Company's marketing executive; Beefeaters had for centuries been part of England's heritage and at the time the opera was conceived, the Tower had only just reopened to visitors after 35 years' closure for restoration. Nonetheless, as with the falling sword and its supposed inspiration for *The Mikado*, it seems somehow appropriate that a librettist noted for the absurd twists and turns in his plots should be inspired by a purely chance event. It might also encourage the budding contemporary writer to pay more attention to the posters being displayed at his local station as he awaits the arrival of the wrong-type-of-snow-bound 7.38 to London Bridge.

Having decided on the subject matter, Gilbert had in mind a frivolous piece, but then decided to turn it into a romantic and dramatic opera set in the

Elizabethan era. He may have been influenced by a paragraph in the *Sporting Times* which suggested that a genuine dramatic story, rather than a fairy tale or further journey into the ridiculous, would find favour with the public. He shared his ideas with Sullivan on Christmas Day 1887. Sullivan, who was yearning to write a grand opera, was delighted with the proposals, and, inspired by Wagner as well as masters of French and Italian opera, set about writing music which matched the mood and atmosphere of the setting and the story. In assembling the libretto, Gilbert drew inspiration from constant visits to the Tower and also perusal of the King James version of the Bible; much of the opera contains speech which might have been heard in the sixteenth century. There were similarities in the story to William Wallace's 1845 opera, *Maritana*, although the principal source was Ainsworth's 1840 novel, *The Tower Of London*. Whilst there would be comic touches in the opera, it was essentially to be a serious work. Despite the enthusiasm of the partners for the task, this was new territory for both of them, used as they were to writing comic opera together; perhaps inevitably a number of difficulties and disagreements emerged. Sullivan had to set the first Act solo for the tenor, "Is life a boon," three times before Gilbert pronounced himself satisfied with it; furthermore, Sullivan had the greatest difficulty in setting Gilbert's lyrics for the song of "The Merryman and his Maid" (this song title became the alternative title of the opera) and eventually Gilbert himself obliged by humming a tune which he felt would be suitable. As Gilbert recalled, "Only a rash man ever (asked) me to hum, but the situation was desperate." Sullivan, in turn, requested Gilbert to make various alterations, to which Gilbert only agreed after some protest. Once again, Sullivan worked feverishly hard during the weeks leading up to October 3rd 1888, when the opening night was scheduled. Often he would work all night before finally retiring at 6 a.m. The strain began to tell; at the rehearsal on 28th September there was a massive *contretemps* between them, fortunately made up before the opening night. Even on the morning of 3rd October Gilbert wrote to Sullivan stating that in his view the success of the play was imperilled unless certain numbers were shortened or withdrawn. Indeed some changes were made to the Act 1 finale just minutes before the first performance was due to start. One of the disagreements was over the title of the piece. Gilbert had in mind *The Beefeaters* but Sullivan rejected this as ugly, and suggested the change to the title with which G & S devotees are familiar. Although Hesketh Pearson's asserts that Gilbert "was never happier in his partnership with Sullivan than when he was engrossed in this plain tale of the Tower," the librettist was assailed by doubts as the first performance approached. He was well aware that in what was a supposedly comic opera, the first four songs in the work were in turn tearful, serious, grim and sentimental! The first number in the opera, following the overture,

165

was a solo, to be sung by Jessie Bond; she recalls how on the opening night Gilbert fussed and danced distractedly around her as the overture neared its end, continually asking her if everything was all right, in a manner which she states she found "intolerable!" Eventually he left her to it, and hurried off to a play elsewhere in London. Despite his apprehension, the notices were kind, one reviewer saying that Sullivan's music was "of a higher form" than hitherto. The only really discordant note came from the *Punch* reviewer who accused Gilbert of stealing the plot from *Maritana*. The reviewer also felt that the opera could have been trimmed by 35 minutes!

In fact the composers realised the opera was on the long side, and cut a solo (Sergeant Meryll's "A laughing boy but yesterday") after just one performance. The composers themselves regarded it as their finest work together. However, the opening run of 423 performances, whilst comfortably longer than for *Ruddigore*, was still far shorter than that for *The Mikado* or indeed *Patience*. Its opening run in New York was 100 performances, compared with 250 in New York for *The Mikado*. Hesketh Pearson suggests that seriousness did not become the composers and that their happiest combination was on a plane of facetiousness; whilst some may have found the combination of grim storyline and ending, intermingled with splashes of comic relief, a moving and exhilarating theatrical experience, others may have found it, to quote Geoffrey Smith, "forced and diffuse...a series of not quite coherent, though impressive effects...an attempt perhaps to do too many and even contrary things" and maybe a little less than satisfying. One Savoyard in the 1920's had the temerity to state that he regarded the piece as overrated and the central character a sentimental bore.

The plot is contrived and, although devoid of supernatural influence, still highly improbable. Colonel Fairfax (tenor) is in the Tower of London under sentence of death for alleged sorcery. Anxious to avoid his fortune passing to his accuser, who has fabricated the allegation, he undergoes a marriage ceremony to a strolling player Elsie Maynard (soprano) who needs the money he promises her in exchange. Fairfax is loved by Phoebe Meryll (soprano), who is in turn loved by the odious jailer Wilfred Shadbolt (bass-baritone). Phoebe succeeds in obtaining from him the key to Fairfax's cell. Fairfax escapes, masquerading instead as Phoebe's brother Leonard (tenor) who has come to join the Yeomen but who agrees to go into hiding. Elsie is loved by the jester Jack Point (baritone), but he has no objection to Elsie's marriage to Fairfax on the basis that he is to die. When Fairfax escapes, Point plots with Wilfred – facing death at the hands of the Lieutenant of the Tower (bass-baritone) for allowing the prisoner to escape – to pretend that the escapee has been shot. By this time, however, Fairfax is successfully

166

wooing Elsie in his new guise as Leonard, until his reprieve comes through and he is able to reveal himself to her as the same man she married. Their joy contrasts with the sadness of the conspirators Phoebe and her father Sergeant Meryll (bass), forced – on pain of death – into unwelcome marriages with Wilfred and Dame Carruthers, the Tower housekeeper (contralto) respectively; it was the Dame's niece Kate (soprano) who provided evidence to Fairfax that Elsie was the woman he married. The one who suffers most is Point, who on realising that he has lost Elsie for ever, collapses insensible at her feet.

Like the majority of G & S operas, *The Yeomen Of The Guard* begins with an overture. It is well known that, although Sullivan did not compose all the overtures for the operas himself, he did compose this one. How well an overture is received by the audience will depend on the skill of the orchestra and the imagination of the producer. The best overtures are those in which the orchestra manage to stay in time with the conductor and produce a pleasing melodic preview of some of Sullivan's choice tunes to come, whilst the curtain opens to reveal various members of the chorus engaging in business, both comic and straight, which hints at their function in the forthcoming action, whether as sailors, fairies or pirates. The most painful overtures are those in which the curtain remains coyly closed and the audience are forced to sit in darkness, the Stygian gloom depriving them of the chance even to read their programmes to pass the time, while the strings scrape their way funereally through what may be several pages of uninterrupted scoring, producing a sound that radiates as much musical appeal as that of a group of Siamese cats being forced through an industrial shredder.

When the overture finishes, the audience will not witness, as they will witness in any other G & S show, at least one section of the chorus either present on stage or marching resolutely on to it. They will see instead a disconsolate Phoebe Meryll sitting at her spinning wheel on Tower Green, singing a sad song of apparently unrequited love ("When maiden loves"). In many ways, quite apart from the big responsibility that this opening number carries, the part of Phoebe is more demanding than that of Elsie; whilst she does not have the big operatic solos that Elsie does, her character combines the loving, the crafty and the resourceful, and she must display every range of emotion from gleeful high-spiritedness to deep sadness. After Phoebe has finished her song, the jailer Wilfred Shadbolt appears. This is a truly wonderful role for the overactor; Audrey Williamson describes him variously as "lugubrious...macabre.... (and) inwardly naïve" with a pride in his professionalism and efficiency, and a longing to be a wit and a jester.

Traditionally the part is played by a large, oafish-looking individual. In his conversation with Phoebe, he makes no secret of his liking for her – which is certainly not reciprocated – and his jealousy "of everybody and everything." He also speaks with apparent relish of the impending death of Colonel Fairfax who has been found guilty of sorcery. Phoebe, on the other hand, speaks glowingly of the condemned prisoner, and it becomes clear that he is the man with whom she is in love. Both exit, and a crowd of townsfolk enter, followed by Yeomen of the Guard. There follows a splendid double chorus; with one tune the townsfolk express their admiration of "Tower warders under orders" and with another the Yeomen, now in the autumn of their lives, think back on past glories. Included within the Yeomen's chorus is a brief solo for Second Yeoman (baritone); both he and First Yeoman (tenor) get short solos in the Act 1 finale, but otherwise merge into the chorus. The tunes of the townsfolk and Yeomen are then combined to provide a rousing and satisfying ending. All this, of course, will be played out with the impressive backcloth of the Tower of London, now one of England's principal tourist attractions. It may be therefore somewhat easier than in other G & S operas for mementoes of a happy show to be obtained. In many societies it is customary for the principals to provide cards and presents to each other, and indeed those who pride themselves on the quality and originality of their gifts may wish to make a special journey to the Tower itself where all kinds of highly appropriate items can be purchased. A solo singer who is new to a society where present-giving is a tradition may feel somewhat embarrassed as, on the opening night, he arrives in the dressing room to find a heap of "have a great week – break lots of legs" cards awaiting him; on the final night his embarrassment will deepen as an assortment of "well done – nice working with you" cards, combined with an assortment of gifts, are thrust into his hands. Rather more sad than embarrassing is the discovery, when the dressing rooms are being tidied up on the morning after the final performance, of a gift or gifts that have been left behind by the intended recipients. It is as well that the donor who so lovingly prepared such tokens of a happy show week is not aware that they are shortly to be consigned to a black Economy Superdeep bin liner, particularly if to obtain them she had to straphang all the way from Dagenham Heathway and queue behind a party of thirty Turkish students merely to get inside the souvenir shop.

The townsfolk exit; Phoebe reappears and Dame Carruthers, one of Gilbert's crustier contraltos, appears for the first time. She is housekeeper to the Tower, and talks in a matter-of-fact way about the hideously cramped conditions some prisoners are suffering after last night's fire. Phoebe again speaks admiringly of her beloved Fairfax, deeply resentful that he should

168

meet his death in "old Blunderbore" as she calls the Tower. Dame Carruthers sternly rebukes her and in song with chorus ("When our gallant Norman foes") she reflects with awe, and an almost unhealthy satisfaction, on the timeless quality of the Tower and those who have perished within its walls. The orchestral introduction to the solo is the same as for the overture, and symbolises magnificently the stern grandeur of the "grim old fortalice." After her solo, Dame Carruthers and the Yeomen exit but Phoebe remains and she is joined by her father, Sergeant Meryll. He tells her that Leonard Meryll, her brother, has come to join the Yeomen and is due shortly; it is hoped that he may have a reprieve for Fairfax. Leonard then arrives but has no such reprieve with him. However he speaks of Fairfax in such glowing terms that his father suggests a plot that will require his cooperation. In exchange for a financial consideration, Leonard will make himself scarce. Once Fairfax has freedom from his cell – which Phoebe believes she can effect through her influence on Wilfred – he (Fairfax) will assume the disguise of Leonard, presumably for as long a time as he remains under sentence of death. In the conspiratorial trio that follows ("Alas! I waver to and fro") the Merylls acknowledge the risks attendant on the plan, but determine to proceed nonetheless. The trio ends with a heartfelt farewell to Leonard, who is now consigned to the dressing room for almost the whole of the rest of an opera which has barely begun. He can of course remedy this situation by transposing certain words in his line "I have here a despatch for the Lieutenant but no reprieve for the Colonel," thereby neatly wrapping up the plot before half of the principals have as much as troubled to open their mouths. If such a ploy fails, he can at least have the consolation of first place in the queue for tea and chocolate digestives, and ample time to study the noticeboard with its selection of patronising messages from the self-important Chairman (ANYONE FOUND LEAVING THE THEATRE WITH MAKE-UP STILL ON WILL BE BARRED FROM THE NEXT SHOW), action photos from the dress rehearsal (*60p each, orders to Bob and Rita by Fri please*) and good luck cards signed simply "Doris" and "Alf" neither of whose names would mean anything to anyone who joined the society after 1970.

As Leonard leaves, Phoebe is in tears. She and her father have a brief conversation, Meryll pointing out that Fairfax is now being led out from his cell under guard towards the Cold Harbour Tower to await his death peacefully. As luck would have it, his journey brings him on to the stage. Colonel Fairfax is one of the best tenor roles in the operas; not only does he have two fine solos, and some delightful quartets and ensemble work, but he has a stature and presence denied to most of the other G & S tenor leads. He is met on stage by the Lieutenant of the Tower, Sir Richard Cholmondeley.

169

Thankfully for those who might have to speak or print his name, this upstanding somewhat humourless character his usually just referred to as the Lieutenant. He appears impressed by the philosophical way in which Fairfax, in a long speech, contemplates his impending death; indeed Fairfax is so calm that he is able to offer comforting words to Meryll, whose daughter is so distraught. As the prisoner says, "we are soldiers, and we know how to die." There shortly follows the first of his solos ("Is life a boon?") in which he reflects that a man should not complain about the timing of his death; if life is pleasurable his death could have come earlier, but if life is wretched, he "might have had to live another morn." Gilbert incidentally chose the words "Is life a boon" to be inscribed on Sullivan's memorial in London. It is a charming ballad, although Audrey Williamson points out that it can be spoilt by "gutsy bellowing!"

At the end of his solo, Phoebe exits, weeping, with Meryll. Fairfax then explains to the Lieutenant that his death sentence arises from a charge of sorcery brought against him by a Secretary of State, Clarence Poltwhistle, who will benefit from his estate if he dies unmarried. Fairfax wishes to frustrate his evil intentions by marrying at once, and he asks for the Lieutenant's help in finding a wife. He tells him that her reward will be a hundred crowns. (It is not suggested she might be entitled to his estate as well!) The Lieutenant is dubious at first, but then agrees after Fairfax makes it clear that in an hour's time the chosen lady will be a widow and free to marry once more. Both exit, and immediately the townsfolk reappear, led by Jack Point, a strolling jester, and Elsie Maynard, a strolling singer. Geoffrey Smith regards Point as epitomising Gilbert's view of the travail of the humorist's life, and in fact one can see many traces of Gilbert in the character of Point. As the townsfolk enter they sing a boisterous song – part of which has the unusual time signature of 5 crotchets in a bar – in which they introduce Point ("Here's a man of jollity"). There follows some banter between Point and the crowd, Point offering his own witty response to some horseplay in which Elsie is an unwilling participant. He proposes some entertainment for the townsfolk, and even provides a menu of the songs and dances he and Elsie can provide. Elsie suggests the singing farce of "The Merryman and his Maid" and there follows that most moving of all the songs in the operas ("I have a song to sing"), which gave Sullivan so much trouble in composition – the song of the merryman "who sipped no sup, and who craved no crumb, as he sighed for the love of a ladye." The construction of the song is interesting, with each verse building on the previous one as in "The House That Jack Built." At this point in the opera the words mean little, but later they will assume heart-rending significance. The song is sung by Elsie and Point, the chorus joining in the final refrain. In the ensuing dialogue the townsfolk acclaim the song a little too enthusiastically, and Elsie is far from happy with the suggestion of "a kiss all round" proposed by one of the citizens. Her protests reach the ears of the Lieutenant, who arrives with a guard and demands to know "what is this pother." The word "pother," meaning bustle, confusion or fuss, sounds like another piece of now obsolete Elizabethan language used freely by Gilbert in the opera to give the work a truly authentic feel. It would certainly be unusual nowadays to hear a police superintendent report that "there was a lot of pother outside the kebab house last night." However, despite the suggestion in the *Concise Oxford* that the word has passed into merely literary rather than colloquial use, it still appears in modern dictionaries and, being composed of two smaller words, is a useful secret weapon for the cryptic crossword compiler as well as the budding *Countdown* contestant.

The rabble are duly cleared by the guards, leaving the three principals alone on stage, and giving Elsie the chance to introduce Point and herself to the Lieutenant. Point raises a laugh by denying that he is married to her, saying "though I'm a fool, there is a limit to my folly;" it is interesting to compare this Gilbertian observation on married life with similar wry comments by Frederic and Mabel in *The Pirates Of Penzance*, or Strephon and Phyllis in *Iolanthe*. It is Point's next remark that interests the Lieutenant; he says Elsie's mother is sick, and he and Elsie are trying to raise money to buy her medicine. The Lieutenant, seizing on this opportunity, asks Elsie to become the wife of Fairfax for the period of his last hour. Point is worried, but reassured when the short duration of the marriage is confirmed. In a trio ("How say you, maiden, will you wed") the three principals articulate their thoughts in song; the Lieutenant is detached, businesslike and pragmatic, Elsie ambivalent but mindful of the benefits of the marriage, and Point contented, providing the money is paid and the groom's impending death inevitable. During the song, Wilfred appears, and on the Lieutenant's instructions he blindfolds Elsie and takes her to the Cold Harbour Tower to meet her new husband, who will also be blindfolded. The Lieutenant says to Point that he has a vacancy for a jester and, presumably with a view to engaging him, asks him what his qualifications are. Point responds with a list of his capabilities, some of which he sets out in speech and others in a solo ("I've jibe and joke"). Bidden by the Lieutenant, who is anxious that his jesting should not give offence, he then gives some spoken examples of his humour. Two of the three "jokes" are feeble and the third barely comprehensible to modern audiences. The dialogue ends with Point putting to the Lieutenant what is supposedly his "best conundrum;" namely, why a cook's brainpan is like an overwound clock. The Lieutenant is not interested in the answer, and bids Point follow him to the library; thus do the pair exit without the solution being revealed. In response to enquiry by Henry Lytton, Gilbert promised to leave the answer in his will, but he never did! Imaginative editors of the show programme or concurrent society newsletter may invite cast or audience members to submit their own solution ("Most ingenious answer wins presentation pack of genuine Tower of London strawberry preserve and elderflower cordial"). Unless the auditorium has more than its fair share of G & S connoisseurs, the programme competition may not necessarily elicit a huge response, particularly if constraints of space and the desire to generate much-needed revenue squeeze the relevant details between the list of patrons "with special thanks to Dr & Mrs Arnold Stentiford-Heath who are reinstated as patrons after their ten-year stay in Botswana" and a half page panel proclaiming SNODGRASS WASTE DISPOSAL SERVICES WISH F.L.O.S. EVERY SUCCESS - FIND US IN GUSSET STREET (TEL 725843) AND LET US DO YOUR DUMPING.

Elsie now enters the empty stage following her marriage ceremony; she is led by Wilfred who removes the bandage from her eyes and exits. Left alone, she then sings one of the most technically difficult soprano pieces in the operas, a recitative ("Tis done! I am a bride!") followed by an anguished song ("Though tear and long-drawn sigh") in which she makes it clear that, far from being pleased that by her marriage she has earned the money needed for her mother, she is intensely sad for the death of her groom in his youth, and the speed with which she will become a widow. The tension is broken only when she leaves the stage and Wilfred reappears and speaks to the audience. He is apparently aggrieved at having been unable to witness what went on between Elsie and Fairfax because the keyhole of the cell was stopped up! He is joined by Phoebe and her father, who in dialogue now set the wheels of their own plot in motion. Phoebe begins to "go to work" on Wilfred, firstly flattering him, then teasing him, leading him on, and making him believe she really loves him. She is of course careful not to say she does! On the contrary, she chooses her words carefully, as she does in her ensuing song ("Were I thy bride") in which she paints a wonderful picture of a couple totally at one with each other. Only at the very end does she deliver the punchline: "But then, of course, you see, I'm not thy bride!" If the two actors interact well together, this is the funniest scene in an essentially serious opera, as the lumbering, unlovable oaf is pursued with mock gestures of affection by a pretty yet cunning young woman; his facial and bodily reaction to what is obviously a new and highly pleasant experience for him is G & S opera at its very best. During the dialogue she is so effective in maintaining his undivided attention that he fails to notice her removing his keys from her waistband; these are passed surreptitiously to her father who goes off into the Tower, once again unnoticed by Wilfred. As the song is in progress he reappears with the keys that Phoebe must then replace – once more without Wilfred knowing – whilst her father exits and she continues to sing. This calls for coordination of the highest order; not only is it a tricky manoeuvre to be performed but it must give the audience the clear impression that Wilfred not only does not, but could not know what is going on. Unfortunately a prop which maintains a blissfully inanimate state during rehearsals may choose the moment when the auditorium is occupied by the paying public, as well as the video recordist, to develop a little personality of its own. If this metamorphosis is undergone by Wilfred's key fob, and a certain amount of tugging at or fiddling with his girdle becomes necessary as a result, the lack of sincerity in his expressions of ignorance will be obvious to any audience member who has recently experienced either a by-election or a visit from a door-to-door life insurance salesman.

Phoebe exits, leaving Wilfred to reflect ecstatically on what he erroneously sees as attempts by her to woo him. It is not the only soliloquy in G & S opera, but potentially it is one of the funniest, and often generates applause. Wilfred exits, and Meryll reappears, delivering a soliloquy of his own. He reflects on Wilfred's gullibility at Phoebe's hands, but more importantly reveals that he has freed Fairfax. Fairfax then appears, his beard and moustache shaved to make him look like Leonard, and dressed in a Yeoman's uniform. As Meryll says to him in the ensuing dialogue, "remember, you are my brave son, Leonard Meryll." A moment or two later, the Yeomen appear; their chorus "Oh, Sergeant Meryll, is it true" is the start of the Act 1 finale. They have arrived to welcome the new recruit, believing him to be Meryll's son Leonard. They give him a hearty reception, and with small solo sections from the First and Second Yeomen they recall his previous acts of heroism. Fairfax graciously accepts the compliments, but modestly suggests that the tales of his bravery are somewhat exaggerated. Phoebe and Wilfred then appear; Phoebe wastes no time in introducing herself to Fairfax and it is left to him to ask "What! little Phoebe? Who the deuce may *she* be?" which should raise a titter from lovers of doggerel in the audience.

Wilfred, in answer to Fairfax's query, points out that Phoebe is his sister. Fairfax quickly acknowledges her as such, but the hugs which follow certainly seem a good deal more passionate than that one might expect of siblings. Wilfred infoms Fairfax that he is betrothed to Phoebe, and, unsurprisingly, Phoebe is not keen to acknowledge this. However, she is more than ready to adopt Wilfred's suggestion, in the ensuing trio with chorus ("To thy fraternal care thy sister I commend") that her "brother" should take her in hand. Fairfax, for his part, is happy to agree this, and in the final verse of the trio there is more kissing between them which is far from fraternal in nature. It is surely inconceivable to the audience that Wilfred could fail to realise who this "Leonard" really is; indeed any one of the Yeomen would see through his disguise as soon as he had opened his mouth to acknowledge their welcome to him, had they heard the tenor voice of Fairfax warbling, or even bellowing gutsily, from his cell.

The happy family gathering is rudely interrupted by the tolling of the bell of St Peter's, the church within the precincts of the Tower. The time for the execution of Fairfax has come. The orchestra play a mournful dead march whilst the bell continues to toll. It will enhance the scene enormously if the bell stays in time and also in tune with the other players. The chorus of townsfolk, together with Elsie, assemble on stage, the block is brought on and the Headsman takes his place. It may also be appropriate for a priest to come and stand by the block, ready to administer the last rites, although there is no provision for this in the libretto. The Lieutenant arrives and sends Fairfax and two others to bring the prisoner to execution. Accordingly they go off, accompanied by Wilfred. The chorus together proclaim "The prisoner comes to meet his doom;" in a solo, echoed by the chorus, Elsie acknowledges that of all the prisoners kept in the Tower "today the very worthiest falls." Suddenly, Fairfax and the men rush in and reveal that the prisoner has escaped. Solemnity gives way to agitation, in the words and the music, as the chorus assert in alarm that "the double gratings open were, no prisoner at all they found." Meanwhile the Lieutenant goes off and returns with Wilfred, who himself is condemned to death and led away. Meryll and Phoebe feign ignorance, and even the hardened Dame Carruthers confesses she cannot explain it. As she sings, Point appears; at once he realises the awful truth that the prisoner's escape means that Elsie's marriage has *not* been terminated by the expected execution, and he quickly reminds the others that "woe is *me*, I rather think." The finale ends with an ensemble section ("All frenzied with despair") in which those present demand to know who is responsible and offer a substantial reward for the person who effects the prisoner's recapture. All hurry off the stage at random, leaving only the Headsman, Elsie, and Fairfax, into whose arms Elsie has fainted. The effect is most striking; the prisoner for whom everybody searches is now seen cradling the woman, who, unbeknown to him, is his wife, while the executioner stands impotently, his axe raised before a block that sees no prisoner kneeling beside it. Despite the dearth of chorus members in the picture, the dress-rehearsal photo of the scene may be in demand from Bob and Rita, even if a heatwave is in progress and the decorum is slightly marred by the musical director dominating the middle distance in his psychedelic green and orange T-shirt and knee-length Bermuda shorts.

Act 2 takes place two days later, by moonlight, still on Tower Green. The curtain opens to reveal the lady townsfolk and the Yeomen. The ladies observe in song that "Night has spread her pall once more" and then proceed to berate those whose negligence has allowed the prisoner to go free. Dame Carruthers enters with her niece Kate and in a brief solo adds her acerbic comments in similar vein. The Yeomen insist, still in song, that they have searched everywhere, but this fails to appease the women who repeat "Warders are ye, whom do ye ward?" and the number ends with the women's mocking and the Yeomen's pleading being combined in magnificent musical ensemble. Everyone exits, and Point appears, reading from a huge volume which he states is a book of jests. He selects a joke and reads it, but seems to derive little pleasure from it; he remarks that the Lieutenant, who has engaged him, is proving difficult to please. Wilfred then appears, also in low spirits. One is moved to inquire how it is that he has escaped the death sentence announced to him by the Lieutenant two days before!

In the conversation that follows, Point initially tries to cheer Wilfred up, but his true feelings get the better of him, and a moment later he is sharing with Wilfred the absurdity of the life of the salaried wit. Wilfred is undeterred and indicates his interest in becoming a jester himself. In a patter song ("Oh! A private buffoon is a light-hearted loon") Point explains to Wilfred some of the pitfalls of his profession. This very wordy song, preceded as it is by several long speeches – including a real tongue-twister involving a succession of words starting with the letter j – goes to emphasize the challenges of the role of Point. Because his character is so crucial to the success of the show, a poor performance will inevitably colour the newspaper review of the show. A good review, particularly if published during the show's run, will be carefully cut out and pinned to the noticeboard, boosting the confidence and morale of the company and inspiring them to even greater heights of excellence. A bad review will simply be dismissed by the chairman with an assertion that he was sure he saw the reviewer leaving the auditorium twenty minutes from the end and so is hardly in a position to judge the show as a balanced whole; alternatively the unpleasantness of the write-up will be explained by someone pointing out that the reviewer has a grudge against the society and always has had since his wife was turned down for the part of Yum-Yum by that society four years ago at the age of 67.

Point sees how he can turn Wilfred's desire to be a jester to good advantage. He proposes that, in exchange for his assisting Wilfred to become a "jester

175

amongst jesters," Wilfred must swear that he has shot Fairfax whilst attempting to swim across the river. Wilfred is happy to agree, and in a joyful duet reflected by suitably lively music ("Hereupon we're both agreed") they confirm the arrangement to "tell a tale of cock and bull." It is one of the best comic sequences in the opera, and may merit an encore, particularly if the players delight the audience by imitating a cock (of the feathered kind) and bull as they hurry off stage. The dark mood soon returns, however, as Fairfax enters. In a lengthy spoken soliloquy, and his second solo ("Free from his fetters grim") he reflects that whilst he is free from his cell, he is confined in the much more formidable fetters of matrimony, and to a girl he has never seen. Meryll then appears and in dialogue informs Fairfax that Elsie, entrusted since her fainting to his (Meryll's) care, is fit enough to leave. Meryll complains that Elsie's stay has unfortunately given Dame Carruthers, whom he dislikes, an excuse for taking up quarters in his house as well. Dame Carruthers and Kate then enter. Fairfax must remind himself that in their eyes he is Meryll's son! In the presence of Fairfax, Dame Carruthers then reveals, and Kate confirms, that Elsie spoke in her sleep about having undergone – in exchange for money – a wedding ceremony to one she had never seen and who was to die in an hour. Fairfax must, of course, feign ignorance, but this revelation is sufficient to tell him the identity of his wife. Dame Carruthers, Meryll and Kate join him in a madrigal quartet ("Strange adventure") in which each reflects on the curious marriage which Elsie has undergone. There is a serenity and Englishness about the madrigal which is somehow very reassuring amidst the increasing tension in the story; Leslie Baily comments that the quartet "might well belong to that age when Henry VIII could despatch a wife to the axe at one moment and write a madrigal at the next." The madrigal, which requires no props or movement, is another obvious favourite for charity concerts, where the tension amongst the singers may have nothing to do with the story or indeed their musical competence, but may arise from the interminable wait for the musical programme to commence or resume following the obligatory raffle draw. The heart of the dinner-jacketed performer will sink as he sees some twenty or twenty-five assorted bottles, boxes of chocolates and plastic flower arrangements laid out on a table top, and plummet even further as each number that is called out is met with a deafening silence from the ranks. When somebody does eventually find tucked in their handbag, hip pocket or other available receptacle a ticket with a corresponding number and colour, it is more than likely that that person will already have won a prize, or be one of the organisers, and so refuse the prize and prolong the draw even more. The performer's most painful experience will be reserved for the moment when the last number is called and, after a silence even more protracted than for the previous 22 calls ensues, he suddenly realises that he has the winning ticket. Not only will he no longer be able to boast to his friends that "I never win anything at raffles" but he will find himself the proud owner of some hideous makeweight, such as a bar of chocolate-coloured novelty soap or a plastic statuette of an armadillo last seen in the GIFTS FOR UNDER £2 display in the nearby sweet shop.

All but Fairfax leave, while Fairfax remains to ponder on his good fortune in landing such a winsome bride as Elsie. His difficulty, of course, is that he cannot tell her who he is, so he decides he will "test her principles" by wooing her in the guise of Leonard. Elsie arrives at that moment, and a conversation ensues in which Fairfax does indeed express his great love for her. Not surprisingly, Elsie is shocked, and hastens to explain to the man she believes to be Leonard about her existing marriage. Fairfax rashly suggests that he and Elsie marry anyway, on the basis that her husband, facing the death sentence, would never dare to return to claim her. Elsie is outraged by this suggestion, but further discussion is forestalled by the sound of a shot off stage. Meryll hurries in and a complex musical sequence begins; in recitative ("Hark! What was that, sir?") he and Fairfax ask what prompted the shot, and when the townsfolk, the Yeomen and Phoebe enter a moment later their conversation too is full of questions and speculation. The Lieutenant then enters, as do Point and Wilfred, and the Lieutenant demands to know "who fired that shot" (or possibly, if prone to spoonerism, "who shired that fot!")

The Lieutenant's brusque enquiry results in a duet between the jester and jailer, with chorus ("Like a ghost his vigil keeping"), in which Point and Wilfred state they have been responsible for the death of Fairfax and describe the manner of his death in the river. In this graphic description of a fictitious death, there is more than a hint of similarity to "The criminal cried" in *The Mikado*. The fast-moving duet is one of the most entertaining sections in the opera, with both conspirators apparently confused over small details such as whether the dead man sank like stone or lead; however in a rip-roaring ending, they hastily agree that "it is very, very certain that he's very, very dead!" (It is traditional for Wilfred and Point to continue their "stone/lead" argument in speech after the duet has finished.) The Lieutenant insists that the body is recovered at once, then exits. Wilfred is acclaimed as a hero, and to a chorus of admiration ("Hail the valiant fellow who") he is carried off on the shoulders of four men. The Lieutenant's instruction to recover the body appears to be ignored. The fact that there is no evidence that anybody does search the river adds fuel to the argument levelled at the opera by critics that the plot of the show is too contrived and leaves too many questions unanswered. Purists may abound not only in high academic circles but amongst the cast of a production. A female cast member and self-styled costume expert will look scornfully at the apparel provided for the female citizens and vociferously claim that "an Elizabethan woman would never be seen wearing anything like that." It would take a brave fellow-thespian to point out to her that it is also unlikely that an Elizabethan woman would divert her attention from the growing drama on Tower Green to check that her sister-in-law Connie and her nephew Darren were safely ensconced in row B seats 21 and 22.

Everybody then exits except Elsie, Point, Fairfax and Phoebe. Dialogue once again takes over from the music, as the four principals contemplate the significance of the "death" of the escaped prisoner. Not surprisingly, Elsie is tearful, but Fairfax and Point are in the happy position of being able to woo her without the spectre of the escaped prisoner hanging over them. It is Point who makes the first move, but barely has he begun, relying upon what he calls his pretty wit, than Fairfax brusquely interrupts and tells him there is more to wooing than "time-worn jests and thread-bare sophistries." In a trio that follows for Elsie, Phoebe and Fairfax ("A man who would woo a fair maid") the three singers give Point a lesson in how to a lady should be wooed, and how to interpret the response. In the dialogue after the trio has ended, Fairfax gives Point a practical demonstration, using Elsie as his lady. Point is content at first, thinking that Fairfax is doing his work for him, but to his dismay and to Phoebe's horror, it soon becomes clear that Fairfax is winning Elsie for himself. There is nothing Phoebe can do, having told the world that Fairfax is her brother, and she now bursts into tears. Meanwhile, Point is directed by Fairfax in no uncertain terms to apply his new-found learning elsewhere. A quartet follows in which each singer reflects on their situation ("When a wooer goes a-wooing"). The emotions for each are very different; there is joy and happiness for Elsie and Fairfax, and utter misery for the tearful Phoebe and the broken Point. The subsequent exit of Fairfax, Elsie and Point is an especially poignant moment. It is to be fervently hoped that one of any number of extraneous noises which can distract a performer will not occur here, be it hail crashing on to the corrugated iron roof of the performance hall or the jangling tones of the front-office telephone.

Phoebe remains on stage and as she sobbingly reflects on the ingratitude of the man she loves, Wilfred enters. In dialogue he asks why she is crying, and she confesses her love for the one who is to marry Elsie. Wilfred is puzzled, and points out that that is her brother Leonard. Too late Phoebe realises that she has blown the gaff; immediately Wilfred is aware that Elsie's lover is Fairfax, the one of whom Phoebe had earlier spoken so admiringly. Thinking quickly, Phoebe reminds Wilfred that he too is guilty of trickery, in falsely claiming to have shot the prisoner. Nonetheless, her own secret is out, and in order to preserve herself, and presumably her family too, she agrees to marry Wilfred. As Wilfred embraces her, the real Leonard arrives and informs Phoebe that the long-awaited reprieve for Fairfax has come, having been held back by Secretary Poltwhistle. Phoebe's joy at this news contrasts with Wilfred's anger as he sees her showering kisses on her brother; not unreasonably he asks how many more brothers she has got!

Leonard leaves them and Phoebe pacifies her new fiance by reminding him that although she is guilty of deceit, he, Wilfred, has got her, and that should be enough for him. Meryll enters joyfully, having heard the news of the reprieve, but his face falls as he is told the price Phoebe has had to pay for Wilfred's silence. The newly-engaged couple exit, and Meryll reflects, aloud, on the unfortunate consequences of Phoebe's indiscretion. To his horror, he realises that Dame Carruthers had followed him on to Tower Green, and knows everything. Now it is Meryll's turn to submit to a most unwelcome engagement as the price of *her* silence. There follows a spirited duet, "Rapture, rapture" (as opposed to "Rupture, rupture" as waggish cast members are wont to rename it), in which Dame Carruthers contemplates with joy, and Meryll with dread (his first words are "doleful, doleful"), their future lives together. Some might say the duet offers welcome comic relief amidst the increasing tension, whilst others regard it as an unnecessary addition – originally put in to allow Elsie and Fairfax more time to change costume – that spoils the atmosphere of the opera. Indeed it is not unknown to cut this item from productions of the work, particularly if the costume change can be effected sufficiently speedily. There are of course shades of *The Mikado* in *this* duet, as one is reminded of Ko-Ko's marriage of convenience to Katisha to prevent his little conspiracy being detected. As the "Rapture, rapture" duet ends with the exit of the couple in similar vein to that in "There is beauty in the bellow of the blast" one is reminded of the three ages of male participation in G & S opera. First, the raw recruit, restricted to cameo parts only and being lectured by every member of the society aged over 45 on how to do them; second, the confident romantic lead, hoping the girl playing opposite feels the same way about him in real life as she does in the story; third, the ageing comic, doomed to spend his declining years being chased around and then off the stage by feisty contraltos.

As Dame Carruthers and Meryll exit, the women townsfolk and the Yeomen enter to commence the most dramatic finale of all the G & S operas. In a chorus ("Comes the pretty young bride") the women set the scene for the wedding of Elsie to "Leonard." Elsie then appears in her bridal dress; she is accompanied by Phoebe and Dame Carruthers, and states, supported by the full chorus, that "this is my joy-day unalloyed." The Lieutenant then appears and, to everybody's horror, announces that Elsie's supposedly deceased husband is not only still alive but has been reprieved and is on her way to claim his bride. Elsie is distraught, and in a dramatic ensemble section the company proclaim this to be a "day of terror! day of tears!" Fairfax then appears, attended by other gentlemen, but Elsie does not see him and thus has no idea that he and her beloved are one and the same. In true operatic style, she is not permitted to turn and face him until she has sung a tense recitative and brief aria in which she mournfully submits herself to her reprieved husband. Of course, this heightens the joy she feels when finally she is allowed to look up and discover the true identity of her "Leonard." The chorus echo their expressions of elation, and all seems set for a happy ending – until Point enters and is aghast to see Elsie with Fairfax. His brief recitative ("Oh, thoughtless crew") is followed by a reprise of two verses of "I have a song to sing" with Elsie and chorus. As the song approaches its end, Point, heartbroken at having lost the lady he loves, is directed to fall insensible at the feet of Elsie and Fairfax as they embrace. Much ink has been spilt on the question of whether Point is supposed to die at this point. George Grossmith, the first Point, having fallen to the ground at the end of the first performance, raised a leg and waggled it in the air, literally getting the last laugh. By contrast, Henry Lytton, who succeeded him, gave the opera a tragic ending by "allowing" Point to die; Gilbert expressed approval of this approach, and Martyn Green, a more recent Point, adopted it also. Nonetheless, the word "insensible" was never changed by the librettist, despite there being ample opportunity for such a change; it has been suggested that he himself was unsure what he wanted, and it must be for each producer to decide what effect he wishes to achieve. However, whether or not Point does "die," the sight of a lonely broken-hearted man seen pathetically lying at the feet of a loving couple, fingering and kissing the hem of the bridal dress, until the dress – like his hope of requited love – slips through his fingers, will generate pathos of a special kind with potential, if skilfully staged, for the audience and cast to be quite affected by what they have witnessed. The curtain will close and, after the actor playing Point has risen to his feet, it will reopen moments later for what must inevitably be a more subdued curtain call than in other G & S operas. The cast may welcome this, especially if they are used to more elaborate curtain calls being hastily set and rehearsed eight times between 1.10 and 1.35 a.m. on dress rehearsal night, and which for their effectiveness depend upon the audience's applause continuing throughout the period during which the players are regrouping in the wings. A protracted closure of the curtain, while the cast all jostle anxiously off stage trying to locate the person who is supposed to lead back on, may result in some spectators believing the night's entertainment to be over, and halfway home to their firesides long before the society chairman has come forward and exhorted the customers to book early for the May production of *Expresso Bongo*.

"No, we've not got the wrong night – that's the Producer, the Stage Manager and the M.D. in there"

Many would say that *The Gondoliers*, the eleventh surviving G & S opera and the final real masterpiece of the series, was the best and loveliest work ever composed by the partnership. With its combination of sparkling music, lovable characters, witty dialogue with a dash of satire, and unashamed *joie de vivre*, nobody who attends a well-directed production of the opera can fail to leave it feeling truly enriched and elated by the experience. Victorian audiences loved it too, and its opening run was one of the longest of all the operas. Yet just months previously the partnership had yet again been in deadlock. Following *The Yeomen Of The Guard*, a far more serious work than any of the other G & S operas, Sullivan had turned his face completely from comic opera, stating that regretfully he felt unable to co-write a comic piece again. Gilbert, by contrast, felt that the public preferred the "more reckless and irresponsible pieces." An acrimonious exchange of letters ensued, in which Sullivan made it clear that if he were to collaborate with Gilbert again, he wanted a far greater role in the musical construction of the libretto, with words that would give him the chance to fully develop musical effects. What particularly hurt Gilbert was Sullivan's suggestion that he (Sullivan) was a mere "cipher in the theatre, " and effectively subservient to the librettist. Following the intervention of Carte, however, tempers cooled and Sullivan relented, apparently satisfied with Gilbert's assurance that he should have a hand in staging and planning the pieces, and that words and music should assume equal importance. In May 1889 Sullivan felt moved to write to Gilbert and encourage him to continue work on a subject Carte had told him was in the librettist's mind – a subject with a Venetian theme. That spring Sullivan had been to Venice and had thoroughly enjoyed the experience. Gilbert further pacified the composer by presenting a libretto with proportionally far more music and less dialogue than almost any of the other full-length operas, including an unbroken musical sequence of nearly 20 minutes at the start. There was, however, sufficient dialogue to convey the two satirical elements of the piece; firstly, republican fervour and the thirst for egalitarianism, and secondly, the exploitation by the nobility of bourgeois snobbery. Gilbert demonstrated true egalitarian principles, not only by giving greater musical rein to Sullivan, but by creating a large number of solo roles with no particular prominence given to any of them. George Grossmith was not among the soloists, having left the company, and one Frank Wyatt took the "Grossmith role." Meanwhile, a young newcomer named Decima Moore was introduced to the solo line-up. Gilbert asked if she had ever acted before; when she replied that she had not, Gilbert responded with feeling: "So much the better for you. You've nothing to unlearn."

Sullivan was also working extremely hard; at the same time as he was composing the lengthy score, he was also writing his grand opera *Ivanhoe*! It took him the whole summer of 1889 to complete the score of *The Gondoliers*. The final preparations were, as usual, hectic; the first orchestral rehearsal was convened just five days before the opening performance on 7th December 1889. The dress rehearsal lasted a massive 7 hours. However, judging by the critics' reaction, the efforts were worthwhile. Both audience and press were captivated by the show's festive, movement-filled, innocent celebration of youth, happiness, love and marriage, with hints of satire and topsy-turvydom. It appeared that, perhaps more than with any other opera in the series, the partners had got the perfect balance between entertainment, burlesque and social satire. The opening run consisted of an impressive 554 performances. Gilbert and Sullivan were famously fulsome in their praise of each other's contribution to the success of the show. One reviewer wrote "It is simply entertainment; the most exquisite, daintiest entertainment we have seen." Another, commenting on the short skirts worn by the lady chorus, remarked that "the gratifying fact is revealed to a curious world that the Savoy chorus are a well-legged lot." Contemporary writers have also been generous with their praise; Audrey Williamson writes that the opera has a "specially sunny quality almost entirely devoid of shade" and Ian Bradley states "In some ways *The Gondoliers* stands as the supreme achievement of the distinct yet united talents of Gilbert and Sullivan." The *Punch* critic was less kind, observing that "there would not be a chance for the opera had the authors' names been Smith and Brown." The opera was far less successful in the States where the poor box-office returns earned the opera the nickname *The Gone Dollars*!

The action of the opera begins in Venice, where two handsome gondoliers Marco (tenor) and Giuseppe (baritone) Palmieri begin the story by choosing their wives, the pretty *contadine* Gianetta (soprano) and Tessa (mezzo-soprano). As they go off to get married, the Duke of Plaza-Toro (baritone) arrives with his wife the Duchess (contralto), their "suite" Luiz (tenor) and their daughter Casilda (soprano). They have come to find the man who was betrothed in infancy to Casilda and who is now heir to the throne of the island kingdom of Barataria. (The opera is alternatively titled *The King Of Barataria*; Gilbert borrowed the name Barataria from the work of the writer Cervantes.) The Grand Inquisitor Don Alhambra del Bolero (baritone) tells them that the heir in question is plying a trade as a gondolier, having been smuggled from Barataria many years ago. Apparently it is either Marco or Giuseppe but nobody knows which. It is agreed they will reign jointly until the question is finally resolved by the true king's foster-mother Inez (mezzo-soprano), and they sail to Barataria to begin their reign. Casilda is far from keen to marry either of them, as she loves Luiz. Fortunately Inez reveals that following some baby-swopping it was her own son that was smuggled to Venice while the real king remained in her custody. That is of course Luiz, so Casilda may claim him after all, and the gondoliers can return to their beloved *contadine*.

Act 1 takes place in the Piazzetta, Venice, and starts, as has been intimated, with an unbroken sequence of nearly 20 minutes' music. The ladies, or *contadine*, are seen on stage, each tying bouquets of roses. In the opening chorus with a brief solo for soprano Fiametta ("List and learn") they explain that this is in honour of the two most handsome gondoliers for whom "every maid in Venice sighs." A number of gondoliers now enter, among whom are Antonio, Francesco and Giorgio, and they commence a charming musical dialogue with Fiametta and her fellow *contadine* Giulia and Vittoria (both mezzo-soprano). The girls explain to the men that the floral tributes are meant for Marco and Giuseppe Palmieri, who are on their way to select two brides from amongst them. The men react somewhat jealously to this, but the girls reassure them that they will still have plenty to choose from after Marco and Giuseppe have taken their pick; until then, they should enjoy their "*dolce far niente*." This Italian expression, which also crops up in *Iolanthe*, effectively means "sweet idleness" but cast and audience members without this information might be forgiven for believing it to be a local pasta dish or a sickly dessert involving a lethal mixture of liqueur and chocolate ice cream. Antonio then sings a solo, with choral backing ("For the merriest fellows are we"), in which he and the gondoliers rejoice in their carefree and uncomplicated lives. No sooner have they finished than Marco and Giuseppe are noticed approaching, and indeed after a brief recitative from Fiametta and a chorus of welcome the two principal gondoliers are seen to arrive in their gondola and jump ashore. It will then be necessary for the gondola to return from whence it came in order to convey the next set of principals on to the scene at a later stage in the opera. The slow and graceful appearance of the gondola on to the set, as with its subsequent removal, is one of the hardest logistical problems the stage manager will have; yanking too enthusiastically on the rope that is used to heave the boat on to the stage may either result in the gondola being upended, tipping the immaculately-dressed principals unceremoniously into the canal, or alternatively failing to stop where it should, so that both gondola and occupants are despatched summarily into the opposite wings. This will cause some distress to the principals who were reliant upon that boat to convey them to the Piazzetta and who now see walking on water as their only hope of making their stage appearance. Moreover, it will cause the hapless erstwhile occupants of the vessel to regret partaking of that extra helping of *dolce far niente* before setting out.

Assuming the two men arrive safely, they greet the girls in a sensual outpouring of Italian which is readily reciprocated (*"Buon giorno, signorine"*). As they sing to them, they are inundated with the bouquets the girls have been preparing for them. The need to sing or speak with an accent or in a foreign language may pose a very considerable challenge to performers of G & S opera, and a producer can make life extraordinarily difficult for soloists by insisting that the accent adopted is absolutely consistent with the character's country, or possibly even county, of origin. In *The Gondoliers*, a cast member with some knowledge of Italian will, however lowly their status in the production, suddenly become extremely popular – or unpopular – as the intricacies of Italian pronunciation are painstakingly explained to the performers. The Italian teacher's contribution to the proceedings is, however, likely to be more welcome and more valuable to the cast than a potentially futile debate about whether the Hampshire accent adopted by a performer for *H.M.S. Pinafore* is in fact unacceptably reminiscent of a West Country burr not normally heard east of Budleigh Salterton.

The Italian greeting leads into a joyous duet (*"We're called gondolieri"*) in which Marco and Giuseppe introduce themselves and their contented lifestyle which combines the hard work of gondoliering with happy music-making. Either, or both, of the gondoliers may seek to demonstrate the latter with the strumming of a mandolin. If the performer is lucky he will be entrusted with a real mandolin and be able to perfect a few simple chords that keep in tune with the orchestra. The less fortunate performer will find himself with a piece of wood with strings painted on to it, and will be forced to stand uneasily before the admiring crowd of *contadine*, self-consciously brushing his fingertips against the strips of paint on as many occasions as he remembers to do it. As the song ends to enthusiastic applause – if not from the audience, then at least from the *contadine*, who are instructed to applaud anyway – the two men announce in a recitative, with chorus ("And now to choose our brides!"), that the time has come to make their selection. As the girls all preen themselves in the hope of being selected, Marco and Giuseppe announce that they will leave the decision to Fate, by being blindfolded and making a selection at random. There follows a charming piece of business in which Fiametta and Vittoria apply the blindfolds to the two men, and together with the chorus accuse them of cheating by peeping either over or under the handkerchiefs that have been used for the purpose. The exchanges are, however, very good-humoured and devoid of any malice. A game of Blind Man's Buff follows, the upshot of which is that Marco picks out Gianetta and Giuseppe picks out Tessa. It is, of course, purely coincidental that they have the strongest singing voices and acting abilities of any of the girls! It is said that rehearsals for this one piece of business took Gilbert three days when the show was originally produced. Certainly a scene like this can be a nightmare for the producer; perhaps the only thing more galling for him than a cast unable to perfect the choreography given to them is to drive home happily one evening having satisfied himself after twelve attempts that they have got it perfectly right, only to have to start from scratch the next week after second soprano Millicent de Lacy Adams is reported as having tendered her resignation from the cast on the grounds of a conference in North Carolina during the week of the show. It will be of little consolation to him to hear the shrill hoots of laughter when Ms Adams' absence, of which only the chairman at that stage is aware, causes the careful plotting to go awry and Marco to fall straight into the arms not of Gianetta but of Avril Plunkett, an aged second contralto whose chances of playing the lead in anything would appear to be restricted to performances of *Lassie Come Home*.

Both the principal gondoliers seem very happy with their choice, Marco proclaiming that Gianetta is "just the very girl I wanted," and there follows some good-natured teasing between the two couples. The happiness of the two couples is then articulated more fully in a rousing ensemble ("Thank you, gallant *gondolieri*"). This begins with solos from Gianetta and Tessa and ends with a joyous chorus, the girls singing the main melody and the men contenting themselves with "la las" to a cross rhythm. As with "A nice dilemma" in *Trial By Jury*, this contains a succession of silent downbeats and may provoke an outburst of sniffing or toe-tapping as the men strive to find a way of perfecting it. The sequence ends with more straightforward block harmony, following which the all the gondoliers and *contadine*, principals included, hurry off to prepare for the double wedding. There is now a complete change of personnel as four new principals are introduced: the Duke and Duchess of Plaza-Toro, Casilda their daughter, and Luiz their attendant who carries a drum. Like Marco and Giuseppe before them, they arrive by gondola. However, they have none of the youthful charms of the gondoliers, and are in fact dressed in pompous but old and faded clothes. They begin by introducing themselves in a quartet, singing that they have come "From the sunny Spanish shore." They have apparently come by sea – which study of a map would indicate to be an excessively long journey – and indeed as the song continues they vow not to repeat the experience! In the first piece of straight speech in the opera, the Duke bemoans the fact that he cannot ride through the city's waterlogged streets, while the women deplore the lack of respect Luiz appears to show to him. The Duke appears more concerned that nobody, not even a band, appears to have come to welcome or escort the party. Luiz points out that the band are "sordid persons who require to be paid in advance." The Duchess, one of the less endearing G & S contraltos, makes the acid retort "That's so like a band!" which will invariably generate some titters if directed to the members of the real-life orchestra. Although many societies successfully rely on keyboard and percussion to provide instrumental accompaniment to the voices, it is usual for a G & S amateur production to include a full orchestra. They will often meet for the first time at the band call during the weekend immediately preceding the show. The musical director, who has for the past few weeks been firing broadsides at the cast at every opportunity, will at the band call suddenly become a model of politeness and decorum however cacophonous the sound that the instrumentalists initially produce. Long pauses will inevitably be occasioned whilst the conductor makes handwritten alterations to illegible or misprinted band parts, and then tries to impress his listeners by warning of a "*poco rit* three bars after E" and a plea for "*allargando* from the strings six bars before letter Q." The politeness and decorum does not, however, extend to those cast members whose presence is required for the band call; they, of course, will be expected to know exactly what the conductor means when he says "we'll pick it up at the upbeat to letter X" and will be open to the strongest criticism for failing to make an entry, notwithstanding that the flautist who provides the cue music is at that time lying in bed with a hangover after a heavy night at the Frog and Truncheon. The singers' only consolation is that budgetary restrictions may limit the duration of the band call; the utter tedium of spending the first three quarters of an hour on the opening number can at least be offset by the eager anticipation of the second Act which, in each of the past five band calls, the conductor has completed within a snappy seventeen and a half minutes.

After Casilda has scornfully dismissed Luiz' offer to compensate for the orchestra's absence with farmyard impressions, the young attendant is despatched to fetch the Grand Inquisitor of Spain, whom the Duke and Duchess have come to see, and demand an audience. Luiz exits and the Duke discloses to Casilda for the first time that, as a baby, she was married by proxy to the heir to the throne of Barataria. As a result of the King's conversion to Methodism, the Grand Inquisitor conveyed the infant heir to Venice to avoid his embracing this creed; now, Casilda is told, the King has been killed in an insurrection and the Duke has come to Venice with his wife and daughter to find the heir and install him on the throne. Luiz reappears in time to hear Casilda protest that as Queen she has nothing to wear and her

188

family has no money. The Duke consoles her by saying that he is being turned into a public limited company which he trusts will improve his financial position. He goes on to proclaim himself a pioneer of fashions, as well as a soldier noted for his unorthodox tactics; his catchy solo ("In enterprise of martial kind"), with martial accompaniment and refrain for the other three principals, recalls a certain lack of enthusiasm on his part to face the enemy. As has been stated, Frank Wyatt was the first Duke of Plaza-Toro following the departure of George Grossmith; Ian Bradley suggests that the absence of a traditional "Grossmith" patter song from the opera may have been attributable to the fact that his successor was a newcomer who might have had difficulty in coping with such a song. Many societies will rely heavily on certain faithful members to successfully execute the traditional G & S operatic roles – the young tenor, the ageing contralto, the funny man, and so on – and trust to Providence that no misfortune will prevent their taking part in a performance and force the production team into reliance on an unknown. Some societies will have a team of trained understudies; if no understudy exists to fill a gap which unexpectedly opens up as a result of a missing principal, and no acceptable substitutes from other societies are available, a desperate appeal may need to be made to other cast members. Whilst many would shrink from such an ordeal, most societies will contain at least one member who relishes the thought of filling the vacancy and the unending gratitude that will be heaped upon him as a result. Safe in the knowledge that the cast and audience will forgive him every error he makes, he will stride to the wings in preparation for his entrance without a trace of nerves. The heartbroken sense of anticlimax he feels when, two seconds before he is due to enter, the missing principal barges past him on to the stage can be likened to that felt by the man who just as he is about to get into bed with Jane Fonda is rudely awoken by the jolt of his train as it draws up at East Didsbury.

The Duke and Duchess exit, leaving Casilda and Luiz together. To the surprise of the audience (or at least those who do not know the story) they rush to each other's arms and sing a passionate duet ("Oh, rapture") in which Casilda explains that her apparent coldness towards Luiz is merely for appearances, and really she is in very much in love with him, as he is with her. It is not surprising, therefore, that Luiz reacts in horror when in the ensuing dialogue he is informed by Casilda of her infant wedding. Luiz attempts to salvage the situation by seeking some retrospective declaration of love, and an embrace to go with it, but it is hopeless. After the passion of the first duet, there then follows a much more sombre one ("There was a time") in which the couple reflect on the fact that their romance is necessarily dead. The Duke and the Duchess then reappear, accompanied by

Don Alhambra del Bolero, the Grand Inquisitor of Spain, who in the dialogue that follows is introduced to Casilda. Don Alhambra immediately presents as a rather smarmy character, eyeing up Casilda in a lecherous manner until she scornfully rebuffs him. Momentarily her hopes are raised when the Duchess suggests that there is a doubt as to where Barataria's heir is to be found; Don Alhambra, however, states the position is not in any doubt at all. In a song, with refrain from the other principals ("I stole the prince"), he informs the others that on stealing the heir he left him with a gondolier in Venice who already had an infant son of his own. Unfortunately the adult gondolier to whom the prince was entrusted had a liking for alcohol, so that when he died nobody could tell which of the infants, each of whom have become gondoliers, was actually the prince. In the conversation after the song Casilda expresses dismay, believing that it will therefore be impossible to ascertain her husband's identity. Don Alhambra states that Luiz' mother, the nurse to whose care the prince was entrusted in babyhood, will be able to tell the prince from the gondolier, and if not, he says nonchalantly, the torture chamber will assist her in her deliberations! A recitative by Casilda and Don Alhambra ("But, bless my heart") follows, which highlights the unfortunate Casilda's position and confirms what a complicated tangle life is. The recitative leads straight into a quintet involving all principals present ("Try we life-long") in which each philosophically reflects that one might as well enjoy life, even though one cannot understand it. This positive and carefree outlook is very much in keeping with the exuberance and cheerfulness of the whole opera. The harmonies are intricate, and it is essential that each principal has the musical ability required to hold his or her particular line, but the end result is well worth the effort. It has been known for the actors to consume plates of spaghetti during the recitative preceding the quintet, as well as during Don Alhambra's previous solo, rendering Don Alhambra's words "Life is one closely complicated tangle" particularly appropriate! Where there are adequate cooking facilities backstage to provide a proper hot meal on stage, this could prove a pleasant experience for lovers of spaghetti amongst the principals. If however the pasta has had to be conveyed from the home of the assistant stage manager, who happens to live closer to the hall than anybody else, it may well have lost its appeal by the time it reaches the stage, and as the Duke grimly manoeuvres an assembly of cold white wormlike objects on to his fork, he may well have special cause to rue his pre-performance meal of garlic eclairs and sticky toffee pudding in front of one of the schmaltzier episodes of *The Waltons*.

The five performers exit – Luiz will not be seen again until the very end of the opera – and the stage fills with the gondoliers and *contadine*. In chorus

("Bridegroom and bride") they all welcome Marco and Giuseppe who themselves enter with their new wives. Tessa then sings one of the loveliest mezzo-soprano songs in the G & S operas, with chorus ("When a merry maiden marries"), in which she reflects on the happiness that attends a bride on her wedding day. Sullivan was accused of plagiarising the tune for this song from another composer, and famously retorted that he and the other composer had only the same seven notes to choose from! The chorus disperse, leaving Marco, Gianetta, Giuseppe and Tessa on stage. They speak enthusiastically about their new lives and new partners, and even when Don Alhambra enters they continue to be exuberant, appearing to mock his pomposity and self-importance. Giuseppe explains that he and Marco are republicans, abhorring inequalities, rank, wealth and of course royalty. However, he is forced to adjust his position somewhat when Don Alhambra informs the two gondoliers that one of them is himself heir to the throne of Barataria! Both gondoliers are then only too willing to embrace royalist principles, and to accept that their earlier opinions may have been ill-advised. Their new enlightened attitutes are particularly timely, as Don Alhambra tells them that both shall go off to Barataria and reign jointly until the true king can be identified. This tilt at the egalitarian idealist, who accepts principles of equality only as long as it suits him, is of course an echo of a similar theme in *H.M.S. Pinafore* and was to be developed much more intensely in such works as George Orwell's *Animal Farm*. However, one suspects that the degree-level student of politics or social science will look elsewhere for authorities in support of his thesis on the subject than his local operatic society's production of *The Gondoliers*. It would be unfortunate if having taken up valuable study time to attend it, he found that the acoustics of the hall and the nervousness of the performers combined to render the chances of their lines being heard, let alone appreciated, as great as the possibility of a killer shark suddenly emerging from the canal depicted on the backcloth, and devouring Mrs Pettigrew, the portly and grossly overworked prompt, in a single gulp.

There is, however, a drawback which Marco and Giuseppe had not foreseen; for some reason which is not explained to them, they are not to be allowed to take their new wives with them. Gianetta begins the finale of Act 1 by singing of her sadness at this situation ("Kind sir, you cannot have the heart"). Don Alhambra comforts them by saying that she and Tessa will be reunited with their husbands once the identity of the true king has been ascertained. He chooses not to inform them that the actual king is now guilty of bigamy! In all innocence, therefore, the two couples embark on a glorious quartet ("Then one of us will be a Queen") in which they reflect on the pleasures that await the lucky lady – whoever she may be. Their joyful

191

singing and dancing cause the chorus to hurry on to the stage demanding to know the cause of this "unmitigated jollity." Marco and Giuseppe respond with a duet ("Replying, we sing") in which a song is created by each taking it in turns to sing a bar of music. Not only must one singer constantly pick up the music from the other, like a baton in a relay, but one singer may often have to complete a word started by the other, for instance "indi-vidual," "ob-ject" and re-publican." The gist of their song is that they recognise that their fellow gondoliers – who are to be invited to Barataria with them to make up the royal court – will as republicans object to the trappings of royalty. However the joint kings indicate they are prepared to make some concessions. When the chorus query this, Marco and Giuseppe launch into another boisterous duet, assisted by the gondoliers and *contadine* ("For everyone who feels inclined"), in which they promise equality to everybody, whether the aristocrat, grate-scrubber or coachman. This passage of music throws up another G & S trivia question, as the chorus serenade the two Chinamen "Sing high, sing low," and offers a possible spoonerism for Marco, who in attempting to serenade the "aristocrat who hunts and shoots" may instead offer a vision of a noble citizen who would seem more at home in the sidings at Willesden Junction than in the sun-drenched piazzas of Barataria.

After the king, whoever he may be, has been suitably hailed by the approving crowd, Marco and Giuseppe decide in a recitative ("Come, let's away") that it is time to set sail. A beautifully touching duet from Gianetta and Tessa ensues ("Now, Marco dear") in which they instruct their husbands to behave themselves and to keep their wives uppermost in their thoughts, perhaps sending "words by little birds to comfort me." At the end the two men join in to create a positively churchy quartet as they implore each other, despite the distance between them, "do not forget you've married me." This rather sad spell is broken by a spirited orchestral introduction which is reminiscent of rolling waves, and this is followed by an ensemble ending to the finale, "Then away we go to an island fair." In this section Marco and Giuseppe, accompanied by as many gondoliers as Venice can manage without, anticipate and then effect their departure for Barataria, and the ladies bid them goodbye. A splendid skit on grand opera is to be found in this section; amidst the rousing words of farewell, set to suitably florid music, there is the wonderfully banal statement "When the breezes are blowing, the ship will be going; when they don't, we shall all stand still!" It is of course possible that the irony will be lost on earnest chorus members, many of whom will have been involved in the town choral society's recent rendition of *Judas Maccabaeus*, and who, conditioned to producing a tight turgid sound, will deliver Gilbert's ridiculous words with as much mischievous spontaneity as might be found in a government report on the health and safety issues inherent in the disposal of liquid manure.

Act 2 is set in Barataria, in a pavilion within the palace. The curtains open to find the two new kings with their new court, consisting of the gondoliers they have brought with them. In attempting to pander to the principles of equality, Marco and Giuseppe are doing some housework, while the members of the court are enjoying themselves. In a chorus ("Of happiness the very pith") they rejoice in their happy position of absolute equality; between sections of chorus there is sandwiched a duet for the two kings who remark that they "put their subjects at their ease by doing all they can to please." In the conversation that follows, Marco expresses pleasure at his court's expression of gratitude, which the members of the court, immersed as they are in their amusements, cannot even be bothered to acknowledge. They do, however, react aggressively when Giuseppe endeavours to venture a grievance. Having pacified them, he complains that, because only one king is allowed for in the rationing of food, the amount of food provided to the two of them is inadequate. A nice touch here might be for a single egg on toast, or some other less than generous repast, to be brought on stage and placed in front of the two hapless and hungry monarchs!

Annibale, one of the members of the court, points out that the joint monarchy is a "legal fiction" and the question of extra supplies should be argued in front of a tribunal. However, having heard further representations from the hungry kings, he agrees to an interim order for double rations – with an indemnity clause in case the kings' claim is unsuccessful! Giorgio, Annibale's colleague, indicates that the kings should expect to work hard in return. Giuseppe fully accepts this, particularly since – as he himself acknowledges – he and Marco enjoy such luxuries as having their salutes returned and being nodded to in the streets. In a solo, with chorus ("Rising early in the morning"), Giuseppe proceeds to inform his listeners of the rigours of a day in the life of a king who is also champion of equality. The list of chores is endless, from lighting the palace fire to running errands for the Ministers of State, refreshed by luncheon consisting merely of sherry and a bun. Nonetheless, as the chorus echo later in the song, Giuseppe states that "of pleasures there are many and of worries there are none." As well as being a very catchy number it does, of course, highlight the absurd consequences of egalitarianism taken to extremes. It is totally in keeping with the mood of the scene for Giuseppe to be quite upstaged by the frolicsome antics of those members of the chorus whom the musical director has not garrotted for their insensitive musical slide from the word "Oh" at

193

the start of the refrain. The stage directions suggest that games such as cup and ball could be played, but depending on the amount of space available, even more ambitious contests such as impromptu tennis or cricket could take place, or members could endeavour to impress the audience by performing tricks with string or juggling. There are of course dangers in encouraging a profusion of hard, round objects on stage; it would be unfortunate if the batsman in a game of stage cricket happened also to be the opener for the town's first XI and impulsively despatched an on-drive into the capacious cleavage of the second bassoonist.

The chorus members exit, leaving Giuseppe and Marco to reflect happily in dialogue on the pleasures of their monarchical existence. Marco does, however, point out that something is still missing; he is referring to their wives from whom they have now been parted for three months. There is only one recipe, he states, for perfect happiness. In that most famous of all G & S tenor arias ("Take a pair of sparkling eyes") he proceeds to sing of those things that make a beautiful woman, including a trim figure, rosy lips, tender hands, dainty fingers and, of course, sparkling eyes (not, as some are wont to suggest, sparkling thighs). With its seductive lilting melody, and not excessive demands on the singer, it is a favourite piece for tenors. The only people for whom the song is emphatically not popular are accompanists, since the song is in the unappetising key of G flat and consequently a key signature of 6 flats. Although, as has been stated, the song is not especially difficult, the coda requires the singer to hit a very exposed top A flat on the awkward word "can." If the inexperienced singer does not hit this correctly or with sufficient support, the voice may crack at the crucial moment, resulting in mortification for the singer, a sad sigh from his singing teacher, and a gleeful grin in the wings from the other cast member who unsuccessfully applied for the part. The satisfaction of the latter will be all the more complete if instead of Marco he was given the part of the gondolier Francesco, carrying no more than twelve words of solo, and even worse, a pairing-off with one of the other minor lead sopranos whose armpits exude the aromatic appeal of a gents' lavatory in The Road To Mandalay following the town rugby team's curry night.

As soon as the solo is over and the applause has died down, the girls hurry on to the stage, announcing in chorus "Here we are, at the risk of our lives." Led by Fiametta and Victoria, who have brief solos, they explain that they are missing their menfolk so much that they have come to Barataria to join them. Tessa and Gianetta are joyously reunited with Giuseppe and Marco, and the two principal girls then begin a breathless musical interrogation of their husbands concerning their new lives – "Does your human being inner

194

feed on everything that nice is? Do they give you wine for dinner, peaches, sugar-plums and ices?" Without giving the men a chance to respond, all the girls sing "Tell us, tell us all about it!" Even after the singing has stopped, Tessa continues in dialogue by explaining that it was their longing for their husbands, and fears about how they were looking after themselves, that has prompted them to cross the seas. However, Giuseppe has to inform them, in response to the girls' questioning, that it is still not known which of the men is king. That uncertainty does not temper the girls' enthusiasm over Giuseppe's suggestion that their arrival should be marked by a banquet and a dance. Without further ado, the assembled company embark upon the most celebrated singing-and-dancing number in the opera, popularly known as the Cachucha but in reality, as set out in its opening line of song, an invitation to make merry and "Dance a cachucha, fandango, bolero!" It is unlikely that even the most ambitious producer will actually ask his cast to do this; indeed some producers will take the sensible decision to limit to the bare minimum the amount of dancing that the company should have to learn, and engage a troupe of specialist dancers to do the job properly. The more agile chorus member may be disappointed at such a decision, but the performer, particularly in the male chorus, who is not gifted with such a degree of rhythmic vitality will be only too delighted. This is partly because his responsibilities will thereby be limited to such innocuous activities as clapping to the music and shouting "*Ole!*" at irregular intervals, which even the most uncoordinated performer can probably manage, and partly because he can enjoy drooling lustfully at what may, in contrast to the ageing society membership, be a young and extremely attractive dance team. Of course it is unlikely that his feelings will be reciprocated, and in any event the girls in question will regard their performance as merely a prelude to more fulfilling activity at the Juice Factory in Curzon Road, where their serious drinking and dancing will begin long after their stage admirer has repaired to his sleeping quarters with the *Readers' Digest* and two chocolate Hobnobs.

It is Don Alhambra who breaks up the party; his appearance causes the chorus to hurry off, leaving only Marco, Giuseppe and a drummer boy on stage. Don Alhambra wastes no time in dismissing the drummer boy, then in dialogue asks the joint rulers what is going on. He seems unimpressed that a footman has been seen dancing, and no less perturbed when informed that the footman has been elevated to the level of Lord High Footman and the drummer boy to the rank of Lord High Drummer Boy! Don Alhambra, having declined Giuseppe's offer of light refreshment, explains that in each court there are distinctions that must be observed, and such distinguished personages as the Lord High Chancellor should not be cavorting with the cook or be forced to "tuck in his tuppenny" (which apparently means "tuck in his head") other than by someone of his own rank. In his ensuing solo, with interjections from the two monarchs ("There lived a king"), Don Alhambra then tells the story of a fictional state where the elevation of even the lowest to positions of wealth meant that a premium was put on things of no value at all. His assertion that "when everyone is somebody, then no one's anybody" is Gilbert's final and perhaps most obvious tilt at the absurdities of egalitarianism. The song shows Sullivan at his subtle best, providing a snatch of hornpipe to accompany the words "With Admirals all round his wide dominions." It is during the dialogue after this song that Don Alhambra chooses to drop the bombshell, as he tells Marco and Guiseppe that whichever is the true king has been married in infancy and is thus an unintentional bigamist. Tessa and Gianetta have during this dialogue crept on to the stage, unobserved, and hear this for themselves. Not surprisingly, they are aghast, and burst into tears, curtly rebuffing the attempts of the ex-gondoliers to comfort them. Fortunately, it seems, they will not have much longer to wait to find who is the lucky – or unlucky – gondolier, since the true king's former nurse and foster-mother with the all-important information has arrived and is in the torture chamber. When Giuseppe expresses concern, Don Alhambra reassures him that "she has all the illustrated papers." Imaginative producers may however substitute something more topical at this point, thus allowing contemporary royal nurses to be engaged in anything from e-mailing concerned relatives to answering ads in the *Barataria Herald* lonely-hearts column using Don Alhambra's mobile telephone.

After Don Alhambra has gone, the two couples appraise the situation grimly; there are indeed problems of dividing three wives into two husbands, or two-thirds of a husband to each wife. This leads on to one of the most remarkable quartets in the operas ("In a contemplative fashion") in which each takes it in turns to make their own personal observations on the difficulties they are in, while the other three sing of the need to exercise "quiet calm deliberation." As the song continues, the individual protestations get more animated, until all four become embroiled in argument. Although each sings entirely different material and words at the same time, there needs to be absolute control and strictness of timing. The "punchline" is at the end, where all four, having become more and more passionate during the song, round it off by singing in perfect unison, "Quiet calm deliberation disentangles every knot." There is a pregnant pause before this final unison section, which the musical director may wish to make as long as he can get away with. He should however recognise that the spell may be shattered by boisterous handclapping from the wife of the chairman of the town's chamber of commerce, who has awoken from her Row C seat 8 reverie and, believing the song has ended, is only too keen to lead the applause as if in the belief that this will encourage the cast to apply themselves with renewed vigour to that remaining part of the show that separates her from her vodka and tonic.

The four singers leave the stage – which Marco and Giuseppe have occupied since Act 2 began – and the male chorus take their place to announce, in song ("With ducal pomp and ducal pride"), the arrival of the Duke, the Duchess and Casilda. Having been acclaimed in suitably majestic terms, the trio duly make their appearance. The Duke graciously acknowledges the courtiers before they once again reiterate their words of welcome, then when (in dialogue) he requests an audience with the king of Barataria, the courtiers exit. Unlike in Act 1, the ducal party are all dressed magnificently. It also appears that the Duke has formed himself into a limited company, and he may raise a laugh by announcing himself, not as the Duke of Plaza-Toro, Limited, but the Duke of Plaza-Toro P.L.C.!

Casilda points out that she is still uncertain who her husband really is. Although the Duke tries to reassure her that the king's (and therefore her husband's) true identity will in due course be revealed, she confesses that she will never be able to love him, whoever he may be. The Duke suggests that it is possible, with mental effort, to love even the least attractive of people, and the Duchess immediately remarks that her love for her husband is a prime example! Having acidly told Casilda "I *loved* your father" which the Duke not unnaturally finds upsetting, she then proceeds to sing a solo with a distinctly martial flavour ("On the day when I was wedded") in which she implies that in order to win her husband and achieve the rank of Duchess she had to tame his fierily tyrannical personality. The audience are not, of course, supposed to believe a word of it; whilst almost every word uttered by the Duchess suggests she is an arrogant, domineering dragon, the Duke presents as meek, submissive and ineffectual. At least one commentator has likened him to Ko-Ko in *The Mikado* in this respect, and it may well be appropriate for a slight, short man to play the part. The Duke may, however, have the last laugh as the Duchess reaches the end of her song. The score gives the soloist the option of finishing either on the F just above middle C, which is comfortably within the contralto range, or the F an octave above that, which is high even for a soprano. Many singers will try and finish the song with a blaze of glory by opting for that top note. Whilst some will hit it impeccably, others will fail miserably, their desire to attempt it being motivated either by pure stubbornness or a morbid fascination for seeing just how many people in Rows E to G seats 14 to 22 would be showered with glass fragments were the Town Hall chandelier to shatter as a result.

When the solo has finished and dialogue recommences, Casilda, whose thoughts have clearly been elsewhere, expresses the hope that her future husband will try and cancel the wedding contract on the basis of her somewhat disreputable background. The Duke is shocked at this suggestion; he reminds his daughter just how sought-after he is, and that as a result he has profited handsomely. In a recitative ("To help unhappy commoners") and duet with the Duchess ("Small titles and orders") he explains how he has achieved this. Essentially, he and his wife have cashed in on middle-class snobbery – recognised by Gilbert as a prevalent trait in the Victorian age, and an obvious target for his satire – by offering their exalted names as endorsements to a wide range of bourgeois business ventures. After they have finished singing, Marco and Giuseppe arrive and present themselves to him; it is the very first time in the opera – with just three musical numbers to go – that the principal gondoliers and the ducal party have shared the stage. After a rather awkward greeting ceremony, in which the joint kings seem unsure how to welcome their guests, a conversation ensues in which the Duke has some fatherly words intended for his future son-in-law – whoever he may be! He goes on to protest at the paucity of ceremony with which his arrival in Barataria was marked. Marco and Giuseppe explain that their off-handed subjects would not tolerate such things as guards of honour and triumphal arches. The Duke is unimpressed with this, and points out that each, as a possible king, should impress the court with their importance, and put on suitable airs and graces. Assisted by his wife and daughter, he goes on to demonstrate this in a quintet ("I am a courtier grave and serious") which is essentially a lesson in royal deportment. Marco and Giuseppe struggle with his instructions at first, but by the end of the song have become so skilled that they are able to join in a gavotte and demonstrate their new-found gracefulness. Whilst it is delightful entertainment, it adds nothing to the plot, and after the not inconsiderable demands of them earlier in the opera, the characters playing the parts of Marco or Guiseppe may consider the necessity to learn a gavotte to be something of an imposition. However, they may not have far to turn for assistance. For every young performer in an amateur G & S society (young in this context meaning under 40) who takes on a demanding role of this nature for the first time, there is likely to be at least one older member, almost invariably female, and nothing to do with the production team, who may – unprompted by the producer – want to assume the role of "taker-in-hand." She will sidle up to her intended victim as the show week nears, and begin with the dreaded words "I think you're doing extremely well and I don't want you to take what I have to say the wrong way" before damning every aspect of his performance in a manner that would stun even Dorothy Parker into a mortified silence. Several earnest conversations, four rounds of drinks in the Crown & Cushion, and three evening tuition sessions in her suburban bungalow later, his confidence in his performing ability will be back at the same level as it was when after eight years of marriage his wife suddenly announced that as far as their love life was concerned she was more aroused by the teatime shipping forecast.

The Duke and Duchess exit, leaving Marco and Giuseppe with Casilda, and the awkward task of telling her that her husband, whoever he is, is in a bigamous relationship. Casilda interrupts their feeble attempts to break the news gently by telling them that she is "over head and ears" in love with another – a somewhat dated expression which may be discreetly amended to "head over heels" by the performer if not the producer. Gianetta and Tessa enter, and Giuseppe, who sees no point in prevaricating any longer, informs Casilda that they are the wives of the joint monarchs. A quintet follows in which all the singers reflect on the awkwardness of the situation ("Here is a case unprecedented") and this leads straight into the finale. Spurred by Don Alhambra's musical invitation to "now let the loyal lieges gather round" the full company enter. The assembly includes Inez, the prince's former nurse and foster-mother, who is now in a position to disclose the identity of the rightful king. The chorus, led by the principals, urge her "Speak, woman, speak!" In response, she informs the listeners that in order to prevent the prince being snatched away in infancy, she swapped her own son for the prince; her son was therefore conveyed to Venice, and it is in fact Luiz who is the rightful king of Barataria! Immediately she finishes speaking, Luiz ascends the throne and is crowned. There is joy for Casilda as she embraces the man she loves; for Marco and Giuseppe and their wives, there is sadness that there is no royal blood amongst them after all, but joy in the discovery that the men are not bigamists after all and that they can be reunited with their partners and presumably return with them to Venice. Luiz remarks that "while others claimed thy dainty hand, I waited – waited – waited" to which the Duke adds "as prudence (so I understand) dictated – tated – tated." It is the first time that listeners are made aware that Prudence, whoever she may be, has been responsible for the prolonging of the suspense and thereby the action; well may she cower before Mr Crump the janitor, who is standing sullenly at the back of the hall looking meaningfully at his watch.

To a fanfare and acclaim from the assembled company, Luiz crowns Casilda and the finale ends with an ensemble musical reprise of the gondoliers' Act 1 duet ("Once more *gondolieri*") and the Cachucha during which the company state that "We leave you with feelings of pleasure." Amidst this joyful and typically Gilbertian resolution of the plot – it is of course far from the first heavily-contrived ending in the operas – neither

Marco nor Giuseppe appear interested to discover which has the honour of having Inez for a mother. In any event it is likely that they will be far too preoccupied with the task of peeling their regal garments from their persons and stocking up the cool box of their Venice-bound boat with sufficient supplies of ready-cooked pizzas and frozen portions of *dolce far niente*.

If a layman is ever asked to cite a setback in the fortunes of the Gilbert and Sullivan partnership, then assuming he has a fair grounding in G & S history, and the question is not asked during chucking-out time at the Coach & Horses, he is more than likely to refer to the Carpet Quarrel. Put simply, Gilbert was outraged to find that, unbeknown to him, a very considerable sum of the partners' money had been spent on new carpets as part of a big bill for preliminary expenses for *The Gondoliers*. As a result of the consequent rift with Richard D'Oyly Carte, he and Sullivan stopped collaborating altogether. It was only through pressure from Carte that composer and librettist came together again. In January 1893, after three whole years without a new G & S opera, Sullivan invited Gilbert to Roqueburn, near Monte Carlo. Here Gilbert read him the sketch plot of *Utopia Limited* (the word *Limited* was initially bracketed but the brackets were subsequently dropped). Sullivan liked it, and agreement was reached in April 1893 for work to begin on what would be their thirteenth collaboration. Sullivan worked slowly, varying his labours with, among other things, attendance at race meetings, boating, and rides on his tricycle! As with many of the other G & S operas, progress towards opening night was not always smooth. In its uncut form, the first Act lasted an hour and three quarters, and some trimming had to be done. Gilbert was not always at ease with the libretto, and actually had to ask Sullivan to compose the music to the Act 2 finale before he fitted the words to it. A severe attack of gout meant that the librettist had to direct many rehearsals on crutches or in a wheelchair; at one point he admitted that he had been "unable to do anything but swear for the last eighteen days." Sullivan objected to Gilbert's portrayal of yet another ageing contralto in love, and Gilbert was forced to change her character so that she was, in Audrey Williamson's words, "more pursued...than pursuing." On one occasion the lady playing this particular character had to go to the dentist, and this affected her speech; when an actor playing alongside her fluffed a line, Gilbert was heard to remark "I wish those two would change teeth and try again."

After four G & S operas in which there was little emphasis on social satire, in *Utopia Limited* it returned with a vengeance. The opera is a tilt at almost every aspect of Victorian England, and in particular her business methods, her party system, the Royal household, the armed services, the law, the theatre, and courtship. The opera opened on 7th October 1893, and with the two partners coming on stage at the end of the evening to take a bow together, Leslie Baily remarks that "it was just like the grand old days." Gilbert had taken what was an unprecedented step in the history of G & S opera by inviting the Press to the dress rehearsal. As though in gratitude for this concession, many of the notices were very favourable. *The Times* ranked it above *The Gondoliers*. George Bernard Shaw, no less, wrote a most complimentary article in the *Saturday Review*, stating that he "enjoyed the score of *Utopia* more than that of any of the previous Savoy operas." Not all the reviewers were so kind; the *Pall Mall Gazette* called it a "mirthless travesty of the work with which Gilbert's name is most genuinely associated." More recent commentators have felt that Gilbert was trying to be too clever; Geoffrey Smith desribes the libretto as "hectic and diffuse" and other critics suggest that Gilbert simply lost control of his material and overreached himself. Another problem was that the lady playing the lead soprano, Nancy McIntosh, had been adopted by Gilbert as his daughter, and many felt that Gilbert, in his desire to give her plenty to do, upset the balance of the piece. It was not only the book which came in for criticism; some reviewers also felt that Sullivan's music, perhaps starved of inspiration by the poor libretto, was below his usual standard. Despite the immense amount of money that was invested in the production – over £7000 – the initial run consisted of just 245 performances, less than half that for *The Gondoliers*. In the States it flopped completely, running for just 55 performances. It was not professionally revived in England until 1975. Rupert D'Oyly Carte considered a revival in the 1920's but abandoned the idea. Leslie Baily points out that "it requires at least five first-rate comedians, all of them good comic actors, really good singers and accomplished dancers. It demands a brilliant soprano and a fine tenor and baritone. Even the smaller parts are more than usually exacting." These words of warning have not stopped some amateur societies giving the show an airing. A large and flourishing amateur society, with a loyal following in the local community, a reputation for doing good G & S, healthy competition for principal parts, a bank balance sizeable enough to withstand the inevitably disappointing box office returns, and a highly-skilled producer with a well-sharpened blue pencil ready to delete large chunks of indigestible libretto, will proceed with little difficulty. The enthusiastic hard-working society, although perhaps lacking depth in talent, might just get away with it on the basis that next year's production of *The Mikado* will recoup any losses. An operatic society lacking both talent and commitment, but motivated merely by a desire to give the membership the chance to boast that they have sung in all the G & S operas, may not be so fortunate. Indeed the unfavourable reaction of the audience to the pages of uncut libretto, the unsuccessful attempts at imitating Christy Minstrels, and the way in which uniformed guardsmen are forced through manpower shortage to become reincarnated as lawyers and company promoters, may be such that it would be foolish to pin too much hope on good houses for *The Mikado* for loss recoupment and more prudent to devise a rigorous programme of weekly raffles, monthly car-boot sales and quarterly sponsored parachute jumps.

The plot of *Utopia Limited* is barely a plot at all; the show has been likened to a revue. The opera is set on the South Sea Island of Utopia, the monarch of which is King Paramount (baritone), assisted by Calynx his Vice-Chamberlain (baritone). The King is constantly under surveillance from the Wise Men Scaphio (baritone) and Phantis (bass), and the Public Exploder Tarara (baritone). The monarch has decided that Utopia should be modelled along English lines. His eldest daughter Zara (soprano) returns from Girton College, Cambridge, bringing with her a number of representatives of British institutions – the soldier Captain Fitzbattleaxe (tenor), the company promoter Mr Goldbury (tenor), the lawyer Sir Bailey Barre (baritone), the Lord Chamberlain Lord Dramaleigh (tenor), and the county councillor Mr Blushington (tenor). These are collectively known as the Flowers of Progress, which is also the alternative title of the opera. It is decided that the island shall be floated as a Limited Company, and, in the second Act, other Anglicisations occur which delight the King, not to mention his younger daughters Nekaya (soprano) and Kalyba (mezzo-soprano) but enrage the Wise Men and Public Exploder. Finally they orchestrate a rebellion against the dull perfection. Zara saves the situation by advocating government by party, which she knows will cause a drift to chaos but plenty of work and therefore prosperity for the professionals. Thus everyone is happy, not least the King, who is successful in wooing his younger daughters' English governess Lady Sophy (contralto).

The opera opens in a Utopian palm grove in the gardens of King Paramount's palace where a number of maidens, including Phylla, Melene and Salata (all sopranos), are discovered. They reflect on their lazy and idyllic state in the opening chorus with solo from Phylla ("In lazy langour motionless"). Following this opening number, the Utopian Vice-Chamberlain Calynx enters and excitedly says to the girls that the King's daughter, Princess Zara, is on her way home from Girton in England. He confirms that with her new-found knowledge she will assist in the process of Anglicisation of Utopia. While Salata is enthusiastic, Melene points out that the maidens are quite well as they are. Calynx asks the maidens to reflect on how much better their conversation would be if, as in England, everyone thought for themselves rather than having their minds made up by the journals, as in Utopia! At this point Tarara (originally known as Tarara Boomdeay after the popular song) enters, uttering furious Utopian language. He explains (in English) that he is angry because as Public Exploder he is under a duty to blow up the King if informed by two Wise Men of any indiscretions on the King's part; and although he has become aware, through a leaked copy of a generally unavailable "Society" paper known as the *Palace Peeper*, that the King is guilty of a number of indiscretions, he can do nothing, because the Wise Men refuse to denounce the King and even appear to condone his behaviour! In his anger he produces two explosive crackers which Calynx pulls. It would perhaps be prudent to guard against the possibility of the failure of the crackers to produce the desired report. The presence of a starting pistol or inflated paper bag in the wings may act as an adequate insurance policy. If the society's budget or depth of forethought will not stretch to this, there is the perennial standby of the frustrated pyrotechnical operator on stage, to wit the exclamation of the word BANG in suitably stentorian tones.

To suitable music, a guard enters, escorting the Wise Men, named Scaphio and Phantis. The chorus of guards and maidens welcome them and eulogise about them in chorus ("Oh, make way for the Wise Men!"). Following this welcome, Scaphio and Phantis sing a very catchy duet ("In every mental lore") in which they introduce themselves and explain that their function is to spy on the King and make sure he "minds his P's and Q's and keeps himself respectable." The chorus repeat their greeting to the Wise Men, then exit, leaving Scaphio and Phantis alone on stage. In the ensuing dialogue Phantis confides in Scaphio of his great love for Princess Zara, and is overjoyed when Scaphio agrees to assist him in his wooing. In another lively duet ("Let all your doubts take wing") Scaphio confirms his willingness to help Phantis, who in turn rejoices that his wooing must surely now be guaranteed to succeed. Both singers are directed to dance alone during the duet; this will require some expert choreography and not a little rehearsal, but, if well thought out, it will give the singers the chance to demonstrate their footwork as well as the opportunity to kick into touch any stray toilet-roll cylinders and other remnants from Tarara's explosive crackers.

The Wise Men exit and the full chorus of guards, nobles and maidens appear, this time accompanying the King. In a brief chorus ("Quaff the nectar") they express their contentment under his rule. The King then sings a solo, with chorus ("A King of autocratic power we"), in which he boasts of his tyrannic will and awesome presence, but he states – and the chorus agree – that this does not interfere greatly with the happiness of his subjects. A recitative section follows for the King and chorus; the King confirms that, with the approval of his people, Utopia will from now on be modelled on Great Britain "to which some add – but others do not – Ireland" – these last words then prompting a brief Irish jig from the orchestra! As the recitative continues, the King states that it has been arranged that his two younger daughters, duly coached by a gracious English lady, will exhibit themselves in public. The twin daughters, Nekaya and Kalyba, then appear; these girls, aged about fifteen, are described in a short choral section as "How fair! How modest! How discreet! How bashfully demure!" There follows a duet for the twins ("Although of native maids the cream") in which they describe themselves as "demurely coy, divinely cold." They also liken themselves to clockwork toys, and invite onlookers to observe them so they may see "what good young ladies ought to be." At the end of their duet, Lady Sophy, their governess, appears. She is described as being of mature years with extreme gravity of demeanour and dress. But for Sullivan's insistence, she might have become yet another ageing lovesick contralto. As it is, a rather different character emerges, with characteristics that are sufficiently attractive to excite the King's admiration. After a brief recitative ("This morning we propose") she gives the spectators a musical course in maiden courtship ("Bold-faced ranger"). Whilst she sings, the two Princesses illustrate her description in gesture, and the chorus echo the last few lines of each verse. The song is an obvious tilt at the absurdly stiff formalities and traditions of courtship in Victorian England; at the end there is even the suggestion that two girls in love with the same man would toss a coin to decide who should accept him! There is little for the chorus to do through the lengthy verses, each identical in musical content, other than echo the words of Lady Sophy. Responsible chorus members will do their best to please the producer by alternately listening intently to Lady Sophy's wise words, and exchanging knowing nods, smiles and whispers with their neighbours towards the back of the stage. The less responsible trouper, whose supply of knowing nods, smiles and whispers begins to run out after six full runthroughs of the number within a single rehearsal, may find his train of thought moving to rather weightier issues such as the origin of mankind, the possibility of life after death, or whether it is more economical to drive 2 miles to Tesco or walk to the all-night grocery to replenish his depleted supplies of semi-skimmed milk.

After her recitative that promises a repeat of the lecture in 10 minutes' time, Lady Sophy exits with the twins, and all but the King exit as well, rejoicing (in a musical reprise of "Quaff the nectar") at the rosy future that awaits young girls who follow Lady Sophy's advice. Scaphio and Phantis enter, as bidden by the King, and dialogue commences. The King produces a copy of the *Palace Peeper* and reflects on the humour of the fact that all the damning articles that are written about him have been contributed by himself, at the command of the Wise Men. However, he is less happy about the celebrated English tenor, a Mr Wilkinson, burlesquing his personal appearance, and giving what Phantis describes as "grotesque imitations of (the King's) Royal peculiarities." When the King states that he fails to see the humour in this, Scaphio explains that the humour lies in the fact that by day thousands tremble before their monarch, only for them to laugh at him by night. The King is won round, sees the humour in the situation, and philosophically reflects that in reality all life is a farce. To illustrate this he sings a solo, with refrain for the Wise Men ("First you're born"), in which he takes the listener through life – from birth through to courtship, married life, child-rearing, payment of bills, and death – and sings of the absurdities inherent in each stage. The tune is jolly and lively, but by contrast with the similarly philosophical "Try we life-long" in *The Gondoliers*, the King's song has a note of irony and despair. Scaphio and Phantis exit after the song, and the King soliloquises on the damage that might be done if Lady Sophy were to see the *Palace Peeper*. He points out that it is necessary for him to buy every copy himself! It is thus to his chagrin that a moment later Lady Sophy enters and tells him that Tarara has shown his leaked copy to her. She puts to him some of the allegations contained within it, which he strenuously denies. Not only does he refute them but states that he is in constant communication with the Mikado of Japan with a view to devising a suitable punishment for the scandalmonger responsible. A duet follows ("Subjected to your heavenly gaze") in which Lady Sophy challenges the King to deal with the culprit, if the allegations are false; the King however refuses, even though he knows he will thereby remain unacceptable to her, and both exit with the issue still unresolved. Desperate for some sort of gimmickry which might make the show more appealing or accessible, some imaginative societies may name the programme for *Utopia Limited* the *Palace Peeper*; it might also serve as a good title for a G & S society's newsletter. It is sad to think that often these lovingly-prepared documents will be condemned to sit unread inside the back cover of hired scores, only to be discovered by the society's librarian some months later along with a subscription reminder, a scrawled invitation to Denise and Phil's summer barbie, an assortment of unopened Christmas cards, and the running order for last October's concert at St Augustine's to raise funds for a member's daughter's sponsored bicycle ride around the entire coastline of Madagascar.

A fanfare and march signal the arrival of Princess Zara, accompanied by Captain Fitzbattleaxe and four troopers, all in the full uniform of the first Life Guards. The full chorus enter, and an impressive musical section begins, the girls greeting Zara in chorus ("Oh, maiden rich in Girton lore") and inviting her to shed her learning on them. In recitative Zara introduces herself and acknowledges the troopers who with Fitzbattleaxe have taken care of her on her long journey. To suitably martial music, they in turn then introduce themselves as smart, well-drilled and courageous, defying the elements in tight tunics and hot helmets. Then, whilst the chorus sing in admiration of them, Zara and Fitzbattleaxe sing of their great affection for each other. It is quite appropriate that the troopers should sing of their "helmet hot" and "tunic tight" for it is an occupational hazard for those cast in certain G & S roles to have to wear costumes that are so uncomfortable as to render it virtually impossible to give a perfect performance. The donning of costumes is a significant milestone as the show nears; many will relish the excitement of trying on period clothing, and the opportunity, at last, to get fully into the character being portrayed. Their skill with needle and thread, their adeptness at always finding the best-fitting garments, and their assertiveness with the wardrobe staff will always ensure that they embark on a production with total confidence in the material that clothes them. For the less fortunate, the experience will be a thoroughly unpleasant one. He (or she) will inevitably find that a piece of costume is missing, and is forced to place his reliance on the wardrobe mistress' assurance that "I'll see what I can find." Those items that are available will not fit properly, and when tried on will either split, necessitating further attention from the W.M., or cause so much humiliating hilarity amongst fellow cast members that the wearer's sole preoccupation is the desire to revert to his T-shirt and jeans as soon as possible. He will discover that, of all the cast, he has the most accessories to remember to put on, from tights, braces and buckles to jabot, wing collar, waistcoat and cummerbund, so that he ends up feeling less like an amateur actor than a Christmas tree. Anything that is left in the dressing room overnight will, of course, disappear, to be discovered five minutes before curtain-up either stuck behind a radiator or attached to another cast member. At last, after a lengthy session with the W.M., the unlucky thespian will tentatively proceed to the stage for the dress rehearsal, terrified that any sudden movement will cause any one of the various fixtures and fittings to dislodge themselves and collapse about his person. At the very end of the evening, at some time after midnight, the producer will release the cast and almost by way of afterthought turn to the performer in question and publicly say "Your costume looks awful. You can't go on like that." The performer will slink miserably away, the assertion by the W.M. that "I think I might have something else that may fit you" as reassuring as the money-back guarantees offered by Honest Pete's Car Mart in Shady Lane.

The King appears with the twins and Lady Sophy, and dialogue begins. Zara embraces her father and her two sisters, and presents Fitzbattleaxe who immediately impresses the King with his politeness. Meanwhile the troopers are being much admired by the young ladies. Lady Sophy, scandalised by this, marches the twins off, and the King too expresses his concern; in what is a clearly deeply ironical reference to the morality of the armed services, he refers to their "puritanical British sensitiveness." In another splendidly martial ensemble number ("Ah! gallant soldier, brave and true") the troopers once more acclaim Zara, and she and Fitzbattleaxe bid each other an emotional and loving farewell. All exit, the King and Zara in one direction, the others in the opposite direction, and the Wise Men return. Scaphio is under the influence of strong emotion, and in his conversation with Phantis makes it clear that he himself is now in love with Zara, whose exit the two of them have just witnessed. At the same time he expresses anger that Phantis will not reciprocate the emotional support that he (Scaphio) promised to Phantis earlier. Fitzbattleaxe and Zara enter, and they learn of the rivalry of the two Wise Men for her hand. Fitzbattleaxe suggests that an English law, the Rival Admirers' Clauses Consolidation Act, be applied whereby a cavalry officer (i.e. himself) will look after her until it has been decided – presumably by a duel to the death – which of the rivals will have her. Zara is not surprisingly happy to cooperate. In an animated quartet ("It's understood, I think, all round") the two rivals accept Fitzbattleaxe's proposal; the guardsman and Princess realise that since the rivals are both cowards, and will not take the risk of losing their lives, they will never reach a decision and Zara is thus safe from both. The Wise Men exit, leaving Zara and Fitzbattleaxe to sing a passionate love duet ("Oh admirable art!"). The only thing which, according to Zara, stands between the lovers is Fitzbattleaxe's bright breastplate, although even this need not necessarily pose a problem if the breastplate in question has been manufactured not from unyielding metal but from silver-painted malleable card that would be pushed to offer protection from the impact of a ping-pong ball let alone two rounds of buckshot. It is likely to pose more of a problem if it has worked loose from the fitting hastily applied by an overworked W.M. and is protruding outwards to such an extent that the hapless Fitzbattleaxe resembles not so much a dashing guardsman as the champion of the Pie-Eating contest organised by the Three Crowns Pudding Club.

Fitzbattleaxe exits, and the King enters. During the dialogue that follows, Zara produces a copy of the *Palace Peeper* which Lady Sophy has given to her. Like Lady Sophy, she is most indignant at its content. The King confesses to her that he is totally under the control of the Wise Men, and he knows they will denounce him to the Public Exploder if he objects to his situation. Zara has other ideas; she informs the King that she has brought from England six representatives of English life (the so-called Flowers of Progress) who she says will reorganise Utopia in such a way that will enable him to defy his persecutors. The King is happy to agree, and he summons Calynx who in turn is sent to summon the Court. All then enter save for the

Flowers of Progress. Massed entries are always difficult for a producer to manage. At rehearsal in the church hall, the cast can simply bunch up at either end of the room and then hurry excitedly into the centre with no apparent obstructions. By contrast, the first rehearsal on the stage itself, with scenery, will find the progress of some chorus members obstructed by stage flats or by an irate stage manager who is still finishing off the set construction. As a result, tardiness in arrival on stage is virtually guaranteed. Anyone in the cast with a predisposition towards gambling may choose to have a flutter on how many times they enter the stage only for the producer to send them off with instructions to do it all over again. The likelihood of fitting in a swift pint at the Goat & Compasses will recede even further when any instruction to repeat the exercise is followed by an explosion of questions from various individuals as to where, when and how they should personally come on stage. Those whose drinking money has in any case been squandered on a losing bet will have to wait for the first night and count on reclaiming the money by wagering that second bass Arthur Plumtree will make at least two stage appearances with his spectacles still firmly wrapped round his ears.

The entry of the chorus signals the start of the Act 1 finale, with no more spoken dialogue for the remainder of the Act. The finale begins with a choral section ("Although your royal summons to appear") in which the subjects ask their monarch why they are wanted. The King briefly explains what Zara has done, and Zara then calls for attention, addressing the Utopians as "viviparians." (No such word appears to exist in the OED; presumably it is a Gilbertian invention arising from the word "viviparous," meaning "bringing forth young in a live state.") The Flowers of Progress then enter; presented by Zara, they introduce themselves in turn and are acclaimed by the chorus. First there is the gallant soldier Fitzbattleaxe, who is the embodiment of the perfect military machine. Then comes Sir Bailey Barre, Q.C., M.P., who is a master of logic, arithmetic and philology, and who has a flair for confounding the simple meaning of a word; Lord Dramaleigh, a Lord High Chamberlain, who guards the moral cleanliness of the Court, and censors plays before they are allowed to be performed; Mr Blushington, a County Councillor with responsibility for the upkeep of streets and squares and the sanitation of houses; Mr Goldbury, a company promoter, traditionally dressed in loud checks and with more than a touch of Jewishness about him, who extols the virtues of what he calls "companification;" and lastly an old friend from *H.M.S. Pinafore*, Captain Corcoran (now K.C.B.) who boasts of the British dominance of the seas and the fact that the Navy never run a ship ashore. This whole sequence shows Gilbert at his most acid, as he attacked the ways in which the leaders and administrators of the time were deluding themselves. Whilst the Victorians *liked* to believe that their Royal family and armed forces were above reproach, their streets spotless, their laws applied fairly and impartially, and their criteria for censorship not abused, the shrewder observers of the age knew that the reality was very different. Corcoran's song "never run a ship ashore" leads into the "What, never? Well, hardly ever" exchange that had been so popular in *H.M.S. Pinafore*, and reminded the listeners of a recent incident involving the British Navy in which a ship had indeed been run ashore! If in addition the producer inserts some suitably nautical movements for the cast at this point, be it some smart saluting or a brisk hornpipe, the delighted audience may momentarily forgive the excessive length of this first Act. Because the opera is performed so rarely, and the great majority of its material so unfamiliar, even a society which executes it with consummate professionalism will be somewhat apprehensive as to the reaction of the paying customers. Of course, the apprehension will be nothing compared with what it was for Gilbert on first performance of one of his operas. He stated he had an "effective method of dealing with first nights which I can strongly recommend. As the curtain rises on Act 1, I leave the theatre and do not return until 11.15. I usually spend the interval at some other theatre, if possible – where there is a dull and highly unoriginal comedy with plenty of platitudian dialogue and a violent plot."

Now that the six Flowers have been presented, they are invited by the King, Zara and Lady Sophy to give instruction in legislation. Each of the Flowers offers initial suggestions, of which Mr Goldbury's is perhaps the most revolutionary; he suggests that Utopia be floated as a Limited Company. Everyone reacts quizzically to this, especially Scaphio, Phantis and Tarara who growl "What does this mean?"as they have been doing at irregular intervals during the finale. In a wordy but jaunty song ("Some seven men form an Association") Mr Goldbury then explains how promoters go about establishing a company. They begin, he asserts, by putting up a sum which may be as big or as little as they wish; if their enterprise is successful, their profits are unlimited, but if it fails, their loss is restricted to the amounts they have put up. Moreover, promoters of a failed company can file a winding-up petition and establish a new company at once. Mr Goldbury's words did reflect the legal position of companies in England, which Gilbert regarded as monstrously unfair. Nonetheless, in the ensuing recitative the King expresses satisfaction with it, stating that "if it's good enough for virtuous England, it's good enough for us." Not heeding the objections of Scaphio and Phantis, he decides that Utopia itself will become a Limited Company. The recitative gives way to a vigorous ensemble number, begun by the King ("Henceforward of a verity") and although the Wise Men threaten terrible

211

reprisals if he persists, the rest of the assembled company are delighted and fully support their King. The finale ends with a serenade to the Act under which Utopia will be registered as a Company – the Joint Stock Company's Act of Parliament, Sixty Two! The prosaic language of the chorus in this sequence contrasts with their frequent interjections of "Ulahlica!" during the finale, but since the programme is unlikely to contain a glossary of useful Utopian phrases, it will be for the audience to decide whether it is another word for "terrific" – which one assumes it is – or an attempt to boost sales of native laxative powder.

Act 2 is set in the Throne Room in the Palace by night. As the curtain opens, Fitzbattleaxe is discovered, singing to Zara. In a recitative ("Oh Zara, my beloved one") he confesses that the fervour of his love affects his voice, and then expands on this in his ensuing song ("A tenor, all singers above"). This is possibly the highlight of the opera, as Fitzbattleaxe demonstrates that distracted as he is by his devotion to Zara, he cannot hit a top note cleanly or execute a cadenza satisfactorily despite his awareness of what is needed for good voice production and technique. As a tilt at the precious, as well as pretentious amateur tenor, it has arguably never been bettered in the world of opera. If a small group of soloists are putting together a compilation programme with an item from each G & S opera, this is the ideal choice as far as *Utopia Limited* is concerned. Its one drawback, if sung out of context, is that the audience may not realise that the singer's fluffing of the high note or cadenza is deliberate rather than a reflection of his own incompetence. (Of course the singer may be incompetent anyway, but the audience will not need to know that.) If an audience member or fellow cast member does decide that the performer is incompetent, careful choice of words is essential if the performer is so foolish as to angle unsubtly for compliments and seek an opinion from the onlooker in question. Since a tactless "You were b***** awful" is unlikely to boost the singer's confidence, and the observer may feel uncomfortable about telling a lie, he can resort to a half-truth ("You looked as though you were enjoying it"), an evasion of the question ("I think the acoustics of this hall make it very difficult for even the best singers to be heard properly"), or the formula which Gilbert himself famously used on one occasion and which was totally truthful ("Good isn't the word!").

In the dialogue that follows, Zara reassures Fitzbattleaxe that since she has accepted him, he need not trouble himself, and furthermore vocal technique matters little in the scheme of things. She also assures him that "at Girton all is wheat, and idle chaff is never heard within its walls" which recalls the world of Castle Adamant in *Princess Ida*. They then discuss the benefits of the Anglicisation of Utopia – the remodelling of the armed services without interference from the Admiralty or Horse Guards, social reforms brought about without Parliamentary restriction, the application of the Limited Liability principle to every citizen of Utopia, and the adoption of the tasteful fashions of England amongst the common people. Again Gilbert was writing with his tongue in his cheek, knowing full well that none of these things had happened in England at all. Zara announces that she must leave Fitzbattleaxe in order to try on her dress for a "Drawing Room" reception, to be held that evening. Anguished that she is to leave him, Fitzbattleaxe passionately declares his love for her. Zara replies that the voice of true love is sweet and soft – a sentiment she declares, and Fitzbattleaxe adopts, in their second love duet, "Words of love too loudly spoken." After the duet Zara exits and the King appears, dressed as a Field-Marshal. A moment later the other five Flowers of Progress arrive for a meeting of the first statutory cabinet council of Utopia Limited. The luxurious setting of Act 2 of *Utopia Limited* perhaps goes some way towards explaining why the opera when first performed was so expensive to stage. In modern amateur productions, the necessarily opulent surroundings will pose a significant challenge to the set construction crew. A fortunate society will boast a team of dedicated, experienced workers, mingling creative and technical skill, briefed expertly by a producer who knows exactly what he wants and how much money is available to do it, and sufficiently organised and focussed to complete the job well within the allotted timescale. A less fortunate society will depend far more on the assistance of willing but inexperienced volunteers from among the membership. Consciences of members will be constantly pricked at rehearsals with such announcements as "If people don't help, we won't have a set and the show can't go on." Thus instead of their usual Sunday morning dates at the rugby club, at the leisure centre, in the church choir or in bed with the colour supplements, members will be found foregathering at the garage, hangar or farm outbuilding where set construction operations are in progress. Those with a fair degree of manual skill will quickly be put to work, but those whose willingness is not matched by their ability will spend most of the session standing impotently on the periphery of the action, engaging in jobs that do not need doing such as holding an object steady that is perfectly capable of standing on its own, or being given tasks that the taskgiver could do himself in less time than it takes to delegate them. Nonetheless the useless worker can reflect smugly that he at least made the effort to turn up, and when, at the end of the show, thanks are extended to "all who assisted in constructing the scenery" he can bask in the glory of knowing that he is included in this assembly of worthies even if his sole contribution was attending four Sundays ago, passing a nail up to the assistant stage manager and downing a tepid cupful of Bovril.

In a brief section of dialogue the King calls upon Dramaleigh to organise the council in such a way as to reflect the organisation of an English cabinet council. The Flowers, having been invited by Dramaleigh to bring their chairs forward, arrange them across the stage like Christy Minstrels. The original Christy Minstrels, who came together in 1843, consisted of a troupe of American musical entertainers with blackened faces. Other companies were later formed which also called themselves Christy Minstrels, and one of these companies performed at St James' Hall in London. They were known as experts in the art of buffoonery and were extremely popular in the late Victorian age. It is this particular entertainment which the King and the Flowers burlesque in the ensemble musical number that follows ("Society has quite forsaken all her wicked courses"). Appropriately enough, the introductory music was the tune of a negro plantation song. In early performances, each singer had a banjo or some other instrument to play, but if that is not feasible for an amateur society, some business involving the chairs may be equally acceptable. Not only is the song a skit on cabinet and court procedure (which could be seen as Gilbert's revenge for the exclusion of his name from the programme of the Royal Command Performance of *The Gondoliers* at Windsor) but the words to the song again show Gilbert at his most sarcastic. The King lists all the changes for the better in Utopia as a result of his country's Anglicisation, and the Flowers respond that all these things have happened, or will happen, in England – the absence of slummeries, the decline in the divorce rate, the proposal to abolish hunger, and the recognition of true literary merit – and of course they are wrong. The Flowers must be extremely careful in their enunciation of their chorus "We're going to abolish it in England;" failure to do so will lay them open to accusations of making a pledge which even the most perfectly governed country could not hope to honour.

This colourful scene immediately gives way to an even more splendid one, as the Drawing Room, a lavish and elaborate royal reception, is about to commence. Upon being told by Dramaleigh that his daughters are ready, the King requests them to enter. Then, to the accompaniment of a march from the orchestra, the whole royal household come in, followed by the King's three daughters and Lady Sophy. *Utopia Limited* is one of very few G & S operas where it is necessary for the ladies' chorus to change their identity, from grass-skirted Utopian maidens to ladies-in-waiting; the gentlemen of the chorus, who may have served with distinction as escorts for the Wise Men and also possibly acted as troopers, will have to re-enter in such guises as Master of the Horse and Master of the Buck-hounds. After they have entered, there is some brief dialogue in which Dramaleigh informs the King that he must embrace the debutantes (who have yet to enter). Lady Sophy is shocked, and the King realises that this will provide plenty more material for the *Palace Peeper*. To more orchestral accompaniment, the debutantes come in. As each lady comes forward to be presented to the King, Dramaleigh reads out her name. Much amusement will be generated both in rehearsals and performance by the use of suitably topical names from the world of fashion and popular culture. The King in a recitative ("This ceremonial our wish displays") states that his aim is to imitate the courtly ways of Great Britain, and this leads into a splendid unaccompanied chorus ("Eagle high in cloudland soaring"). This musical pledge to pursue excellence and cast fear aside, in order that "glory then will crown the day," is arguably the best-known chorus in the opera. After the chorus, everybody exits to suitably regal music from the orchestra. With its elaborate set, suitably extravagant costumes, large array of principals and chorus, and some intricate movement, this Drawing Room scene is one of the most demanding sections to rehearse and perfect in any of the G & S operas. Whilst the wise producer will not attempt to work on it without a reasonable number of personnel present, a less flexible director will decide that, come what may, the evening's work will commence at 7.30 with that scene. It may be that at 7.32, a mere one third of the cast have arrived, the others delayed by icy roads, a three car pile-up on the bypass, a thrilling finish to that night's *Emmerdale*, the need to get the coffee cups out and put the urn on, and the need to raise the temperature of the rehearsal hall above the nine degrees Celsius that is registering on the wall thermometer. Undeterred, the director may press ahead, calling out unsuspecting members of the chorus to fill in the more important roles. Thus it is that when Dramaleigh reads out "Miss Scary Spice" it is not a stunning-looking debutante of that name who will step forward, but 66-year-old Albert Potts whose ability to set the onlookers' pulses racing is about as great as that of the packet of stale Bourbon biscuits which the assistant secretary is withdrawing from her B & Q carrier bag.

After everyone has departed, Scaphio and Phantis appear dressed as judges. Having come down the stage melodramatically, they sing a duet ("With fury deep we burn") in which they proclaim themselves to be dissatisfied with the present state of affairs, and state it is time for the Flowers to return to England. The King enters at the end of the song, and dialogue ensues in which Scaphio and Phantis explain that, as a result of the Anglicisation, their own business interests have been totally undermined. The *Palace Peeper* has suffered because of the new libel laws, the burlesque theatre has failed to meet approval from the Lord Chamberlain, and debts are not paid because of the Limited Liability principle. The King refuses to do anything about it, but merely suggests that the grievances are placed in writing for consideration at

215

a future meeting. A trio follows ("If you think that when banded in unity"), incorporating musical material already heard in "Let all your doubts take wing." In it Scaphio and Phantis hint darkly at reprisals for the King and engage in a furious dance, but the King appears indifferent, indulging in a little dance of his own and claiming that "it means unruffled cheerfulness." He exits and the Wise Men are left fuming; in dialogue they remind each other that because the King too is a corporation, and no longer a human being, they cannot touch him. Providing he confines himself to his Articles of Association, their threats are empty. Tarara appears and the three of them agree that they will need to devise a plot of what Phantis calls "superhuman subtlety" to end the current state of affairs. An extraordinary trio follows ("With wily brain upon the spot"). It begins with staccato block harmony, which is followed by a succession of rapid exchanges between the singers to a playful orchestral accompaniment, including a series of whispered suggestions from Scaphio. The song ends with the trio confirming together "At last a capital plan we've got." The object of the whispering is of course to ensure that nobody, not even the audience, can hear what is proposed. However, a waggish Scaphio in the course of his *sotto-voce* asides may, far from talking of frustrating the King, take the opportunity to share more interesting titbits such as informing Tarara that one of his braces is showing, or telling Phantis that the conductor's toupee has moved forward by at least three inches since the start of the performance.

The trio exit, Scaphio and Phantis in one direction and Tarara in the other, and Dramaleigh and Mr Goldbury enter. In dialogue they express satisfaction with the Drawing Room, particularly the provision of tea and biscuits which was Dramaleigh's own touch (it was later adopted by the real Royal Court in England as a result of this opera!). Nekaya and Kalyba then enter, having been sent into the Throne Room by Lady Sophy because Fitzbattleaxe and Zara were "going on" in the garden (whatever that may mean). Dramaleigh expresses pleasure at seeing the girls, and both he and Mr Goldbury come closer to them and look admiringly at them. Kalyba responds by pleading that the men should not take advantage of their "unprotected innocence." Both she and Nekaya confess to feeling unsettled by the attentions of the men, not because it is in the nature of Utopian maidens, but because of the teachings of Lady Sophy; she has told them that such attentions are improper and contrary to English principles. Mr Goldbury responds by attempting to refute the idea that English girls are so ridiculously demure; to demonstrate, he sings a song in praise of the independent, active, sporty English girl ("A wonderful joy our eyes to bless"). The song immediately leads into a joyful quartet ("Then I may sing and play?") in which the men confirm that there is nothing objectionable and

216

indeed everything to be gained by the girls if they simply act naturally. The girls express delight at the suggestion that they can be themselves, with Kalyba looking forward to rowing and fishing, and Nekaya to happy laughter. The joyful refrain calls for a merry dance to go with it, and, as with all dance numbers in the operas, painstaking rehearsal by the four principals is necessary to perfect it. Failure to do so may not only meet with critical comment from the reviewer and supposed experts within the cast; any exhibition of two-left-footedness will be preserved for ever by means of that comparatively recent – and, to some, repugnant – phenomenon, the Show Video. If the incompetent performer is very unfortunate, a Video Evening will be convened, in which all the members – their inhibitions and tongues loosened now that the show has finished and diplomatic restraint no longer applies – will gather round the screen and spend the evening laughing uproariously at every *faux pas* and solecism that proceeds from the lips, hands and feet of the artistes. Less unpleasant for the champion of woodenness is the simple offering of copies for sale without a general viewing. Not only will he be spared the humiliation that such a viewing would entail, but it is quite possible that any purchaser will never actually get round to playing it, and in due course it will be quietly consigned to a drawer of tapes full of half-recorded-over episodes of *Neighbours,* and interminable footage of assorted juvenile relatives building sandcastles on Southend beach.

After the quartet, all four singers exit and Lady Sophy appears. In a recitative ("Oh, would some demon power") and subsequent aria ("When but a maid of fifteen year") she sings of her long-felt, but totally frustrated, desire to be united with a blameless King, and her wish that her "over-conscientious heart" could now be quelled. There are obvious similarities to the ageing female's laments in *The Mikado* and *Patience;* this time, however, the mature contralto has a genuine admirer in the form of the King. He has entered and heard her song; at the end of it he comes forward and in a recitative ("Ah, Lady Sophy") he interprets her lament as expressing love for him. Lady Sophy indignantly produces the *Palace Peeper* and says that while its rumours about his indiscretions remain uncontradicted, she will have nothing to do with him. Still in recitative, the King reveals, much to Lady Sophy's amazement, that all the offending articles were written by himself, under pressure from Scaphio, and that is why no action has been taken against the contributor! The recitative gives way to a jolly duet ("Oh, the rapture unrestrained") in which the couple sing of their joy that, with the *Palace Peeper* problem solved, and the King blameless after all, they have each been granted their heart's desire. Dramaleigh and Mr Goldbury are then directed to enter with the twins followed by Fitzbattleaxe and Zara. Their attention is drawn to the fact that the King and Lady Sophy are dancing together, and the King is kissing his new partner. After the initial surprise, all four couples then break into a wild Tarantella, and then exit. The two Wise Men together with Tarara and the chorus hurry in. They are in a rebellious mood, and together in song ("Upon our sea-girt land") they express anger at the reforms brought by the Flowers of Progress. As with many chorus numbers in G & S opera, the ability to hold a musical line in this short but dramatic piece of choral writing is important to the success and effectiveness of the piece. It will be for individual producers and musical directors to decide on whether it is better for the chorus to learn all their words and music first, and then start plotting, or whether "floor work" should go hand-in-hand with the musical preparation. In some ways the latter may be preferable, as it may help to keep the nicer points of musical interpretation in perspective. Many musical directors will be familiar with the earnest chorus member who, pencil in hand, delays the progress of musical rehearsals with questions such as "would you wish to have some *rallentando* two bars before the *decrescendo* at the top of page seventy-eight" or "is there really supposed to be a double-dot on the first quaver of the second bar of the first stave, or should we do what the first altos and second basses are doing?" Whilst the musical director may be quite happy to share his knowledge and expertise with the questioner, the interruptions will be less welcome for those other singers who realise that all of these points will be forgotten once the books are put down and floor work commences, and who if asked what *rallentando* meant to them would hazard a guess that it might be either a Uruguayan tightrope walker or a new brand of spicy potato chip.

After the chorus the remaining principals then enter and in dialogue the King demands to know what the matter is. Scaphio explains that the reforms have turned Utopia into such a perfect place, free as it now is from war, crime, litigation and sickness, that there is no work for the armed services, the lawyers and doctors. The King and Zara are perplexed, and it is only when prompted by Sir Bailey Barre that Zara realises what is missing – namely, government by party! She points out that under party government reforms will never last because one party will simply undo what the other party has done, and this state of affairs will bring the country to a standstill. Thus there will be ample work for the professionals as crime, sickness and other social problems abound. It is Gilbert's most direct hit at the failings of the English political system and those who would turn these failings to their own advantage, and retains amazing topicality over a century later. In its original form Zara's speech was even more biting, referring to inexperienced citizens governing the Army and also the Navy (with shades of Sir Joseph Porter in

218

H.M.S. Pinafore!) but was later edited down. With a couple more "Ulahlica's" the crowd acclaim Zara's suggestion with enthusiasm, while Scaphio and Phantis furiously admit defeat and are led off in custody. The King proclaims the introduction of government by party and announces that the Monarchy (Limited) is turned into a Limited Monarchy. There then follows the ensemble Act 2 finale, with solos for Zara and the King ("There's a little group of isles") in which both soloists extol the magnificence of Great Britain, the King expresses the hope that her (Britain's) fine qualities may be fully adopted in Utopia, and the company, justifiably, voice their hope that Britain "makes no mistake, that she's all she professes to be!" By now, the audience will doubtless have got the message, the house lights will rise, and the committee will be free to make initial overtures to the manager of the Happy Falling Company in Windy Lane and start taking cast measurements for a bulk consignment of jumpsuits.

The thespian who wishes to boast that he has performed in all thirteen surviving G & S operas must, at some stage in his amateur operatic career, find a society which feels strong enough and confident enough to perform *The Grand Duke*, the last of the fourteen works written by the partnership. Any society contemplating an airing of this work must do so in the knowledge that its opening run lasted just 123 performances (less than a fifth of the number enjoyed by *The Mikado*), it was never performed in the U.S.A., and following its opening run it was considered such a failure that it has never been professionally revived. Even before the work was written, Gilbert himself seemed to think his best days were behind him, admitting in 1894 that "I am a crumbling man – a magnificent ruin, no doubt, but still a ruin." It needed Carte's wife Helen to persuade the pair to work together once more. In August 1895 Gilbert read to Sullivan the plot of a new opera he had devised, based on a short story entitled *The Duke's Dilemma* and an American newspaper article which considered the legal consequences of a dead person being brought back to life. Sullivan agreed to set it, and work on the last G & S opera duly commenced. It is not easy to identify a central theme or object of burlesque running through the opera, as it is in, for instance, *Patience, Princess Ida* or indeed *Utopia Limited*. With its complex plot involving a penny-pinching nobleman, a troupe of actors plotting his downfall, and a person's fate being decided by card-playing, it has been variously explained as a tilt at *fin-de-siecle* decadence, the inviolability of dramatic contracts, and the extent to which an actor's theatrical behaviour influences his role in real life. Other scholars have offered, and will doubtless continue to offer, further interpretations. The artificiality of the plot was matched only by the artificiality of some of the rhyming, with the words "ghost," "discover" and "yellow" being respectively spelt "ghoest," "diskiver" and "yallow" for rhyming convenience!

When rehearsals began in 1896, Gilbert's gout had got so bad that he had to be carried to the stage. His problems did not end there. Nancy McIntosh's limited acting ability prevented her taking part in the opera, and another newcomer had to be recruited. A Hungarian lady, Ilka von Palmay, was appointed to take the soprano lead; until Sullivan intervened she had been engaged by a Berlin company to take the part of Nanki-Poo in a German *Mikado*! Once again Gilbert's desire to keep her busy upset the balance of the libretto. He was, however, able to use her European accent to good advantage in the context of the story; the part she played was that of an actress who was performing in a foreign country, and therefore it was in fact wholly appropriate for her to declaim her lines with a foreign accent. It may have been Gilbert's desire to give her more to do which meant a delay in the entry of one of the lead characters, the Prince of Monte Carlo, until very late in the proceedings. In fact the first Prince, Scott Fishe, did not appear until 11 p.m. on the opening night and had time to go to his club in the evening; fellow club members apparently assumed that Gilbert had sacked him!

The first performance, on 7th March 1896, received a mixed reception. Six encores were demanded, and many of the reviewers were complimentary. Jane Stedman writes of "the exquisite costumes of blue, violet, mauve, grey and grass-green." The *Court Circular* was particularly enthusiastic, saying "Gilbert and Sullivan have added to the gaiety of the nation." Sullivan himself seemed pleased enough with it, recording in his diary "Opera went well, over at 11.15. Parts of it dragged a little, dialogue too redundant, but success great and genuine I think." There certainly is some splendid music in the opera; Ian Bradley is surely right when he says "it deserves to be seen and heard more often," and Michael Hurd, writing in the programme for the 1996 Petersfield Operatic Society production, asserts that "the work is slowly reclaiming its place in the G & S canon." However the majority of the critics have tended to be dismissive of the work and especially of the libretto. At the time of the opening run, *Musical Standards* wrote that "in Mr Gilbert's libretto one of the characters for the sake of rhyme pronounces ghost as ghoest and we may be pardoned if we call *The Grand Duke* a ghoest of a Gilbert and Sullivan opera." Hesketh Pearson states that "the most famous association in theatrical history fizzled out like a damp squib." Gilbert himself, in a letter to Mrs Bram Stoker written two days after opening, said of his new work "I'm not at all a proud mother and I never want to see the ugly misshapen little brat again!" Sullivan did not even bother to discuss possible refinements to the show with Gilbert, but departed almost immediately for Monte Carlo and confessed: "another week's rehearsal with Gilbert and I should have gone raving mad. I have already ordered some straw for my hair."

The story of *The Grand Duke*, alternatively titled *The Statutory Duel*, contains many reminders of other G & S operas, with allusions to the influence of an actor's theatrical behaviour on his real-life role (*Thespis*), infant betrothal (*Princess Ida*), decadent nobility (*The Gondoliers*) and the pronouncement of a living person as legally dead (*The Mikado*). The opera is set in the Duchy of Pfennig Halbpfennig where a group of actors led by their principal comedian Ludwig (baritone) are plotting the downfall of the despised Grand Duke Rudolph (baritone) and the election of their manager, Ernest Dummkopf (tenor), in his place. Ludwig inadvertently discloses details of the plot to Rudolph's detective. The Notary Dr Tannhauser (tenor) suggests that, in order to ensure the plotters' survival, Ernest and Ludwig engage in a Statutory Duel whereby on the turn of a card the loser is pronounced legally dead and the winner assumes his privileges and obligations. The survivor will then go and denounce the dead man to Rudolph. Since the law providing for Statutory Duels is due to be repealed next day, the dead man will then come to life, free from all obligations and liabilities. Ludwig wins the Duel and goes to Rudolph. Rudolph is a miserable man, all the more so when he learns of the plot against him. Ludwig brilliantly offers to engage in a Statutory Duel with Rudolph which they will rig so that Ludwig wins, thereby relieving Rudolph of his weighty responsibilities. Whilst this is more than acceptable to Rudolph, Ludwig has other ideas. As soon as Ludwig wins, he then renews the law providing for Statutory Duels for a further hundred years, so that in effect he will continue as Grand Duke! What he has overlooked is that instead of marrying his soubrette sweetheart Lisa (soprano) he will now have to throw her over and marry the troupe's leading lady, English actress Julia Jellicoe (soprano) whom Ernest loves. However no sooner has Ludwig accepted this situation, to Lisa's dismay, than the formidable Baroness von Krakenfeldt (contralto) appears and reminds Ludwig that as Rudolph's promised bride, Ludwig must consider himself engaged to her. Then, as if that were not enough, the Princess of Monte Carlo (soprano) arrives with her father the Prince (bass) and they remind Ludwig of the Princess' infant betrothal to Rudolph which, as winner of the Duel, Ludwig must now honour. Ludwig is saved when it is discovered that the rules of the Duel were misinterpreted and accordingly he was the loser of his duel with Rudolph. Rudolph is delighted to pair off with the Princess, whose wealth is assured thanks to her father's proficiency at roulette; and with the repeal of the law providing for Statutory Duels, which Rudolph has no reason for wishing to continue, Ludwig may return to his beloved Lisa, while Ernest is accepted by Julia.

The action commences in the market place of Speisesaal, in the Grand Duchy of Pfennig Halbpfennig. It is to be assumed that the Duchy lies somewhere in central Europe, and set designers can enjoy creating a suitable scene, perhaps with a wealth of timber-framed houses and an Alpine backcloth. On the stage itself, players in Ernest Dummkopf's theatrical company are enjoying a meal in celebration of the wedding of two of its members, the company's leading comedian named Ludwig and a soubrette named Lisa. From the words they sing in the opening chorus ("Won't it be a pretty wedding?") it is clear that the wedding ceremony has not yet taken place. Gilbert's cynical view of marriage, evident in a number of other G & S operas, is made clear when the company sing "Man and maid for aye united, *till divorce* or death shall part them!" In between these ensemble sections, four girls from the chorus, Elsa, Olga, Gretchen (sopranos) and Bertha (mezzo-soprano), reflect anxiously in brief solos on the possibility of a bride with ill-fitting dress, cheap gloves and untidy hair who stumbles on her train. Ludwig and Lisa come forward and in duet indulge in some affectionate teasing, but in a rousing end to this opening musical section, the chorus strike another note of ambivalence, advising Lisa that only by turning a blind eye and deaf ear to Ludwig's possible unkindness and rudeness can she hope to keep her marriage intact! Notary Tannhauser then enters and in the ensuing dialogue expresses distress that half of the wedding breakfast has been eaten in advance of his arrival. He is assured, however, that the wedding itself has not taken place. It is explained to him that the guests have had to eat first; all the parsons are in conference until six that evening discussing the arrangements for the wedding of the Grand Duke to the wealthy Baroness von Krakenfeldt, and the company are due on stage at seven! The Notary only finds this out after his initial enquiries are met with a burst of unintelligible chatter. It is a curious feature of almost any amateur operatic society that when a gap of any sort occurs in rehearsal, a buzz of animated discussion commences immediately, infuriating the producer beyond measure; yet when the chorus are actually *invited* to engage in it there is either a coy silence or modicum of conversation so subdued in nature that a neutral observer might suspect some sad or tragic event had occurred, such as the death of a former member, or the failure of the treasurer to purchase last Saturday's tickets for the society's lottery syndicate thus depriving ten members of a share of the week's jackpot prize.

It is clear that, not least because of the indirect disruption to the wedding arrangements, the Grand Duke is highly unpopular with the company. It seems, however, from what Bertha says, that there are plans to dethrone him next day. Ludwig is alarmed that she has alluded to the conspiracy without first having given and received the conspirators' secret sign. He explains in song, with chorus ("By the mystic regulation"), that the sign consists of the eating by one conspirator of a sausage roll in the presence of another; that other, if he is a conspirator as well, must in turn eat a sausage roll himself. It is clear from the song and succeeding dialogue that the company have had enough of eating sausage rolls; nonetheless Ludwig demonstrates his commitment to the cause by eating one himself. Lisa's sympathy for him, although resulting in one of the more unfortunate speeches in G & S opera ("He's always at it, and it's a wonder where he puts it"), is well founded. Not only must Ludwig nightly on stage consume an item of food which is hardly the best aid to keeping the vocal chords uncluttered, but it will almost certainly be cold and chewy, having been prised hastily from a pack with the words BEST SERVED PIPING HOT inscribed on the front. Then, in any social gathering connected with the production, from the band-call tea interval onwards, caterers will wish to enter into the spirit of the show by offering platefuls of sausage rolls to all who are unwise enough to come near them, with the *piece de resistance* – Mrs Anstey's giant home-made concoction – being created for the centre of the buffet table for the reception on the final night. By then the character playing Ludwig might be forgiven for averting his gaze from Mrs Anstey's handiwork and seeking sanctuary amongst the cheese-and-onion Wotsits.

The company turn to happier matters, namely the prospect of Ernest Dummkopf, their manager, being elected to succeed the present incumbent as Grand Duke. Ludwig reflects that Ernest is not particularly competent or adventurous, but after he (Ludwig) has exited with Lisa, Olga reminds the company that Ernest has promised places about the Court for all of them – according to professional position – providing they vote for him. Ernest then enters and confirms his promises to them. Seemingly assured of their support, he proceeds to boast, in dialogue and then in song with chorus ("Were I a king in very truth"), that anyone capable of directing a theatrical company is surely capable of running a country as well. These sentiments must have been very close to Gilbert's heart, after his years of directing often truculent performers! The extent to which any G & S production, whether a lavishly costumed and thoroughly professional affair or a low-budget performance with costumes and sets to match, is enjoyed by its participants will depend very much on the personality of the producer. The new recruit to an operatic society will learn a great deal about him – or her – from his or her reaction to certain incidents within the course of a production, such as the society's "traditional final-night prank;" until it happens, nobody will know how the producer may take to the addition of unscripted dialogue of both dubious origin and taste, or the insertion of extra properties on stage, whether it be a giant teddy bear hanging from the Houses of Parliament in *Iolanthe* or a cigarette placed in the mouth of a sculpted figure within the pavilion of the Court of Barataria in *The Gondoliers*. Another test of a producer is when, two days from opening night, an important and complex dance routine falls apart because either a key player is away, or the performers have simply forgotten what they are supposed to do. The well-adjusted and philosophical producer will count to three and politely suggest that it might be prudent to revisit that routine, charitably attributing the players' forgetfulness to anything from the flickering light at the back of the hall to the sudden appearance in the room of glamorous Giselle Gorringe, an ex-member who broke the hearts of at least six men in the society by taking up a full-time job in New Jersey. By contrast, the producer blessed with a lesser degree of equanimity will fly into a rage, instantly wiping the foolish grins from the faces of those principally responsible for the shambles which provoked it; by the time the producer has in turn threatened to terminate the evening's work, resign on the spot, and/or cancel the entire production, even the least culpable trouper will be left feeling like an inky-fingered second former who has been caught cribbing his Latin prep.

The chorus exit after the song, leaving Ernest on his own. For a few moments he soliloquises about his love for Julia Jellicoe, the talented English comedienne in the troupe who, he sadly believes, does not return his love. Julia then enters, and in dialogue confirms that she feels Ernest to be beneath her. However, she recognises that once he has become Grand Duke, and awarded places about the court according to professional position, it follows that life must imitate art and she will be obliged to become his Grand Duchess! Since she has no strong feelings for Ernest, her love for him will be no more than an act and in a solo, with brief duet at the end ("How would I play this part"), she considers how to go about creating a convincing, but totally phoney, display of affection, just like Phoebe in "Were I thy bride" in *The Yeomen Of The Guard*. The chorus then hurry in again with Ludwig, Lisa and the Notary. They seem very agitated and begin a dramatic ensemble musical section by asking, in song, "My goodness me! what shall I do?" They also appear particularly angry with Ludwig. In a recitative Ernest asks what the matter is, and Ludwig confesses in a solo, with chorus ("Ten minutes since I met a chap"), that he has just been duped into revealing details of their plot to the Grand Duke's own detective. The chorus respond by calling Ludwig a succession of unflattering names, then resolve to disappear quickly in order to save their own skins. They then quickly exit. On the face of it this is one of the easier chorus numbers to set, involving little more than directing the chorus to hurry in and stand in horror at what Ludwig has done. The great danger then, of course, is that members of the chorus will create that *bete noire* of producers, the dreaded Straight Line. The producer may attempt to humour what may be a quartet of offenders by asking if the four of them would stand in a straight line if talking together in a pub or even simply in the street. If this fails to have the desired effect, the guilty should not be surprised if for the next production they find their neat formation repositioned ten paces closer to the car park, if not actually in it.

Julia, Ernest, Ludwig, Lisa and the Notary remain and dialogue begins. Julia and Ernest soundly berate Ludwig (her words "Well, a nice mess you've got us into" could be amended slightly in the style of Laurel & Hardy!) but the Notary has thought of a way out of the difficulty. In the conversation which follows, and in his intervening solo with ensemble refrain ("About a century since"), the Notary explains the concept of the Statutory Duel. By the law of the land, any legal dispute is resolved by the disputants choosing a card from a pack. Whoever draws the lower card is deemed to be legally dead, and all his obligations as well as privileges pass to the winner. By happy coincidence, the law providing for Statutory Duels is to be repealed next day, thus allowing any persons deemed to be "dead" as a result of this law to come to life again. The Notary suggests that Ludwig and Ernest engage in a Statutory Duel; the winner will then go to the Grand Duke and denounce the "deceased" loser as the real conspirator, and since his criminal liabilities will be deemed to have died with him, the loser will have nothing to fear when he returns to life next day. The denouncer, meanwhile, will receive a free pardon for assisting the State in reporting the conspiracy! A quintet follows in the style of a madrigal ("Strange the views some people hold!") in which the singers rejoice at their country's enlightened attitude to the resolution of disputes in contrast to the more barbaric practices found elsewhere. This leads immediately into a more vigorous quintet ("Now take a card and gaily sing") in which the Duel takes place. Ernest draws a King, and Ludwig an Ace. An exuberant dance follows, again extolling the benefits of the card-playing; never, surely have Diamonds, Hearts, Clubs and Spades been so keenly serenaded! If publicity officers attempting to promote *The Grand Duke* baulk at the idea of littering the window of the local bookshop or building society with sausage rolls, some artistic displays of playing cards might be a highly apposite alternative. For a show as unfamiliar to modern audiences as *The Grand Duke* is, it is essential that the publicity is as exhaustive as possible, from the erection of banners across the High Street to announcing, at rehearsal, the registration numbers of vehicles in the car park that are NOT displaying car stickers. The reputable society with an influential chairman may have valuable contacts with the local media; newspapers and radio stations in the area will consequently be prepared to publish or transmit in-depth interviews covering every aspect of the production, from the venue and admission charges down to the wardrobe assistant's favourite variety of packet soup. The less fortunate society, whose media coverage may be restricted to half a column on page seven in the town's freebie journal, will have to resort to less genteel means of marketing its unmissable production as ticket sales struggle to achieve twenty per cent of the break-even figure with less than a week before performances begin. Members may well in that case be reduced to standing impotently in the town's covered precinct, waving handbills towards shoppers and trying to convince them that they are not, on this occasion, drawing potential customers' attention to the fantastic end-of-season end-of-line everything-must-go carpet sale in the Bog Lane Community Centre.

The five performers dance their way off, and a march is played by the orchestra. The march heralds the arrival of Grand Duke Rudolph himself, preceded by seven Chamberlains who hail him in a brief chorus ("The good Grand Duke of Pfennig Halbpfennig"). The words of the chorus, however, reveal that Rudolph is universally regarded as contemptible, and it is only their desire for self-preservation which causes them to go through the motions of praising him. Rudolph then enters, meanly and miserably dressed, and looking weak and ill, but his clothing displays an array of orders and decorations. He will later be revealed as immensely wealthy despite his meanness. He begins by singing his song of introduction ("A pattern to professors of monarchical autonomy") in which he presents himself as a humourless and penny-pinching man with a liking for cheap ceremonial. As if to demonstrate the absurd results of such ceremony about the court, a simple request for snuffbox and handkerchief is met by the passing of these articles in turn from the junior Chamberlain to Rudolph via all the other Chamberlains! Rudolph then launches into one of the longest speeches, if not **the** longest speech, in all the operas, in which he outlines the elaborate arrangements for his wedding to Baroness von Krakenfeldt, involving no expense to him whatsoever but considerable expense to the populace. Each Chamberlain, it seems, will have something to do, from the Lord Chamberlain down to the Acting Temporary Sub-Deputy Assistant Vice-Chamberlain. After each Chamberlain has been briefed the seven of them exit, leaving Rudolph to reflect alone for a while on the fact that his bride is as stingy as he is. With appropriately humorous touches – perhaps involving some business for the Chamberlains – the speech may prove most entertaining, despite its prolixity. Nonetheless, as with much of the dialogue in the *The Grand Duke*, there is considerable scope for cuts, assuming that the society places the desirability of absolute faithfulness to the original script behind the need to finish before the pubs close. Having regard to the length of the show, producers have little to fear from even the most ardent traditionalists, and one can safely assume that it is unlikely that refunds will be demanded by patrons outraged that the producer sought to apply the blue pencil to those hilarious one-liners at Lines 647 or 685 which was the only reason for their buying tickets in the first place.

After Rudolph's speech, the Baroness enters. Rudolph persuades her to show him some affection in public on the basis that he is able to use public love episodes as a basis for raising rents he charges on nearby properties! She produces a report from his detective. For safe keeping she had wrapped it in a newspaper, in which there is an article disclosing that Rudolph is already engaged to another. It seems that he was betrothed in infancy to the

Princess of Monte Carlo. Rudolph endeavours to reassure the Baroness that it is unlikely that he will be held to this arrangement since it is a condition that the ceremony must take place before the Princess is of age. (It is one of the incongruities of the opera that one assumes that Rudolph is already an old man and, as the Princess is NOT yet of age, he is surely several decades older than she is!) Her father, the Prince of Monte Carlo, apparently has no money at all, so the Princess has no means to travel to the Duchy for the ceremony. Naturally, Rudolph has no wish, despite the Prince's entreaties, to assist the process by travelling to Monte Carlo or financing her journey. Moreover, at 2 tomorrow, the Princess will be of age and the arrangement will die. The Baroness is apparently satisfied with this, and in a duet and dance ("As o'er our penny roll we sing") the couple look forward to their married life together, lived with due regard to rigid economy. Another somewhat unfortunate line is Rudolph's "Perhaps we'll have it once a year" which although supposedly referring to the Baroness' vision of clear mock-turtle soup suggests another, and quite unnecessary, form of matrimonial economy altogether.

After the duet and dance, the Baroness exits and Rudolph reads the detective's report which reveals the existence of the plot against him that could result in his deposal the next day. The thought of this causes him to believe, in his own words, that "I'm going to be very ill indeed!" This leads straight on into his solo ("When you find you're a broken-down critter") in which he laments his various maladies with symptoms such as the feeling of having a beehive in his head, a sewing machine in each ear, and a tongue which is "decidedly yellow."(The word is of course "yellow" but has to rhyme with "tallow!") There are obvious similarities with the Nightmare Song from *Iolanthe* in its portrayal of an old man's infirmities. Jane Stedman points out that the reference in Rudolph's song to "black beetles and crawly things never at rest" (with splendidly apt orchestral accompaniment) suggests the visual hallucinations of migraine. At the end of his song he sinks, weeping and exhausted. Ludwig then enters and dialogue begins. Ludwig is about to confess his part in the plot and presumably denounce Ernest as well, but when the miserable Rudolph reveals his wish to put an end to what he sees as an insupportable existence, Ludwig is struck by a brilliant idea. He suggests that Rudolph engages in a Statutory Duel which he (Rudolph) must contrive to lose; Rudolph will then "die" and by the time he comes to life again and resumes his Grand Duchy following the repeal of the relevant law, the plot and attendant explosion will already have taken place and the survivor will have had to bear the brunt of it. Ludwig offers to engage in the Duel with Rudolph which they will rig to ensure that Ludwig wins (Rudolph's line "But suppose I were to lose?" is an uncharacteristic error on Gilbert's part; the line should surely be "But suppose I were to win?"). Ludwig suggests that such an outcome can be achieved if "I'll put an Ace up my sleeve – you'll put a King up yours." The producer may, despite the fact that it will *add* a word to the excessively long libretto, wish to change the word "yours" for "your sleeve" since otherwise Rudolph's part of the bargain might sound excessively onerous even for one whose topmost regions are bulging with an apian enclosure and a brace of domestic appliances.

In order to make the Duel more realistic the parties agree to stage-manage a quarrel immediately beforehand, summoning the townsfolk to act as witnesses. In response to Rudolph's musical command "Come hither, all you people," which commences the Act 1 finale, the chorus together with the Notary and Lisa then enter. They are terrified that the summons might result in their arrest and hanging, and they watch apprehensively as Rudolph and Ludwig square up to each other. In a lightning-fast duet with chorus ("Big bombs, small bombs") they succeed in conveying suitably convincing-looking feelings of hatred towards each other. The Notary immediately recognises the need for a Statutory Duel and in an ensuing recitative section, the Duel is explained to the company and the drawing of the cards solemnly takes place. Ludwig duly wins, as planned, much to the delight and relief of the chorus, who acclaim him by crying "Hurrah! Hurrah! Our Ludwig's won! Give thanks, give thanks to wayward fate!" In between these bursts of acclamation, they round on Rudolph and mock his legal demise in a succession of short solos and then an ensemble section ("My Lord, Grand Duke, farewell"). Amidst this display of ridicule, Rudolph exits in a rage, promising that his subjects will burn in "penitential fires" once the law has expired and he has returned to his ducal duties. Once he has gone and the excitement has subsided, Ludwig sings his inaugural song as the new Grand Duke, with chorus ("Oh, a monarch who boasts"). In this very jolly patter number he announces that he will renew the law providing for Statutory Duels for a further 100 years, which means that he will remain Grand Duke until he dies. In the subsequent recitative he promises to honour Ernest's earlier pledge to give places about the court to everyone in the troupe according to professional position. During the recitative Julia enters and when she hears Ludwig's announcement she is horrified. When asked by the chorus what the matter is, she sings a song with choral interludes ("Ah, pity me") in which she explains that as the leading comedienne, she must by definition become the Grand Duchess, and Ludwig's wife. The song is lengthy and because it is only at the end that Julia's point is properly made, is an obvious candidate for cutting. One of the most thankless tasks for a musical director is trying to explain to the chorus what page numbers and/or bar numbers have been cut, and then waiting whilst pencils are first found then applied to the pages in question. The task becomes even more laborious if certain performers have chosen to purchase or otherwise equip themselves with editions of the score that are different from those loaned to the large majority of the members through the local library. The advantage of purchasing rather than hiring a copy is, of course, that it is possible to make as many markings as is desired, without the necessity of removing the scribbles after the performance. Sadly, however, the fact that a copy is a hire copy will not stop some performers marking them and omitting to erase the annotations afterwards. Such markings may range from drawings of pairs of spectacles at strategic intervals, presumably to remind the performer to look out (for what, it is not clear), to a mass of complex and often seemingly conflicting stage directions which may look as intelligible to subsequent hirers as a treatise in Sanskrit on the properties of sulphanilamide.

A duet then ensues for Lisa and Julia ("Oh, listen to me, dear"). In the duet Lisa pleads with Julia not to pursue Ludwig, since her (Lisa's) heart is set on him. Julia, however, points out that to be a Grand Duchess is "leading business," and since Lisa is only a soubrette she will be unable to cope with that role. Julia's assertion causes Lisa to be overwhelmed with grief. Moreover, the ensuing recitative for the Notary, with chorus ("The lady's right"), makes it clear that nobody else is prepared to help Lisa either; the Notary, in stressing the solemnity of dramatic contracts, points out that Ludwig's elevation frees him from his promise to Lisa. A heartbroken Lisa then sings a sad solo with chorus ("The die is cast") in which she resigns herself to losing Ludwig. After her solo she exits. For a moment Ludwig is sympathetic, asking in recitative "Poor child, where will she go?" but Julia responds that such sentiments do not form part of his new role as Grand Duke! Accordingly, Ludwig snaps out of his mood of anxiety and commences the final, vigorous section of the finale with the words "For this will be a jolly court, for little and for big." In this ensemble section, with solos for Ludwig and Julia, the company look forward to a new regime of merriment and jollity, without state and ceremony, and with court attire that recalls the "dead old days of Athens in her glory." This joyful finale ends with Ludwig being carried round the stage to the ironwork of the well, where Julia stands by him and the company group round him. The curtains having closed, the stage crew will then have the unenviable task of dismantling the public square and creating the entrance hall in the Grand Ducal Palace within the space of 20 minutes. This will be a particularly exacting challenge if the process has taken up to 45 minutes at technical rehearsal. If the set for Act 1 has encompassed a happy mixture of timber-framed houses and Alpine backcloth, the dismantlers may feel more than a tinge of regret to see it removed, particularly if the chalk used by the stage manager to number the rear of the flats has been washed off by rainwater dripping into the scenery dock so nobody will remember how they slot in again next time. Regret may be mingled with apprehension if in the rush to complete the transformation to Grand Ducal Palace, certain bolts are not tightened properly and cast members have to assess their quickest and safest methods of escape should the impact of Mrs Appleyard's ample posterior dislodge the west wall and cause it to crash spectacularly into the stairwell.

Assuming the transformation to the Palace entrance hall has safely taken place, the curtain opens on Act 2 to find the members of the theatrical company, including Ludwig, Julia and Lisa, entering the stage, dressed in costumes from their current production of *Troilus and Cressida*. Carrying garlands and playing pipes and other instruments, the company rejoice at the wedding of Ludwig and Julia which has just taken place, singing a chorus ("As before you we defile"). Their exultant cries of "Eloia!" bring back memories of "Ulahlica" from *Utopia Limited*. This chorus was in fact intended as a tilt at the trendy devotion to Greek costume at that time. Ludwig then sings a recitative ("Your loyalty our ducal heartstrings touches") in which he presents his new Grand Duchess, pointing out that he did not choose her as his wife. He then sings a solo, with chorus ("At the outset I may mention"), in which he explains how he sees the Grecian influence being brought to bear on his court. Though very well received on the first night, just as the preceding chorus was, many of the allusions are now so obscure that only a person of formidable intellect would grasp more than a handful of them. There are a number of Greek words, and one expression, meaning "they'd be turning to the drink," which is actually written in Greek in the score, although there is a helpful footnote which states how it should be pronounced! At one point there is a reference to a Mrs Grundy, described by Ian Bradley as "the personification of strait-laced puritanism and moral outrage;" Bradley points out that Mary Whitehouse would be the modern-day equivalent and perhaps a more sensible name for modern performers to invoke. After a reprise of a section of the opening chorus to the Act, the chorus then depart leaving just Ludwig, Julia and Lisa. For many male chorus members the transformation to Grecian mode will be a painful experience, not because of the abstruse classical allusions or the unintelligible vocabulary, but because of the costume required. If togas are obtained which reach only just below the thigh it is inevitable that generous portions of male legs, complete with knobbly knees and varicose veins, will be on show to the public. However long the togas are, the feet will almost certainly remain open to view, protected from the rough-and-tumble of quasi-Grecian living by nothing more than a pair of skimpy sandals. Thus will ruthlessly be exposed all the corns, calluses, bunions, ingrowing toenails and extraneous hairs which have, at the behest of protective friends and relations, remained closeted from general view by the merciful intervention of socks and shoes since their last infamous public airing on Bognor beach in July 1978.

After the chorus have exited, Ludwig sings a recitative in which he simply reflects that "Yes, Ludwig and his Julia are mated" following which Lisa sings a tender aria ("Take care of him – he's much too good to live"). In this aria, with occasional vocal interruptions from Ludwig, she implores Julia to look after her new husband and attend to his peculiar needs. It is arguably the loveliest, and saddest, moment in the opera. After Lisa has exited in tears, Julia discusses with Ludwig, in dialogue, how she should play the part of a Grand Duchess, rather as she did with Ernest in Act 1. In particular, she stresses how her temperament would demand some strong scenes of jealousy. There then follows a duet ("Now Julia, come") in which Julia acts out the part of the jealous wife who has caught her husband with someone she believes to be a rival. The duet adds nothing to the story whatsoever, and since Julia has already demonstrated her histrionic abilities to the audience in her Act 1 solo, this later number might be a suitable candidate for the producer's pruning shears. Of course if the actress playing the part of Julia were to seek to reflect Julia's character off the stage as well as on it, she would doubtless insist that the duet remain! Having the stage to oneself with plenty of solo work is not, of course, the only reward for the principal with pretensions of grandeur. Other by-products include being singled out by the press photographer for a special solo photograph for the centre spread in the *Weekly Herald*, and being photographed for the foyer and the programme. These pictures may be accompanied by some biographical notes. Thus will readers learn that this will be Jeremy Hyde-Davies' twenty-fifth G & S production, his previous appearance in *The Grand Duke* being his "memorable portrayal" of the Notary in 1966, and that Monica Arbuthnot (whose real name is Monica Mudd) is a "welcome newcomer" to the society after performing "to great critical acclaim" as Countess Kalamazinskaya in the world premiere of the dramatic cantata *The Prince Of Irkutsk* in the locality seven months ago, and winning the Peregrine Phelps Prize in April – whoever Peregrine Phelps may be. These self-congratulatory snippets may be supplemented by attempts at sadly misguided frivolity as if in an effort to ingratiate the cast members with the audience; hence the information that Alison Van Niekirk, playing the part of Lisa, lives with her husband Rob, two children and four cats, and will therefore be hoping to make beautiful "mew-sic" and deliver a "purr-fect" performance without any rival society wishing to "whisk-her" away.

After the duet, the members of the chorus enter in great excitement, and commence a musical section by frenziedly singing that "Your Highness, there's a party at the door." They go on to explain that the "party" consists of a certain lady whom they do not recognise but who has responded to their lukewarm welcome with indignation and a volley of strong language. It is none other than the Baroness, who storms in and, still in song, demands to see Rudolph. Ludwig, also in song, responds that "he isn't at home just now," and the chorus happily add their sung corroboration to his statement, adding that their detested ex-leader is likely to be found in the town cemetery! After the somewhat turgid music of the previous number, this bouncy musical section is a delight. In the ensuing dialogue, Ludwig explains to the Baroness that he has succeeded Rudolph as Grand Duke as a result of the Statutory Duel, and that he has revived the law for a further century. The Baroness expresses considerable joy upon hearing this news, and points out that since Rudolph's responsibilities as well as his privileges have passed to Ludwig, he (Ludwig) is therefore obliged to honour his marriage to the Baroness! Julia protests, but to no avail; in a solo, with chorus, the Baroness proclaims "Now away to the wedding we go" and everybody except Julia hurries off to prepare for this next wedding ceremony. Julia is left heartbroken; in her recitative ("So ends my dream") and her ensuing solo ("All is darksome") she laments this tragic reversal in her fortunes. Only towards the end of her solo does she determine to face the future in positive frame of mind. She exits and Ernest enters; having seen a wedding procession, he says to the audience that is anxious to know what is happening. His initial belief that Ludwig and Lisa have married is proved false when Lisa enters, and, at the sight of the "dead" Ernest, hurries off again. His revised conclusion, which in a speech he also shares with the audience, that Ludwig has married Julia, is also shown to be incorrect when Julia appears alone. The chorus will, in the meantime, be enjoying their last substantial period of inactivity in the opera, thereby providing a golden opportunity for arrangements for the after-show party to be announced. The most straightforward sort of after-show party involves the cast foregathering in the theatre bar and remaining there until Mr Crump, the janitor, signals by unsubtle jangling of keys and switching the bar lights off and on at thirty-second intervals, that it is time to bring proceedings to a conclusion. If "in-house" facilities are unavailable or considered too restrictive, the member of the society with the largest house and most tolerant disposition may feel prevailed upon to accommodate the forty cast members, twenty-five helpers and twelve orchestra members that wish to drive along six miles of road, one mile of driveway and six hundred yards of dirt-track to start consuming portions of ready-to-eat quiche lorraine and Safeway Tortilla Chips at twenty-nine minutes past midnight.

234

Julia is at first horrified at the sight of the deceased theatrical manager, and despite Ernest assuring her that he is physically very much alive, she says how awful it is to be haunted by a "technical bogy." In the dialogue that follows, Ernest, who believes the Statutory Duel law to be expiring shortly, asks Julia to honour her pre-Duel commitment to him. Julia then explains about the extension of the law for another century; at first Ernest is incredulous, then pleads with her to defy the law and elope with him to England. Julia refuses and in the ensuing duet ("If the light of love's lingering ember") she confirms that she regards Ernest as "a spectre appalling." Notwithstanding Ernest's threats to haunt her, she categorically rejects him and both leave the stage in opposite directions. The chorus together with Ludwig and the Baroness then re-enter and sing a brief ensemble number, to music already heard in this Act ("Now bridegroom and bride let us toast"), in which they determine to toast Ludwig and the Baroness in "a magnum of merry champagne." The Baroness then takes up this theme in a rousing solo with chorus ("Come, bumpers – aye, ever-so-many") in which she points out that the best wine is that which the drinker does not have to pay for himself! For the sake of completeness, the producer may ask one or more of the cast to act as a wine waiter during this scene. Such an appointment may have its advantages. If the waiter is to be attired in traditional flunkeys' garb he should be spared the need to expose his bare legs and feet to the public gaze for one section of Act 2 at least; by the constant topping-up of glasses, even those that do not need to be topped up, he is kept busy and is therefore exempt from the often onerous requirement to stand and react to what is going on; and, best of all, he will not have to drink the brew he is pouring for the assembled company. Unless a public-spirited society member has contributed some quality wine, or a more malicious participant has laced the liquid with vodka or some equally potent concoction, the drink provided is likely to be both bland and unappetising. If they are lucky, the cast will be downing fizzy lemonade from the cash-and-carry round the corner, but equally, they may be forced to sup Mrs Samuels' 1993 elderberry, with a bouquet that mingles the seductive appeal of cold tea with the vintage tradition of underarm antiperspirant.

The Baroness exits at the end of the song. As she does so, Ludwig notices somebody approaching and in a recitative with chorus ("Why, who is this") he asks who it might be. A Herald – who may well have been seen disguised as a chorus member in Act 1 – then enters. In his baritone solo, with chorus ("The Prince of Monte Carlo"), he informs Ludwig that the Prince of Monte Carlo is arriving to bestow his beautiful daughter on him. Although some of the rhyming is hideously corny (for instance, "oughter" with "daughter" and "stickler" with "particklar"), this song is one of the catchiest and most memorable in the opera, with a remarkable second verse in which there are four key changes in quick succession. In recitative ("His Highness we know not") Ludwig commands his court to conceal themselves behind the draperies, ready to spring out on the Prince at a given signal. He and they then do so, and the Herald exits. The Prince and Princess of Monte Carlo then enter, accompanied by six theatrical-looking nobles – who will explain that they are in fact supernumeraries – and their Costumier, referred to in the list of *dramatis personae* as Ben Hashbaz. A duet follows ("We're rigged out in magnificent array") with interjections from the Costumier and the supernumeraries. In the duet the Prince and Princess explain that, in order to impress Ludwig and his court with a (somewhat specious) display of wealth and power, they have hired an array of costumes and a set of supernumeraries who masquerade as an assembly of nobles. They explain that the supernumeraries have been hired from the Theatre Monaco but they never speak because their language is so appalling. In the ensuing dialogue, the Prince explains that he has only got out of his financial predicament by virtue of his invention of the game of roulette. This has enabled him not only to pay his debts but to get his daughter to Pfennig Halbpfennig by *" train de luxe"* (surely a century later she would come by Eurostar!) to honour her betrothal to Rudolph. The Prince confesses, however, that he is not altogether satisfied with his collection of nobles, whom he describes as "not wholly convincing." A delightful section of dialogue follows, in which the Prince and Costumier together endeavour to improve the attitude and appearance of the hired company in preparation for the meeting with Rudolph. One "noble," known as Viscount Mentone, is so clueless that he has forgotten his own name (producers may wish to substitute a more topical name for Mentone such as the elusive Lord Lucan!). There is some splendid opportunity here for lesser lights in a society to demonstrate their skills in cameo roles; the part of the Costumier cries out to be camped up, and the supernumeraries can display a considerable range of thespian gaucheness and incompetence, such as false moustaches that adopt a surreal angle over the upper lip, wigs that have worked loose and cover half the face, and liberal outbreaks of nose-picking or fly-button checking. Hardened producers will reflect that this merely reflects the manner in which most chorus members were planning to conduct themselves anyway.

At the sound of a gong, the curtains fly open and Ludwig, together with his court (and presumably Lisa and Julia), rushes on to the stage. The company then engage in a reckless dance, which the Prince, Princess and their entourage join in. Geoffrey Smith describes this surprise welcome for the visitors as "the most embarrassing moment in the Savoy operas!" Ludwig explains that the dance is the court's official ceremonial for distinguished visitors, but, rather like the Cachucha in *The Gondoliers*, this will not stop many producers entrusting the dance to a specialist troupe and leaving the chorus to clap their hands and utter boisterous cries of encouragement when the mood moves them. The Prince attempts to explain, somewhat obliquely, to Ludwig (whom he of course believes to be Rudolph) that his daughter has come to honour her betrothal to him. He goes on to explain how being a roulette banker has solved his financial difficulties, demonstrating the fickleness of the roulette ball in a solo plus chorus ("Take my advice – when deep in debt") in which a brief game of roulette is actually played on stage. Described by Ian Bradley as one of the gems in the opera, it was deliberately written by Sullivan in the French *café chantant* style and has a wonderfully Continental *joie de vivre* and exuberance. There are several lines of French in the song; if the soloist is able to capture the Gallic ambience and bring a taste of "café society" to the stage, it may prove the highlight of the evening. The impact will sadly be ruined if the singer struggles through the piece with all the cosmopolitan self-assurance that might be expected of one whose knowledge of things French is confined to the packet of beans in his fridge-freezer, and the three words *Ooh*, *la* and *la*.

The Baroness has by now reappeared and is outraged to see the Princess displaying affection towards the man she (the Princess) believes to be Rudolph but who is of course Ludwig. In dialogue, Ludwig has to reveal that he is not Rudolph, but accepts that as victor in the Statutory Duel he now has an obligation to the Princess! He remarks that this is his fourth prospective bride in 24 hours. In a fit of sarcasm, he asks the company "Would anybody else like to marry me? You, ma'am – or you – anybody?" (Ludwig may earn a few extra laughs by extending his invitation to members of the audience at this point!) As his other "brides," Lisa, Julia and the Baroness, react in a mixture of outrage and despair, the Princess propels the company towards the exit in order for the wedding ceremony to take place; as they make to leave they sing a reprise of their earlier chorus "Now away to the wedding we go." They are however halted in their tracks by the arrival of Rudolph, Ernest and the Notary who in recitative, echoed by a puzzled chorus, cry "Forbear! The Law forbids the banns!" Rudolph then sings a solo, with choral interjections ("Well, you're a pretty kind of fellow"), in which he furiously chides Ludwig for the shameless way in which he has taken advantage of his victory in the Statutory Duel. The song suggests he knows something Ludwig does not, as he sings that Ludwig's purported revival of the law is "mere empty brag and clatter!" Although the refrain is another jolly tune, it is to be found in the overture and since the song adds nothing to the plot, it can quite conveniently be omitted. (The current libretto states that the song, and indeed the "roulette" song, is no longer used.) At the end of the song, Rudolph sinks exhausted into the Notary's arms, and in the dialogue that follows, it is left to the Notary to explain that the law actually provides that in a Statutory Duel the Ace – which Ludwig drew to beat Rudolph – shall invariably count as the *lowest* card. Rudolph was therefore the real winner in the Duel, so he can be deemed to be legally alive, and may claim the Princess. The fact that Ludwig was the loser meant that he had no power to revive the law; the striking of the clock brings the operation of the law to an end, enabling Ludwig to come to life again and be reunited with Lisa. Rather more curiously, Ernest claims that the repeal of the law will enable *him* to come to life again, and on that basis Julia accepts him; Gilbert seems to have overlooked that Ernest was the legal victor of his earlier Duel with Ludwig and is therefore legally still alive anyway! An ensemble reprise of the first chorus to different words ("Happy couples, lightly treading") sees everybody looking ahead to the multiple weddings and confirming that "this will be a day delightful." Nobody seems to worry that the hated Grand Duke is back in power again; it might also be seen as incongruous that Julia should suddenly find Ernest acceptable despite the fact that the conspiracy by which he was to become Grand Duke (and she Grand Duchess) has been blown. Arguably of far greater concern is the ability to survive the after-show party without being cornered by Mrs Anstey as she endeavours to dispense kingsize portions of unconsumed sausage roll.

The production is over; as the last chorus draws to a close on the final night, however, the performer will have to cope with three challenges. The first is to ensure that he is behind the line of the curtain when it closes. The second is to survive the embarrassment of the presentations which may follow. Well-organised societies will perhaps restrict stage presentations to bouquets for the lady artistes, producer and conductor, distributed expeditiously and before the audience's supply of applause has dwindled to too great an extent. Societies that are less sensitive to the bus-timetables, car-park tickets and bladders of their customers may, however, seek to detain them by several minutes as lengthy and platitudinous tributes are offered by the well-meaning but verbose Chairman, and a seemingly unending supply of gifts appears from the back of the auditorium. The sense of embarrassment is accentuated markedly if a gift is either not forthcoming when it should be, or the presenter cannot immediately recall or recognise its intended recipient. Even if the performer endures this unedifying spectacle to the end without seeking sanctuary in the pit directly beneath the stage, the biggest challenge is still to come, which is to cope with the desperate anti-climax which always follows a happy show. A society may try to mitigate this by the holding of a video evening, or a runthrough of music for the next show, very soon afterwards. Nevertheless, the thespian must still reconcile himself to returning from the excitement of show week to normal life and sadly-neglected household chores and repair jobs. After several weeks in which anything seems preferable to the prospect of rushing the evening meal and braving snow, hail, wind and storm to be bawled at by a temperamental producer, the amateur performer will feel a curious sense of emptiness as he helps to dismantle the set on the following morning. No longer is he a Venetian gondolier, a lofty peer or a smart dragoon guard, but Mr Smith of 12 Apple Tree Gardens with nothing more to look forward to on the Monday except a bulging in-tray, two basketfuls of ironing, and a trip to Sainsbury's Homebase to buy a sack of tiling grout.

The thirteen preceding chapters have taken the reader through the surviving G & S operas. Three other works should be briefly considered for the sake of completeness: the first ever G & S opera, *Thespis,* which can never be performed as it was written because the music has disappeared, and two other works composed by Sullivan, *Cox And Box* and *The Zoo*, with a different librettist in each case. Both are often performed alongside one of the shorter G & S operas. The true G & S aficionado will only be genuinely satisfied when he has appeared in performances of all three as well as the thirteen surviving G & S operas. His air of insufferable superiority when this task is accomplished is liable to leave those poor unfortunates whose achievement stretches to anything less feeling as impotent and inadequate as a prospective Antarctic trekker whose principal protection against the elements comprises a £10.95 C & A cagoule and whose sole nourishment consists of a pack of Boots Low Calorie Prawn and Lettuce sandwiches.

Cox And Box was the first in time and was Sullivan's first journey into comic opera. The lyrics were by F.C. Burnand who intended the piece to be a burlesque of an earlier work, *Box And Cox*. It was written with a view to entertaining guests at a musical and dramatic supper party at his house. Burnand approached Sullivan to write the music, and the composer agreed. Initially it was only performed privately, but on 11th May 1867 it received its first public airing, at the Adelphi Theatre in London, as a "benefit" concert for a member of staff of *Punch* magazine. It was so successful that it later enjoyed a run of 300 performances at the Royal Gallery of Illustration. One of the reviewers, who complimented the writers on the work, was a certain W.S. Gilbert. The private performances had relied solely on piano accompaniment; the orchestral scoring was only completed at 11 a.m. on the day of the first public performance!

There are only three characters in the opera; they are a journeyman printer John James Box (tenor), a journeyman hatter James John Cox (baritone), and the landlord Sergeant Bouncer (baritone). Not only is the show economical on cast, but the outlay on scenery should not be excessive either, since the action all takes place in a bedroom. At the start of the opera Cox is discovered alone in the room. Bouncer enters and, addressing him as Colonel Cox, remarks – in dialogue – that he (Cox) has had his hair cut. When Cox suggests that his haircut now gives him the appearance of a soldier, Bouncer (after Cox has exited) is moved to sing a nostalgic song with suitably martial music ("Rataplan") recalling the excitement of his own army days. Cox reappears and in the ensuing dialogue complains to Bouncer about the smoke which frequently fills his apartment. There follows a duet ("Stay, Bouncer, stay!") in which Cox further complains that his coal is disappearing too. A further bout of "rataplans" from both men end the duet. The word "rataplan" is derived from its frequent use in many operas of the period, most notably in Verdi's *La Forza Del Destino*, to imitate the beat of drums; it is not, as the name might suggest, the latest revolutionary transatlantic diet programme.

Cox exits after the song, and Bouncer says to the audience that – unbeknown to Cox – the reason for the smoky room and the vanishing coal is that he is letting the room not only to Cox by day, but to a certain Box by night. Box enters and as the dialogue continues it becomes clear that he, too, is unaware of this arrangement. Bouncer exits and Box – who also notices that items of his have gone missing – cooks himself some bacon using the fire and the gridiron. As it cooks, he sings a "lullaby" apparently to himself and also to the rasher of bacon reposing on the gridiron ("Hushed is the bacon"). This section of the opera presents the greatest logistical difficulty to prospective performers; there may be a stark choice between cutting out any cooking business at all, or risking the wrath of the local fire inspector. A third option, to cut the song out completely, may particularly appeal to the performer who is loath to compromise his good name in the community by singing soothing words to his cooked breakfast.

Cox then enters and sings a happy song ("My master is punctual"), rejoicing in the fact that he has been given a day off. Box is asleep and Cox does not see him; he does see the bacon, however, and concludes that it is Bouncer's. Cox then places his own item of food, a chop, on the gridiron! Box rises and, after each has asked themselves out loud what is going on, the inevitable confrontation ensues. A brisk duet ("Who are you, sir?") becomes a trio when Bouncer enters and another session of rataplan quickly follows. After the trio comes some heated dialogue as a result of which Bouncer promises to try and sort the situation out. Box and Cox then calm down and agree that there is no point in arguing; they also demonstrate that they each have a musical bent, and in the best-known musical number in the piece they sing a duet serenade ("The Buttercup") in which Box executes a masterly cadenza going from B flat above middle C to an octave below middle C. Meanwhile Cox imitates the sound of a stringed instruments with a succession of "Fiddleiddledums." Leaving aside the infinitesimal saving on typesetting, it is surprising that Burnand did not write "Fiddle*diddle*dum" for it is far more likely that that is what will in fact be sung; that is of course discounting the possibility that what Burnand actually wanted was "Fid-LYDLE-dum" as his spelling seems to suggest. If the producer is having a bad night, however, it might be prudent for the performer not to attempt it if he wants to leave the rehearsal hall with four fully-inflated car tyres and a working set of limbs.

Discussion then moves to relationships. In dialogue Cox informs Box that his *intended* wife is an owner and hirer of bathing machines. Box tells Cox in a kind of story-in-song, with interjections by Cox ("Not long ago"), that he was engaged to be married, but then broke the engagement because he felt himself to be unworthy of the lady in question. After being threatened with a breach of promise action he staged a faked suicide. In the dialogue which follows, it transpires that the lady is the same one that Cox is intending to marry. Moreover, not only does Box not wish to have anything more to do with her, but neither does Cox! Each attempts to offload her on to the other, and things again become heated to the point where Bouncer, as he enters, is told to go off and find suitable duelling weapons. He returns not with the expected pistols but a letter, which he hands to them then exits. The letter bears the welcome news that the lady, named Penelope Ann, is to marry a Mr Knox instead! Not only are the two men now fully reconciled and happy in each other's company, but the *absence* of a strawberry mark on Cox's left arm convinces Box that Cox is his long lost brother. As they embrace, Bouncer re-enters for the final trio ("My hand upon it") and inevitably the opera ends with all three committing themselves to a further stint of rataplan. If *The Sorcerer* is to be the society's other offering on the evening that *Cox And Box* is performed, a strict diet may be most advisable in anticipation of the ham and eggs to follow – that is, if the cast's appetite has not been dulled by the sight of assorted fragments of cooked pig left on the gridiron.

Thespis was, as has been stated, the first joint work of Gilbert and Sullivan, commissioned by John Hollingshead for the Gaiety Theatre as part of a package of Christmas-time entertainment for his patrons. Gilbert was able to engage actors who were already "big names" to play the principal parts. One example was the popular and leggy Nellie Farren who was cast in the male role of Mercury – the only occasion in G & S opera when Gilbert cast a performer of one sex into the role of someone of the opposite sex. Gilbert also emphasized the prominence of the chorus in the work. This represented a significant departure from tradition. Once,when asked by a principal "Why should I stand here? I'm not a chorus girl," Gilbert famously responded: "No madam, your voice is not strong enough or no doubt you would be."

Reactions to the opera, which ran from 26th December 1871 for 63 performances, were mixed. Sullivan, whose brother Fred had a part, said he had "rarely seen anything so beautifully put on stage" but admitted that the music had gone badly and one singer was a semitone sharp. Although *The Times* said the piece as a whole "deserves high praise," another critic felt it was under-rehearsed, while Gilbert, never one to mince words, dismissed it as "crude and ineffective." After its opening run it was never revived, and has never been performed again as originally written, for the simple reason that almost all the music has been lost. One song, "Climbing over rocky mountains," was reworked into the *The Pirates Of Penzance* (nobody knows if any other similar reworkings took place), and another, "Little Maid of Arcadee," was published separately but is virtually impossible to obtain today. Members of an operatic society wishing to perform it must either "borrow" from other music by Sullivan or compose fresh music themselves. Neither is entirely satisfactory; the former brings the inevitable problem of fitting what may be too many syllables into too little music, or vice versa, and the latter course is only to be adopted by those who can combine the patience of a saint with the nerve of a tightrope walker. Failure to satisfy the devotees of Sullivan on the night may leave the more thin-skinned composer wishing he had limited the audience for his ill-conceived compositions to the trio of rubber ducks floating in his bath tub.

For actors fortunate enough to take part in a production of *Thespis*, alternatively titled *The Gods Grown Old*, the story is as follows. The curtains open to reveal the fogbound Temple of the Gods on the summit of Mount Olympus. Through the fog comes a fatigued chorus of Stars who in their opening chorus ("Throughout the night") bemoan the feebleness of the light they give. During the chorus the elderly moon goddess Diana enters, wrapped in cloaks and shawls and with galoshes on her feet, and proceeds to remove these items. In the dialogue after the chorus has finished (one infers that the chorus should leave at this point, although there is no specific direction to this effect) she bemoans the coldness of the night air and rouses the elderly Apollo, who appears in dressing gown and smoking cap. As the sun god, he decides not to bother to come out today but send a fog instead. The fog, duly despatched, clears Olympus to reveal a ruined temple and backcloth of mountains. Mercury promptly appears, and as god of thieves informs Diana and Apollo of his nefarious nocturnal activities. He complains that he feels hard done by; initially in dialogue and then in a solo ("Oh, I'm the celestial drudge") he states that he is abominably treated as the gods' errand boy. After the solo the elderly decrepit Jupiter enters to suitably loud and majestic music. He too wears a dressing gown and also a silk night-cap, and he too is unhappy; he feels that the influence of the gods has dwindled to an unacceptable level, with even the human sacrifices offered to the gods consisting of nothing better than preserved Australian beef. The beef crisis in the latter part of the 1990's might lend this speech, with a little tweaking, a particularly topical air, but even if a performance were to be launched once the crisis had passed, the revolution in convenience foods might well instead prompt a reference to such burnt offerings as a Bernard Matthews turkey breast roast or even a Marks & Spencer microwaveable steak and kidney pudding.

As Mars enters, Mercury comes forward and in a quartet for him, Diana, Apollo and Jupiter ("Oh incident unprecedented!") he states, to the horror of the others, that Olympus is being stormed by thousands of mortals who "seem to be more like a Cook's Excursion." It seems that the terrible retributions available to Diana and Jupiter are ineffective at short distance. The four singers exit; presumably Mars goes with them although there is no stage direction to that effect. Sparkeion and his wife-to-be Nicemis then enter. They announce themselves as two members of Thespis' theatrical company who are out on a picnic together. In a duet ("Here far away from all the world") Sparkeion declares his love for Nicemis but Nicemis warns him of the danger of being too carried away by the exhilarating mountain air. Accordingly in the dialogue after the duet, Sparkeion speaks of redirecting his attentions towards his ex-fiancee Daphne, and Nicemis does not seem to object! Other members of Thespis' company then appear, singing the chorus "Climbing over rocky mountains" which was reproduced, with a few minor word changes, in *The Pirates Of Penzance* eight years later. It is the obvious choice to "represent" *Thespis* in a compilation evening which seeks to provide an item from each of the 14 G & S operas. At its best, such an evening will involve a full chorus, costume and and some spoken introduction or narration. However, the outlay of resources may not be so generous; at its most basic, such a compilation evening will involve a hastily-assembled collection of items sung by a non-costumed chorus of perhaps seven – of which there is sure to be at least one bass whose definition of harmony is a raucous rendition of the tune an octave lower – and linked by introductions that are as captivating as the movement of the dial on the hall's electricity meter.

Thespis himself then enters and whilst a picnic is consumed a lengthy section of dialogue follows, involving the company members Daphne, Pretteia, Preposteros, Stupidas, Tipseion and Cymon. There is a certain amount of animosity between them. Thespis regrets that he has been made a manager of what he calls "these thoughtless revellers" and in a solo ("I once knew a chap who discharged a function") he reminds those present of the story of a director of a railway company whose desire to look after his employees led to his ruin. According to press reports, this number, with whistles in the orchestral accompaniment and the actors imitating railway trains, was especially well received when it was first performed. After the song Jupiter, Mars and Apollo reappear in Olympian costume. Thespis initially fails to recognise Jupiter and snarls at him "Don't know yah!" but when informed as to Jupiter's identity, more civilised conversation ensues and Thespis candidly informs Jupiter that he and his fellow mortals think little of the gods, asserting that "you are not the gods you were." He suggests that the gods need time to help them decide how best to recover their influence. Accordingly he proposes that his company swap roles with them, so that the thespians take the place of the gods, and the gods go to earth as a band of touring players. Jupiter agrees and they shake hands on it. A musical sequence follows which could be said to be the Act 1 finale, consisting of a quartet for Jupiter, Mercury, Diana and Apollo ("So that's arranged") in which the four main gods confirm their agreement; a solo for Thespis with chorus ("While mighty Jove") in which both he and they contemplate the new order; and then solos, supported by chorus, for Sparkeion, Nicemus, Timidon and Daphne in which they appoint themselves god of day, moon god, god of war and muse of fame respectively. The libretto directs the chorus of thespians to enter just before Thespis' solo, although nowhere after their entrance song were they told to leave! Right at the end a procession of old gods enter; all the gods proclaim in a chorus "We will go" and gather together to allow the thespians to bid them farewell. The last line of Act 1 reads simply "TUTTI. Here's a pretty tale!" With no music available, it will be for the arranger to choose whether he wishes to develop this into a dramatic finale in which, as in oratorio, the four words are declaimed again and again in a series of powerful melismas, or whether he will content himself with the line being uttered once only and compensate with a longer interval. The latter course may be especially welcome for the pianist, for whom accompanying the society through *Thespis* may be a particular challenge as he struggles to cope with what may well be several pages of photocopied music from various operas or other works by Sullivan. However many pages there are, it will pay him to bind them securely. Few things are more disconcerting for the nervous performer than to see the keyboard accompaniment, upon which he is steadfastly relying, come to an unscheduled halt as what appears to be reams of white sheets of printed music cascade spectacularly from the piano and turn the surrounding floor area into a passable representation of the upper slopes of K2 in midwinter.

Act 2 is also set on Olympus a year later, but in place of the ruins there is a magnificent temple. The thespians, acting as the new gods, all seem very relaxed and happy, and articulate their happiness in a chorus, with solo for the stage manager Sillimon ("Of all symposia"). All then exit save Nicemis, dressed as Diana, Pretteia, dressed as Venus, and Sillimon. They consider the confusion that has arisen between the role of each thespian as god, and their real-life situation; ironically it was in *The Grand Duke*, the last G & S opera, that this theme would be revisited. During the dialogue Pretteia and Nicemis exit, and Sparkeion enters. Sillimon expresses concern for Daphne as a result of his (Sparkeion's) new affair with Nicemis, but in a solo, the music for which survived and was separately published ("Little maid of Arcadee"), Sparkeion tells the story of a certain young lady who was jilted by one man but was then wooed by another! Sparkeion exits and Sillimon then has a conversation with Mercury who has mysteriously entered the scene. When asked what he thinks of the new regime on Olympus, Mercury replies in a song ("Olympus is now in a terrible muddle") in which he paints a picture of extraordinary confusion on Earth, with people living far longer than they should, marriage becoming obsolete, young men becoming hermit-like and "young ladies popping all over the place." This last image is particularly intriguing; when read with the line about the hermitic young men it begins to make sense, but at first hearing one is bound to wonder whether the chaotic conditions on Olympus had added an extra potency to Earth's stores of kidney beans.

Thespis enters and in the ensuing dialogue, once Sillimon has exited, Mercury confirms that his conduct of affairs on Earth has led to a lot of complaints. After he has gone, Daphne enters in tears, lamenting that Sparkeion has deserted her for Nicemis. Thespis, however, points out that according to *Lempriere's Classical Dictionary*, Apollo is Calliope's husband; since Sparkeion has assumed the role of Apollo, and Daphne that of Calliope, they should be together. Sparkeion and Nicemis then enter and an argument begins, first in dialogue and then in a quartet with Daphne and Thespis ("You're Diana, I'm Apollo") as to which woman is entitled to Sparkeion. All exit having agreed that while they are gods, Daphne is entitled to him; when Sparkeion becomes a mortal, he will be Nicemis' husband! Jupiter, Apollo and Mars then appear in disguise, and in a recitative ("Oh rage and fury!") express dissatisfaction with the topsy-turvydom Thespis has created. A lengthy section of dialogue ensues. Mercury enters and adds his complaints, accusing Thespis of failing to seek his advice, and being thoroughly unreasonable with it. Thespis himself then enters and has to endure a barrage of critcism from the ex-gods, whom of course he does not recognise. However, on the basis that it is apparently usual for the gods to assemble once a year to listen to mortal petitions, the thespians assemble and, with their accusers pretending to be pressmen, a list of complaints is raised. These include the fact that a foggy November Friday in Athens has lasted six months; battles have been abolished, but since the dread of fighting was the only thing that kept nations civil to each other, war is universal; and because Tipseion (as the wine god Bacchus) is an abstainer, the grapes will yield only ginger beer. Thespis' command that all the ginger beer be extracted immediately in order to improve its quality leads into the final musical sequence, and effectively the finale of the opera. The ex-gods proclaim "We can't stand this," prompting Daphne, Sparkeion and Nicemis to call for their removal forthwith. The accusers Jupiter, Apollo and Mars then reveal themselves as the real gods, and Diana then appears with the other gods and goddesses. The thespians in chorus ask to be pardoned for their rudeness and beg to be allowed to stay, but they are driven away by the triumphant gods. Thespis has the final word, pointing out to Jupiter and his colleagues in a solo, with chorus ("Now, here you see the arrant folly"), that he has merely done his best to do what was agreed between him and the gods. It is clear that the music would have been a reprise of the earlier popular number "I once knew a chap." The thespians prepare to descend the mountain as the curtain falls. Anybody either participating in, or watching, the performance should count themselves fortunate to have witnessed a rare event indeed, if perhaps also relieved that if one of the G & S musical scores was to fall victim to the musical Bermuda Triangle, it was this one. There is surely no contest between the cavortings of Titipu's Lord High Executioner, or the matchmaking on the sunny Piazzetta in Venice, and this tale of grapes, ginger beer, goddesses and galoshes.

The Zoo, subtitled *A Musical Folly*, was the result of a collaboration between Sullivan and Bolton Rowe (his real name was B.C. Stephenson), and was intended as a burlesque of the conventions of grand opera. As in *Trial By Jury*, there is no spoken dialogue. The opera opened at St James Theatre in London on 5th June 1875, just over two months after the first night of *Trial By Jury*. Although the critics of the time were not unkind about the work, it failed to achieve the heights of popularity enjoyed by the G & S operas. It was never part of the standard D'Oyly Carte repertoire, but a republication of the score by J.B. Cramer in 1975 has led to a revival of interest in it. A somewhat backhanded compliment was paid to it in the 1993 *Oxford Dictionary of Popular Music* which described the score as "pleasantly inferior!"

The opera is set in a zoological gardens and the curtain opens to reveal a refreshment stall and a bear pit. An opening chorus ("The British public here you see") introduces the audience to the visitors, who as staunch Britons underline their superiority over the lions with a brief burst of "Rule Britannia." As the crowd begins to disperse, Aesculapius Carboy (tenor) is seen at the verandah of the stall with a rope round his neck. In recitative he announces his intention of hanging himself. The tourists demand to know why, and Carboy responds by singing a solo, with chorus ("I loved her fondly"). In it he explains that as an apothecary he was rejected by the father of Letitia (soprano), the girl he loves, as a suitable partner for her. To get his revenge he sent him a painful skin lotion but owing to a misunderstanding the lotion went to Letitia instead. In a further recitative ("And now let's go back") he again threatens suicide, but the stall owner Eliza Smith (mezzo-soprano) enters and flatly forbids him to go through with it. The chorus are directed to "retire." As Eliza proceeds to trumpet her wares, Thomas Brown (tenor) enters and thrills to her voice; there follows a tender love duet for them ("Ah, maiden fair"). They go up towards the stall and Letitia enters. She sings an aria at this point; the words for this have been lost and although some new words in praise of her beloved Carboy are suggested in the current vocal score, they are not Rowe's originals. In recitative she asks Eliza and Thomas where Carboy is. On hearing this, Carboy reveals his presence, and is overjoyed to be told that the lotion went to Letitia's father after all. This leads into possibly the most enjoyable number in the opera ("Once more, the face"), a quartet in which Carboy and Letitia sing tenderly of their love for each other, Eliza then in much faster tempo berates Thomas for eating too much, and the two separate tunes are then sung together. This latter device of Sullivan's would be employed to great effect in the later G & S works. Eliza's tune is one of the catchiest in the opera, and to more prurient members of the cast or audience her accusation that Thomas has "had four tarts" would not be without its entertainment value either.

The chorus come forward again and a big ensemble number follows ("Help! Ah Help!"), an obvious skit on the more melodramatic scenes of grand opera, in which the bloated Thomas faints. As he lies prostrate on the ground, only Carboy offers sensible advice; Eliza looks on uselessly, willing him to recover, while the chorus are of no real assistance and limit themselves to asinine reaction to what is going on. At length Thomas does recover and Eliza then exits. A further ensemble number ("Hoguards! Minions!") follows, in which by his somewhat unorthodox exclamations Thomas reveals himself to be of noble birth. The assembled company put on a suitable show of reverence, insisting, despite Thomas' protestations, that they should kneel before him. An extraordinary number follows ("Ladies and gentlemen") in which Thomas attempts to express his feelings, but is unable to speak articulately, despite the attempts of the chorus to help him. A more straightforward number for chorus, with brief solos from Thomas ("We gather from what you have said"), sees the newly-revealed nobleman being encouraged to press for Eliza's hand. After the chorus Thomas, Letitia and Carboy exit and a furious Mr Grinder, Letitia's father, enters. In a solo, with chorus ("Where is my daughter"), he demands to see Letitia; the chorus by way of welcome slap him on the back, which is particularly painful as that is where Carboy's lotion has been applied! Eliza then returns; she is perplexed because she is unable to locate her beloved and in recitative asks as to his whereabouts. Somewhat cryptically the chorus promise a happy ending then exit with Grinder. Alone on stage, Eliza professes not to understand them, and in a charming solo ("I'm a simple little child") sings of her supposed naivety and lack of sophistication; in fact she reveals she is a woman of considerable wealth who has been dated by several male admirers. The chorus return with Grinder, Letitia and Carboy, and the scene is set for another big ensemble number. Grinder, having at last found Carboy, hurls insults at him ("Found you at last, wretched outcast!") and bids him take his leave. Letitia and the chorus plead for him, and the music builds up to a splendidly operatic climax. As the dust settles, however, Grinder is unmoved and Carboy once again prepares for suicide. The chorus, evidently rather tired with Carboy's melodramatic mopings, try to assist in the location of a rope and obligingly sing "Farewell" in response to Carboy's similarly worded valediction. As he lowers himself into the bear pit, Thomas reappears, dressed as the Duke of Islington, and the finale begins with Eliza's recitative "What do I see in this disguise?" In fact Thomas is not in disguise, but reveals that he is indeed the Duke of that London borough. He proposes marriage to Eliza; initially she is concerned that marrying him will mean leaving her beloved animals, until Thomas reveals he has bought them all. Amid the general euphoria Carboy continues to bemoan the fates; it seems his desire to be torn apart by the bears has been frustrated since the bears have been moved! However, as he reaffirms his commitment to a painful death, Thomas reaches a deal with Grinder; as a result, Grinder withdraws his objection to Carboy as a son-in-law on the basis that the Duke will provide for them handsomely. A reprise of the opening music, with another snatch of "Rule Britannia," sees Carboy reunited with Letitia and all ending happily. The apothecary and his bride can look forward to an income of ten thousand a year from Thomas; Thomas and Eliza, meanwhile, can look forward to such rare marital delights as being lulled to sleep by a cockatoo and woken from it by a rattlesnake on the pillow. At any rate, it would prove a novel case for a marriage guidance counsellor.

BIBLIOGRAPHY AND SUGGESTIONS FOR FURTHER READING

Texts marked with an asterisk have been quoted from in this book.

Ayre, L: *The Gilbert & Sullivan Companion* – W. H. Allen, 1972

* Baily, L: *The Gilbert & Sullivan Book* – Cassell & Company, 1952

* Bradley, I: *The Complete Annotated Gilbert & Sullivan* – Oxford University Press, 1996 (N.B. Ian Bradley's book contains the text of all the surviving G & S operas and a wealth of background information, and is particularly to be recommended.)

Eden, D: *Gilbert & Sullivan; The Creative Conflict* – Associated University Presses, 1986

Fischler, A: *Modified Rapture; Comedy in W.S. Gilbert's Savoy Operas* – The University Press of Virginia, 1991

Ffinch, M: *Gilbert and Sullivan* – Weidenfeld & Nicolson, 1993

* Gammond, P: *The Oxford Companion to Popular Music* – Oxford University Press, 1991

Hayter, C: *Gilbert and Sullivan* – Macmillan, 1987

James, A: *Gilbert & Sullivan* – Omnibus Press, 1989

Jefferson, A: *The Complete Gilbert & Sullivan Opera Guide* – Webb & Bower, 1984

Orel, H (ed.): *Gilbert and Sullivan; Interviews and Recollections* – Macmillan, 1994

* Pearson, H: *Gilbert and Sullivan* – Penguin, 1950

* Smith, G: *The Savoy Operas* – Robert Hale, 1983

* Stedman, J: *W.S. Gilbert; A Classic Victorian & His Theatre* – Oxford University Press, 1996

* Williamson, A: *Gilbert and Sullivan Opera* – Marion Boyars, 1982

Wilson, F: *An Introduction to the Gilbert and Sullivan Operas* – Pierpont Morgan Library, 1989

PERFORMING IN A GILBERT AND SULLIVAN OPERA

If after reading this book you feel that you would like to take part in a G & S opera for the first time, you should join an amateur operatic society. Wherever you live, certainly in England or Wales, you will never be far from such a society. Details of societies in your area can be found in your local public library. Your initial contact should be with the secretary, whose telephone number should be contained in the library details. Many societies specialise in G & S opera; some alternate G & S with other operas and musicals; some take a conscious decision to exclude G & S from their repertoire altogether. If you decide you would like to join the society, you may be asked to do a simple audition; it is unlikely to be excessively daunting, and may consist of nothing more than the first three lines of the National Anthem. Having joined the society, you may have to undergo a further audition to take part in the next production. If you are successful in this regard, you will be expected to attend regular rehearsals which may take place weekly or even twice weekly. To begin with, you will learn the music, then start what is called "floor work" – in other words, learning moves to go with the music. You will need a thick skin to cope with the inevitable criticisms that the show director (producer) and musical director may offer. As the show nears, you may have to attend a number of consecutive evening rehearsals and possibly daytimes at weekends. When in performance, you will be expected to wear period costume and make-up, and observe strict rules to ensure the audience see you "in character" throughout the show. When you have a fair amount of experience, together with some musical and acting ability, you should think about auditioning for a principal part in a production, although you should be warned that society rules may preclude new members auditioning for solo parts. Do not be discouraged – your turn will come. The National Operatic and Dramatic Association (see below) run courses and summer schools to help the prospective performer build up his or her ability and confidence.

Taking part in a G & S show is hard work and demands commitment. However, the rewards are considerable. You will make many new friends; the half-time coffee break and post-rehearsal pub gathering provide ample opportunity for this. You will broaden your own thespian and musical skills, and equip yourself with greater self-confidence and self-belief for all areas of your life. You will enrich and enhance the cultural life of your local community, and provide much happiness for audiences who love the G & S operas as much as you do. And you will have lots of fun!

THE NATIONAL OPERATIC & DRAMATIC ASSOCIATION (NODA)

NODA seeks to further the interests of individuals and societies that enjoy amateur operatics and dramatics. It runs numerous courses, can tell you about societies in your local area, and gives advice and assistance to societies on all aspects of their administration. Its quarterly magazine provides a wealth of information on local productions, publications, and facilities which may be of use both to societies and individual performers. It may be that your own society is affiliated to NODA. Whether it is or not, you may wish to consider becoming an individual member. For further details, write to NODA National Headquarters, NODA House, 1 Crestfield Street, London WC1H 8AU; telephone 0171 837 5655, fax 0171 833 0609.

ALSO AVAILABLE FROM ROMANSMEAD PUBLICATIONS

THE JENNINGS COMPANION by David Bathurst

Fossilised fish hooks!

Crystallised cheesecakes!

The Jennings books of Anthony Buckeridge have become classics of schools fiction not only in Great Britain but also overseas; nearly 6 million copies have been sold worldwide. THE JENNINGS COMPANION is the definitive companion volume to the 25 Jennings titles which have appeared between 1950 and 1994. It provides not only an in-depth study of Jennings and his creator, but lists all the characters that appear in the stories and is packed with quotations and illustrations from the books as well as information for the collector. It is a "must" for the Jennings enthusiast and anyone who has enjoyed the Jennings books.

ISBN 1873475 49 7

AVAILABLE NOW at £5.99 plus £1 postage and packing from ROMANSMEAD PUBLICATIONS, 46 MOSSE GARDENS, FISHBOURNE, CHICHESTER, WEST SUSSEX PO19 3PQ.

....And coming from Romansmead in the year 2000

FLANDERS & SWANN – PORTRAIT OF A UNIQUE PARTNERSHIP